# CliffsNotes®

## RICA®

---

## 2ND EDITION

*By*
*Jerry Bobrow, Ph.D. and Beth Andersen-Perak, Ph.D.*

*Contributing Authors/Consultants*

Rhonda Byer, M.S., M.Ed.

Dana Gottlieb, B.A.

Frieda Bauch, M.A.

Diane Fiello, Ed.D.

Chris Collins, M.A., M.Ed.

Karen Sekeres, M.S.

Joy Mondragon-Gilmore, M.S.

Terri Battenberg, M.Ed.

**Houghton Mifflin Harcourt**
**Boston   New York**

## About the Author

Bobrow Test Preparation Services, founded by Jerry Bobrow, Ph.D., has presented classes at California State Universities and school districts for over 30 years and has published more than 40 national best-selling test preparation books. Using the time-tested teaching techniques developed by Dr. Bobrow, a team of professionally recognized reading and literacy specialists revised this edition of the *CliffsTestPrep RICA*, led by Beth Andersen-Perak, Ph.D., Associate Professor of Teacher Education at Azusa Pacific University. Dr. Andersen-Perak has over 30 years of experience as a reading specialist, school teacher, school administrator, and school reading coordinator.

## Acknowledgments

I would like to thank Donna Wright, project editor for Wiley Publishing, Inc., for her careful review of the manuscript, and Linnea Fredrickson and Cindy Hadash for their assistance in proofreading and assembling this manuscript.

## Editorial

**Acquisitions Editor:** Greg Tubach

**Project Editor:** Donna Wright

**Copy Editor:** Cate Schwenk

**Technical Editor:** Barbara Swovelin

## Composition

**Proofreader:** Leeann Harney

Wiley Publishing, Inc. Composition Services

**CliffsNotes® RICA®, 2nd Edition**

Copyright © 2010 Susan Bobrow

Library of Congress Cataloging-in-Publication Data:
Cliffsnotes RICA / Jerry Bobrow, Ph.D. ... [et al.]. – 2nd ed.
    p. cm.
  Rev. ed. of: CliffsTestPrep RICA, c2006.
  Summary: "Get subject reviews by domain, analyses of question types, a vocabulary list, and two full-length practice tests"—Provided by publisher.
  Summary: "CliffsNotes RICA 2e includes subject reviews by domain, analyses of question types, a vocabulary list, and two full-length practice tests with complete answers and explanations"—Provided by publisher.
  ISBN 978-0-470-58730-0 (pbk.)
  ISBN 978-0-470-88072-2 (ebk.)
  1. Teaching–California—Examinations–Study guides. 2. Reading teachers—Rating of—California. 3. Elementary school teachers—Certification—California. I. Bobrow, Jerry. II. Cliffs TestPrep RICA. III. Title.
  LB1763.C2C58 2010
  372.112'09794—dc22
                              2010028552
Printed in the United States of America
DOO 10 9 8
4500645596

For information about permission to reproduce selections from this book, write to trade.permissions@hmhco.com or to Permissions, Houghton Mifflin Harcourt Publishing Company, 3 Park Avenue, 19th floor, New York, New York 10016.

www.hmhco.com

**Note:** If you purchased this book without a cover, you should be aware that this book is stolen property. It was reported as "unsold and destroyed" to the publisher, and neither the author nor the publisher has received any payment for this "stripped book."

# Table of Contents

# PART III: TWO FULL-LENGTH PRACTICE TESTS

# PART IV: FINAL PREPARATION AND SOURCES

This book is dedicated to the memory of

*Educator and Author*
**Jerry Bobrow, Ph.D.**
December 4, 1947–November 11, 2007

*Coach*
**Foster Andersen**
March 11, 1940–April 26, 2004

*Architect/Engineer*
**Jim Collins**
November 29, 1943–October 22, 2005

*Their wisdom, caring, insightfulness, and humor*
*continue to nourish and give strength to those who knew them.*

# Preface

**Be Prepared for the RICA!**

The Reading Instruction Competence Assessment (RICA) Written Examination is designed to assess the candidate's knowledge about effective reading instruction in the five RICA domains and the candidate's ability to apply that knowledge. This test includes 70 multiple-choice questions, four regular essays, and one case-study essay.

Because the RICA requires you to use some skills and knowledge that you might not have used in a few years, thorough preparation is the key to doing your best. This fact makes your study time more important than ever; it must be used wisely and effectively.

In keeping with the fine tradition of CliffsNotes, this guide was developed by leading experts in the field of test preparation and reading instruction to give you the best preparation possible. The strategies, techniques, and materials presented in this guide have been researched, tested, and evaluated in RICA preparation classes at many leading universities, county offices of education, and school districts. Bobrow Test Preparation Services, a leader in the field of teacher credential exam preparation, is continually offering RICA classes at the request of many California state universities and school districts. This book uses the materials used and developed in these programs.

This guide is divided into an introduction and four parts:

# Introduction

A general description of the exam, format, commonly asked questions, and some basic overall strategies

# Part I: Analysis of Exam Areas

Focuses on introducing and analyzing each question type with an emphasis on suggested approaches and samples

# Part II: Review of Exam Areas

Short intensive reviews include a review of the Content Specifications—the Five Domains, Key Terms and Concepts, and Vocabulary

# Part III: Two Full-Length Practice Tests

Two complete full-length practice tests with answers, in-depth explanations, and review charts

# Part IV: Final Preparation and Sources

Some final tips and reminders to help you do your best

This guide is not meant to substitute for comprehensive courses in each subject area, but if you follow the Study Guide Checklist on the following page, review subject areas, and study regularly, success on the RICA examination is possible.

Good luck!

# Study Guide Checklist

❏ 1. Read the RICA information materials (registration bulletin) available at the testing office of most undergraduate institutions.

❏ 2. Review the information and sample problems available online at www.rica.nesinc.com.

❏ 3. Become familiar with the test format, page 1.

❏ 4. Read General Description, RICA Scoring, and Questions Commonly Asked about the RICA, on pages 1–5.

❏ 5. Learn the techniques of A Positive, Systematic Approach to multiple-choice, essay questions, and the case study, starting on page 6.

❏ 6. Carefully read Part I: Analysis of Exam Areas, starting on page 13.

❏ 7. Read Part II: Review of Exam Areas, starting on page 105.

❏ 8. Strictly observing the time allotment, take Practice Test 1, starting on page 157.

❏ 9. Check your answers and review the explanations, starting on page 206.

❏ 10. Read the sample responses, starting on page 215, and use the evaluation sheet pages 221–225 to evaluate your responses.

❏ 11. Fill out the Analysis/Tally Sheet for Questions Missed, page 220.

❏ 12. Review weak areas as necessary. Remember to review by domain and content areas.

❏ 13. Strictly observing the time allotment, take Practice Test 2 in its entirety, beginning on page 227.

❏ 14. Check your answers, review the explanations, evaluate your essays, and fill in the analysis sheets for Practice Test 2.

❏ 15. Review weak areas as necessary. Now focus your review.

❏ 16. Review Part I: Analysis of Exam Areas, starting on page 13.

❏ 17. Carefully study the Content Specifications to decide which strategies you will be using, page 105.

❏ 18. Carefully read The Final Touches, page 301.

# Introduction

## Format of the RICA Written Examination (Not Video Exam)

*Time: 4 Hours for Complete Exam*

| Format of the RICA Examination | | |
|---|---|---|
| **Question Type** | **Domain** | **Number of Questions** |
| **Multiple-Choice Questions** | Multiple-choice questions address content from all five domains. | 70 questions<br>(only 60 count—10 are experimental) |
| **Written Essay Response Assignments**<br>Focused Educational Problems and Instructional Tasks | **Domain 1**—Planning, Organizing, and Managing Reading Instruction Based on Ongoing Assessment | No written essay response for Domain I |
| | **Domain 2**—Word Analysis | 1 Long Essay—approximately 150–300 words (2-page response) |
| | **Domain 3**—Fluency | 1 Short Essay—approximately 75–125 words (1-page response) |
| | **Domain 4**—Vocabulary, Academic Language, and Background Knowledge | 1 Short Essay—approximately 75–125 words (1-page response) |
| | **Domain 5**—Comprehension | 1 Long Essay—approximately 150–300 words (2-page response) |
| **Written Case Study**<br>Assignment Based on Student Profile | Case study addresses content from all five domains. | 1 Long Essay—approximately 300–600 words (4-page response) |

Notice that the number of questions and the timing are subject to change.

## General Description

The Reading Instruction Competence Assessment (RICA) is designed to assess the candidate's knowledge about effective reading instruction in the five RICA domains and the candidate's ability to apply that knowledge. The test is composed of the following:

- A Multiple-Choice Section consisting of 70 questions (only 60 questions actually count)
- A Constructed-Response Section that requires candidates to write essays
  1. **Focused Educational Problems and Instructional Tasks** (4 essays: 2 short essays of 75–125 words each and two longer essays of 150–300 words each—each essay covers one domain). Notice that there is no required essay for Domain 1.
  2. **Case Study** (1 essay, approximately 300–600 words in length)

# RICA Scoring

The overall scoring for each domain on the RICA is *approximately*:

sub.3

| | |
|---|---|
| Domain 1—Planning, Organizing, and Managing Reading Instruction Based on Ongoing Assessment | 10% |
| Domain 2—Word Analysis | 33% |
| Domain 3—Fluency | 13% |
| Domain 4—Vocabulary, Academic Language, and Background Knowledge | 20% |
| Domain 5—Comprehension | 23% |

The RICA written examination score is composed of:

1. **Sixty multiple-choice questions from all five domains.** These questions assess your skills and knowledge about reading, as well as draw upon your ability to apply or analyze material related to *specific* reading instructional tasks. Remember 70 multiple-choice questions are on the test, but only 60 count toward your score and there is not a penalty for guessing.

2. **Four constructed-response essays with open-ended questions from Domains 2, 3, 4, and 5.** Assignments are labeled A, B, C, and D, and present you with a reading problem related to an individual student, an entire class, a group of students, or a situation. The table provides numerical values of the raw scores for illustration purposes only.

## Example of Total Possible Constructed-Response Scores

| Specification | Length of Response | Total Possible Raw Score | | Weight | | Raw Score Weighted |
|---|---|---|---|---|---|---|
| Domain 2 | 150–300 word essay | 6 | × | 2 | = | 12 |
| Domain 3 | 75–125 word essay | 6 | × | 1 | = | 6 |
| Domain 4 | 75–125 word essay | 6 | × | 1 | = | 6 |
| Domain 5 | 150–300 word essay | 6 | × | 2 | = | 12 |

sub. 1 (Domain 2, Domain 3)
sub.2 (Domain 4, Domain 5)

(Essays are scored from 1–3 by two evaluators, giving total possible raw score of 6)

3. **One case-study essay addressing all five domains (300–600 words).** In this section of the exam, test-takers will be given a student case study, including the student's reading background, reading performance, and sample case material. You will be asked to evaluate and assess the student's reading performance, describe instructional intervention strategies, and provide an explanation why this intervention might be effective. Case study essays are scored similar to the constructed-response essays above, using two evaluators. The only difference is that there is a greater weighted response because the case-study essays are longer (300–600 words).

The total raw scores for the entire exam are converted to a scaled score of 100–300 possible points. The minimum passing scaled score (the magic number) is **220** to pass the RICA.

Scoring and passing standards are subject to change.

**Score Reports:** When you receive your score report, you will notice that performance indices are provided in order to give you feedback about your strengths and weaknesses on each domain. The index consists of one to four plus symbols (+). The greater the number of plus (+) symbols, the higher your performance on the exam. For example, three to four pluses (+) indicates that your performance is adequate or better. If you receive one or two pluses (+), your performance is less than adequate. A separate performance index is provided for your case study since it includes all five domains.

# General Information

- There is no penalty for guessing on multiple-choice or constructed-response questions. Answer all of the questions. Guess if necessary. Always attempt a response.
- Multiple-choice questions have four choices: A, B, C, and D.
- Essays have room for notes at the bottom of the page.
- The RICA may be taken as often as necessary until a passing score is achieved on one single exam administration.
- The information given above is subject to change.

# Questions Commonly Asked About the RICA

**Q. What is the RICA?**

**A.** The Reading Instruction Competence Assessment (RICA) was adopted by the California Commission on Teacher Credentialing (CTC) "to measure an individual's knowledge, skill, and ability relative to effective reading instruction." The RICA was revised in 2009 to become aligned with the California Reading/Language Arts Framework. The RICA is composed of two different and separate assessments—the RICA Written Examination and the RICA Video Performance Assessment. The candidate needs to pass either one of the two assessments to complete the requirement. **This book is designed specifically to prepare you for the RICA Written Examination.**

**Q. Who administers the RICA?**

**A.** The RICA is administered by Evaluation Systems, Pearson Education with guidelines drawn up by the California Commission on Teacher Credentialing.

**Q. When and where is the RICA Written Examination given?**

**A.** The RICA Written Examination is administered statewide six times a year. You can get dates and test locations from the RICA Registration Bulletin or from www.rica.nesinc.com. You can also contact the California Commission on Teacher Credentialing to obtain credentialing information at the CTC website at www.ctc.ca.gov.

**Q. What materials should I take to the test?**

**A.** Be sure to take your admission ticket, some form of photo and signature identification, several sharpened No. 2 soft-lead pencils with good erasers, and a watch to help pace yourself during the exam. No scratch paper, books, or other aids are permitted in the test center.

**Q. What is included in the RICA Written Examination?**

**A.** The RICA Written Examination consists of two sections: Section I, 70 multiple-choice questions; and Section II, open-ended questions from Domains 2, 3, 4, and 5, which includes 4 essay assignments A, B, C, and D, plus one case study, Assignment E.

**Q. How much time do I have to complete the test?**

**A.** You have 4 hours to complete the entire test. You may work on the sections in any order.

**Q. What is a passing score?**

**A.** Raw scores are converted to scaled scores of 100 to 300. You need a total scaled score of 220 to pass the exam.

**Q. When will I get my score report?**

**A.** Your official test score will be mailed to you about 4–5 weeks after you take the test. Unofficial scores will be available, for your access only, on the Internet. The date for score reporting will be listed in the bulletin. To get your unofficial score go to www.rica.nesinc.com.

**Q. Can I take the RICA Written Examination more than once?**

**A.** Yes. But remember, your plan is to pass on your first try.

**Q. Do I need to take both of the sections at one time?**

**A.** Yes.

**Q. Should I guess on the test?**

**A.** Yes! Since there is no penalty for guessing, guess if you have to. On the multiple-choice section, first try to eliminate some of the choices to increase your chances of choosing the right answer. But don't leave any of the answer spaces blank. On the open-ended assignment section, be sure to give a response.

**Q. May I write on the test?**

**A.** Yes! As scratch paper will not be provided, you must do all of your work in the test booklet. Your answer sheet for the multiple-choice section, however, must have no marks on it other than your personal information (name, registration number, and so on) and your answers.

**Q. How should I prepare?**

**A.** Understanding and practicing test-taking strategies will help a great deal. A focused review of the subject matter listed in the Content Specification Domains is invaluable. This guide gives you insights, review, and strategies for the question types. Some universities offer preparation programs to assist you in attaining a passing score. Check with them for further information.

**Q. How do I register?**

**A.** The RICA Registration Bulletin is available at most college or university testing offices and teacher preparation programs. The registration bulletin is also available on the website at www.rica.nesinc.com. Register by mail with Evaluation Systems, Pearson Education P. O., Box 348150, Sacramento, CA 95834-8150; electronically on the Internet at www.rica.nesinc.com.; or by telephone at (916) 928-4004 or (888) 793-7999.

**Q. How do I get more information about the RICA program?**

**A.** Check the official RICA website. As new information becomes available, it will be posted at www.rica.nesinc.com.

# Taking the RICA Written Examination: A Positive Systematic Approach

## Getting Started: Five Steps to Success on the RICA

1.  **Awareness.** Become familiar with the test—the test format, test directions, test material, and scoring—by visiting the RICA website at www.rica.nesinc.com.

2.  **Basic Skills.** Review the basic abilities required on the test in each domain: planning and organizing; word analysis, fluency, vocabulary and comprehension. Know what to expect on the exam. Review Part I, "Analysis of Exam Areas," to help you determine your strengths and weaknesses so that you can develop a study plan unique to your individual needs. Review Part II, "Review of Exam Areas," to identify key reading terms, concepts, technical vocabulary, and domain content specifications.

3.  **Question Types.** Become familiar with the question types of each domain area on the test outlined in Parts I and II: multiple-choice questions, essay-response questions, and the case study essay response.

4.  **Strategies and Techniques.** Practice using the strategies outlined in the next section of this book, and make a decision about what works best for you. Remember that if it takes you longer to recall a strategy than to solve the problem, it's probably not a good strategy for you to adopt. The goal in offering strategies is for you to be able to work easily, quickly, and efficiently. Remember not to get stuck on any one question. Taking time to answer the most difficult question on the test correctly but losing valuable test time won't get you the score you deserve. More importantly, remember to answer every question, even if you answer with only an educated guess. There is no penalty for guessing, so it is to your advantage to answer all questions.

5.  **Practice, practice, practice.** It's the key to your success on the RICA. In addition to the sample practice problems in Part I, "Analysis of Exam Areas," this book offers you two complete practice tests.

## Strategies for Multiple-Choice Questions

The multiple-choice section appears first, followed by the essays, and finally the case study.

### Applying the "Plus-Minus" Strategy

Many people who take the RICA don't get their best possible score because they spend too much time on difficult questions, leaving insufficient time to answer the easy questions. Don't let this happen to you. Since you have about 1 minute per multiple-choice question and each question is worth the same amount, use the following system to avoid getting stuck on any one question.

1.  **Solvable Question**   Answer easy questions immediately.

2.  **Possibly Solvable Question (+)**   When you come to a question that appears to be solvable but is overly time-consuming (a time-consuming question is a question that you estimate will take you more than several minutes to answer), mark a large plus sign (+) next to that question in your test booklet. Next, make an educated guess at the correct answer on your answer sheet, then move on to the next question.

3.  **Difficult Question (–)**   When you come to a question that seems impossible to answer, mark a large minus sign (–) next to it on your test booklet. Then mark a *guess* answer on your answer sheet and move on to the next question.

If you budget your time as suggested, you have just over 1 minute to 1½ minutes per multiple-choice question. Don't waste time deciding whether a question is a "+" or a "–". Act quickly, as the intent of the strategy is, in fact, to save you valuable time.

After you work all the easy questions, your test booklet should look something like this:

    1.

+2.

    3.

    4.

−5.

+6.

etc.

4. After answering all the questions you can answer immediately (the easy ones), go back and answer your "+" questions. Change your guess on your answer sheet, if necessary, for those questions you are able to answer. You may instead want to return briefly to the "+" questions in the same subject area before moving on to the next subject area. But do not spend too much time taking a second look at the "+" questions, or you will not complete the section.

5. If you finish the section and have rechecked your "+" questions, then you can either:

(A) Attempt those "−" questions, the ones that you considered impossible. Sometimes another problem will "trigger" your memory, and you will be able to go back and answer one of the earlier "impossible" problems.

or

(B) Don't bother with those impossible questions. Rather, spend your time reviewing your work to be sure that you didn't make any careless mistakes on the questions you thought were easy to answer.

6. Allow about 1 minute per question. Never spend more than about 1½ minutes on a question. If it looks like your question is going to take more than 1½ minutes, mark a plus or a minus, take your guess, and move on.

Remember, you do not have to erase the pluses and minuses you make in your test booklet. Be sure to fill in all of your answer spaces—if necessary, with a guess. As there is no penalty for wrong answers, it makes no sense to leave an answer space blank. **Never leave an answer space blank!**

## Using the Elimination Strategy

Take advantage of being allowed to mark in your test booklet. As you eliminate an answer choice from consideration, make sure to *mark it out in your test booklet* as follows:

A̶

?B

C̶

?D

Notice that some choices are marked with question marks, suggesting that they may be possible answers. This technique will help you avoid reconsidering those marked-out choices you have already eliminated and will help you narrow down your possible answers. Remember, you are looking for the best answer of the ones given, which might not be the perfect or ideal answer. This elimination strategy will help you find the best answer. These marks in your test booklet do not need to be erased.

## Avoiding the Misread Strategy

The most common mistake that test takers make in answering multiple-choice questions is the *misread*. This mistake refers to **incorrectly reading** the question, the information given, or the answer choices. In other words, you do not clearly understand what you are being asked, or you misunderstand the information in the passage or the answer choices.

When you misread a question, you are not looking for the answer you should be looking for. When you misread the information given, you are not going where the information and question should be leading you. You are not taking advantage of what is given, and, in fact, you could be working from faulty information. Finally, when you misread an answer, you will either not select an answer you should select, or you will select an answer that doesn't mean what you think it means.

A question could ask,

> "Which of the following should the teacher consider first, before preparing her lesson?"

or the question may instead have asked,

> "Which of the following should the teacher include in her lesson plan?"

Notice that the first question is asking about the FIRST thing that the teacher should consider BEFORE preparing her lesson, whereas the second question simply asks what she should INCLUDE in her lesson plan.

To avoid misreading a question (and, therefore, answering it incorrectly), simply circle or underline what you must answer in the question. In the preceding examples, you would have circled or underlined the questions in your test booklet in this way:

> "Which of the following should the teacher <u>consider first</u>, <u>before preparing her lesson</u>?"

or

> "Which of the following should the <u>teacher include in her lesson plan</u>?"

You should also circle or underline key words in the information given, and you should focus on key words in the answer choices.

And, once again, these circles or underlines in your test booklet do not have to be erased.

## Reviewing the Strategies

When you start reviewing for the multiple-choice section, keep the following items in mind.

1. Remember that the test is composed of 70 multiple-choice questions covering the five domains. The 70 multiple-choice questions appear first. Allow approximately 1 minute per question but never spend more than 1½ minutes on a question. Be sure to pace yourself accordingly.
2. Never leave a question without at least filling in a guess answer. Be careful when skipping questions to make sure that you are marking your answer in the correct space.
3. Try to answer all of the questions but don't deliberate or think too long on any one question or group of questions at great length. Remember, each question is of equal value. If you are uncertain, use a process of elimination to choose your response. Since there are only four choices, if you can eliminate one or two, your guessing odds increase tremendously.
4. A common mistake is misreading the question. Be sure to focus on what the question is asking.
5. You are to select the best answer. This means the best of those given, which might not always be an ideal answer.

## Strategies for the Regular Essay Questions

There are a total of four regular essay questions on the entire exam and one case-study essay. The two essay questions related to Domains 3 and 4 will require essays of approximately 75–125 words each. The two essay questions related to Domains 2 and 5 will require essays of approximately 150–300 words each.

## Approaching the Questions

As you approach the essay questions, always keep in mind that the evaluators are scoring written responses that demonstrate: 1) *purpose* and understanding of relevant content from the domains; 2) effective *application* of relevant content from the domains; and 3) *supporting* examples, evidence and rationales. With this in mind, first briefly scan the four essay questions. Do not attempt to answer an individual question at this point. Simply scan for general content to decide which question you will work on first. Select the one with which you feel the most comfortable. If you take the questions out of order, be sure to write your answer on the appropriate essay sheets and be careful not to skip any questions. Some general strategies include:

1. Read and mark the question. That is, circle or underline what the question is asking. For example, does the question ask you to describe what a teacher should do? Does it ask you to explain why a strategy or activity would be effective? Does it ask you for a series of steps or a number of examples?

2. Restate the question to yourself before attempting to answer the item. It is essential that you clearly understand what the question is asking for.

3. Quickly jot down, in the area provided in the test booklet, pertinent facts and information needed to answer the question. You can make a list of individual words or jot down phrases. Do not attempt to make a complete formal outline of your answer. Time constraints limit the effectiveness of detailed formal outlines.

## Answering the Questions

Follow these guidelines in writing your essay responses.

- Do not restate the question in your introductory sentence. This is considered unnecessary.

- Write in a clear, concise style. Many questions call for an answer to identify a problem or need, recommend a strategy or activity, and explain why this strategy would be effective.

- Answer all parts of an individual question. It's easy to skip part of the question under the time pressure— for example, listing two causes, but forgetting to list the two results.

- Refer back to the question to make sure that your answer is focused. Marking the question will help you maintain focus.

- Essay answers will vary in length from about 75–125 words (for Domains 3 and 4) to 150–300 words (for Domains 2 and 5).

- Specific assessments, activities, materials, key words, and glossary words are essential elements in demonstrating your knowledge of a subject.

- When you write your essay answer, be very specific answering the question or tasks given. Your answers will be easier to write if you use specific examples. For example, if you are asked to give the benefits of reading a variety of books aloud to a class, it might be much easier to base your answer on a few specific books or types of books, rather than discussing a variety of books in general.

- Do not write more than you need to. That is, keep in mind that two of the essays require 75-to-125-word answers and two require 150-to-300-word answers. Since the 150-to-300-word essays have more value than the 75-to-125-word essays, budget your time accordingly. Spend about 15 minutes on each short essay and about 30 minutes on each longer essay. Remember, if you spend too much time on one question, you might not have time to adequately complete your other essays.

- Do not spend an inordinate amount of time on any individual factor in a question that asks for multiple factors. Your overall score will be based on your ability to answer all parts of the question, not simply one part.

- Answer each question. Before skipping a question, read it a few times to see whether you gain insight concerning the question. The questions are generally designed so that you can receive partial credit if you have some knowledge of the subject. Partial answers will get partial credit. Even an answer that receives one point will be added to your total points.

- If you are completely unfamiliar with a question prompt, try a common-sense answer or skip the question. Do not get stuck. Recognize that by skipping a question you know nothing about, you will gain time for other questions, but try to write some sort of answer for each question.

- Unless specifically asked, do not write a conclusion or summary for any question. The question format does not normally require this type of response.

- Remember, these are fairly short essays, not formal three-, four-, or five-paragraph essays. You are trying to show the readers what you know. You may show steps, use bullet points, drawings, and so on.

## Checking Your Answer

Keep the following points in mind.

- Keep track of your time. Pace yourself. Make time to briefly scan your responses to make sure that you've answered the question. Look for major errors in focus. Don't be overly concerned with minor spelling or grammar errors.

- Complete each essay in the proper booklet. Then, if time permits, review or reread your responses. You should give a response to each of the four essay questions.

# Strategies for the Case-Study Essay

The case-study essay follows about seven or eight pages of information and should be approximately 300–600 words in length, or approximately a four-page response. You should leave about 1 hour to evaluate and write your case study essay.

## Approaching the Case Study

When you start reviewing for the case study keep the following items in mind.

1. Read and mark the tasks given. That is, circle or underline what you are being asked to do. Typically you will be asked to identify strengths and/or weaknesses, describe or recommend a strategy and/or activity, and explain how this strategy/activity will be effective.

2. Quickly jot down, in the area provided in the test booklet, pertinent facts and information needed to answer the question. You can make a list of individual words or jot down phrases. Do not attempt to make a complete formal outline of your answer. Time constraints limit the effectiveness of detailed formal outlines.

## Writing the Case Study

Follow these guidelines in writing your case study essay.

- Do not restate the question in your introductory sentence. This is considered unnecessary.

- Write in a clear, concise style.

- Identify the student's reading strengths, weaknesses, or needs; recommend an instructional strategy or activity; and explain why this strategy might promote reading proficiency.

- Answer all of the tasks given. It's easy to skip a part under the time pressure—for example, identifying three weaknesses, describing activities, but forgetting to explain why they will be effective.

- Refer back to the tasks to make sure that your answer is focused. Marking the tasks will help in maintaining focus.

- Specific assessments, activities, materials, and key words (buzzwords) that are used in the field will often help display your knowledge of a subject.

# PART I

# ANALYSIS OF EXAM AREAS

This section emphasizes **how to approach question types** that you will see on the RICA test. Sample questions are followed by important test-taking strategies and complete explanations.

**Read this section carefully.** Underline or circle key techniques. Mark notes in the margins to help you understand the strategies, suggested approaches, and question types.

# Introduction to the Multiple-Choice Questions

| Domain | Content Areas | Percent of Questions |
|---|---|---|
| **Domain 1**<br>Planning, Organizing, and Managing Reading Instruction Based on Ongoing Assessment | **Content Specification 001:** How to plan, organize, and manage standards-based reading instruction.<br>**Content Specification 002:** Purposes of reading assessment, best practices related to standards-based entry level assessment, monitoring progress, and summative assessment. | 20% |
| **Domain 2**<br>Word Analysis | **Content Specification 003:** How to understand and develop phonological and phonemic awareness skills.<br>**Content Specification 004:** How to develop knowledge and skills in concepts about print, letter recognition, and the alphabetic principle.<br>**Content Specification 005:** Phonics instruction and important terminology, concepts, and sight words.<br>**Content Specification 006:** Recognition of sight words to promote accurate word analysis that leads to automaticity and contributes to spelling development.<br>**Content Specification 007:** Understand the role of syllabic and structural analysis, and orthographic knowledge that leads to automaticity in word recognition and contributes to spelling development. | 33% |
| **Domain 3**<br>Fluency | **Content Specification 008:** Understand the role of fluency and factors that affect the development of fluency.<br>**Content Specification 009:** How to promote fluency development. | 10% |
| **Domain 4**<br>Vocabulary, Academic Language, and Background Knowledge | **Content Specification 010:** Understand the role of vocabulary, academic language, and background knowledge.<br>**Content Specification 011:** How to promote vocabulary, academic language, and background knowledge. | 23% |
| **Domain 5**<br>Comprehension | **Content Specification 012:** Understand literal, inferential, and evaluative comprehension.<br>**Content Specification 013:** Understand how to facilitate comprehension by providing instruction that prepares students for reading tasks by scaffolding.<br>**Content Specification 014:** Understand how to promote comprehension and analysis of narrative/literary texts.<br>**Content Specification 015:** Understand how to promote comprehension of expository and informational texts, and the development of study and research skills. | 14% |

The multiple-choice section of the RICA is composed of 70 questions, although only 60 questions actually count toward your score. Ten of the questions are experimental and may be used on future tests. The 70 multiple-choice questions appear first on the exam. Be sure to allow approximately 1 minute per question, but never spend more than $1\frac{1}{2}$ minutes on a question. Since you are given 4 hours to complete the entire exam, pace yourself accordingly to allow no more than 90 minutes or $1\frac{1}{2}$ hours for the multiple-choice questions. Some questions will be single questions, but others may be in groups, that is, two or three questions referring to the same information.

Remember to use the strategies mentioned in the Introduction.

# Sample RICA Questions and Strategies

The following multiple-choice questions are grouped by domain and identified by content area. Read the sample questions, pay special attention to the strategies given for each question, and then focus carefully on the explanation.

## Domain 1

## Planning, Organizing, and Managing Reading Instruction Based on Ongoing Assessment

### Content Specification 001: Understand how to plan, organize, and manage standards-based reading instruction.

1. In a multiple-choice assessment a third-grade student who speaks a second language at home is asked to identify the word that matches a picture of a "throne." The choices are:

   a. thrown

   b. throne

   c. throwne

   The student chooses answer "A" but doesn't understand why his answer is marked wrong. What does this error suggest to the teacher for further instruction to assist the student in mastering ELA content standards?

   A. This student's difficulty is with correct spelling, and the teacher should recognize that the student would benefit from adding this word to his/her weekly spelling list.

   B. This student is confusing homophones, and the teacher should provide individualized instruction and practice to help the student differentiate between words that sound the same.

   C. The teacher needs to provide an environment that promotes independent reading to help this student with vocabulary.

   D. This student's reading and vocabulary development can be furthered by extra classroom lessons provided by a teacher, aide, or parent volunteer.

## Strategies to Use

First, underline or circle key words. Next, focus on the information that is provided with the question. The information states that the student speaks a second language at home and makes an error on a multiple-choice question. Notice the answers that the student has to choose from are homophones. This will help lead you to the best answer to this question. You need to be sure that the answer you choose specifically answers what the question is asking.

## Explanation

The best answer is **B.** Confusing *throne* and *thrown* is a common error for students who hear another language at home. Additionally, they might be more familiar with the word *thrown* and possibly would have seen it in print before. The teacher should recognize that this student needs some additional individualized instruction to clarify these words. Choice A is incorrect because this student is not experiencing a spelling problem. Although independent reading promotes increased vocabulary, as suggested in Choice C, this is not the best solution to this student's difficulty. Choice D contains correct statements but does not specifically address the question.

## Content Specification 002: Understand the purposes of reading assessment and best practices related to standards-based entry-level assessment, monitoring of students' progress, and summative assessment.

2. What are some effective assessments to use in monitoring student oral and written language in order to determine student understanding and use of effective English language structure and conventions?

   A. running records, multiple-choice tests, student reports, individual student conferences, and parent conferences

   B. anecdotal records, teacher observation, student conferences, checklists, and collection of writing work samples

   C. mini lessons, cloze procedure tests, oral reading inventories, book lists, retellings, and writing rubrics

   D. analyzing student-invented spelling, portfolio assessment, student self-assessment, and student work files

## Strategies to Use

Notice that you are looking for effective assessments. You need to be aware of the information that the tests listed provide to the teacher. For example, a running record would help the teacher assess a student's reading level but would not adequately provide information on whether the student is grasping language conventions.

## Explanation

The best answer is **B**. Assessing English language structures is an important Structure of the English Language content specification and is an integral part of the teaching process. The teacher observes his students frequently to determine what they already know and what they need to learn. Authentic assessment can provide the teacher with information about students and the impact of the instructional program in the classroom. Most importantly, authentic assessments inform instruction. The other choices do not adequately address both the oral and written parts of the question.

3. A first-grade teacher administers running records to assess her students' reading. When listening to one of her students read an unknown text, the teacher notices that the student is able to read most of the words in the text accurately and use appropriate decoding strategies to figure out unknown words. After the student has read the text, the teacher asks him questions about the story. The student is unable to provide any correct answers and responds, "I don't know." What does this information tell the teacher about the student's reading ability and what do the results suggest for the teacher's future reading planning?

   A. This information assists the teacher in selecting books for the student at this reading level and suggests that the classroom needs to provide books for students on many reading levels.

   B. The student is able to comprehend what he has read accurately, and the teacher needs to select more challenging text for the student to read.

   C. The student is able to decode the text but has weak comprehension skills; therefore, the teacher needs to provide direct instruction in comprehension strategies and demonstrate what needs to be understood from the text.

   D. This student is able to decode the text accurately and would benefit from paired reading, flexible guided reading group instruction, and small group instruction on specific phonetic skills.

## Strategies to Use

First underline or circle key words. Note that the question includes the grade level of the student—underline "first-grade." The question also provides the information that the student can decode accurately but does not comprehend the text adequately—this is important information. The question also includes two parts: What does the **information provide** and what are the **next steps for teaching**? Be sure that the answer you choose addresses the two parts asked in the question.

## Explanation

The best answer is **C**. The student's comprehension skills are weak if he cannot answer any of the subsequent questions about the story. The teacher will need to address this weakness in planning her future reading lessons. Choice D also mentions correctly that her student can decode accurately but supplies next step strategies that would not wholly address the student's deficits and, therefore, is an incorrect answer. Neither Choice A nor Choice B answers the question correctly. Reading is the active act of combining decoding and comprehension. The goal of all beginning reading programs should be that all students comprehend grade-level material. The teacher should be sure that the student in question is given an opportunity to discuss the meaning of any words or concepts he might not understand, use strategies such as literature circles that promote discussion of text and further facilitate comprehension, support the reader by tapping into any prior knowledge as it relates to the story, discuss the pictures before reading the story, and give clues to the story line beforehand.

Adequate reading comprehension is the ultimate result of effective instruction in reading. If a student is able to decode but not comprehend, then the student is not able to enjoy and understand written language. The knowledge and active application of certain reading strategies are necessary for comprehension.

Additional teaching strategies to develop reading comprehension in all grades, not only first grade, might include the following:

- direct explicit instruction, modeling, and student practice in comprehension strategies such as: preview, predict, visualize, and summarize
- using open-ended questioning techniques
- using drama activities that are good for supporting literacy development
- guided oral retellings
- question the author
- guided reflection
- small discussion groups
- reciprocal teaching (an approach using multiple strategies to support students in understanding text; students ultimately take on the role of the teacher)
- helping students to make inferences
- think-alouds—teacher modeling the mental processing of print

# Domain 2

# Word Analysis

## Content Specification 003: Understand the role of phonological and phonemic awareness in reading development and how to develop students' phonological and phonemic awareness skills.

4. During a phonemic awareness activity, a primary student is unable to blend phonemes said aloud by the teacher. The teacher explains that he will say the sounds in a word very slowly and then the students are to tell him what word he is stretching into sounds. The student listens attentively to the sounds and then orally says an incorrect word, not relying on any of the sounds the teacher has said. For example, after hearing /c/-/a/-/t/, the child says, "kitten." What does this information suggest to the teacher?

   A. It would be beneficial to the teacher to include the use of magnetic letters in small group instruction, and the teacher needs to instruct the student in matching sounds to the letters.

   B. The teacher could help this student with blending skills by assigning independent practice with a volunteer or teacher's aide.

   C. The teacher needs to provide this student with explicit instruction in blending and to select appropriate activities and materials to practice sound segmentation and blending.

   D. This student would benefit from additional instruction in phonemic awareness, since phonemic awareness is an essential reading skill and students need to understand how language works in order to be successful readers.

## Strategies to Use

First, underline or circle key words in the question. Note that the question provides the exact task and the exact response of the child. Knowing that this is a phonemic awareness task will help you narrow down the choices.

## Explanation

The best answer is **C**. Choice A involves matching sounds to letters, not a phonemic awareness task. Choice B would help the student practice the skill with an adult, but this particular student needs more instruction in the skill before practice can begin. Choice D is true; the student would probably benefit from added instruction in phonemic awareness, but this is too general an answer and it does not specifically address what the question is asking. Choice C specifically addresses this student's weakness. Blending is an important prerequisite to reading, and students need practice and explicit instruction in this skill. In teaching this skill, the teacher needs to select activities and materials that are appropriate for this student's stage of development. Some good activities for this student would be oral games such as playing a guessing game by identifying a familiar item in the classroom and say: "What am I thinking of? I'm thinking of something in the room where you can sit and write. I'm thinking of a /d/-/e/-/s/-/k/. What am I thinking of?" Or you can use student's names, stretch them into sounds, and ask the students to tell you what name you are saying.

# Content Specification 004: Understand the role of concepts about print, letter recognition, and the alphabetic principle in reading development and how to develop students' knowledge and skills in these areas.

5. After reading a big book to her students who are gathered on the rug in the front of the room, the teacher asks a kindergarten student to find a word on the page of text and to frame that word with her hands. The student comes to the front of the room where the big book is displayed and uses her hands to frame a whole line of text instead of just one word. After the teacher ascertains that the student has understood the task, what kind of classroom intervention could the teacher plan for this student?

A. The teacher should engage the student in activities that promote understanding of *word*. Some activities that the teacher could use are having the students track print as the teacher reads, counting words, and explaining that there are empty spaces between words.

B. The ability to frame a word needs to be practiced by this student in order to foster her understanding of phonics. Some activities that could help this student understand the concept of a word are writing in sand, singing songs, cut-and-paste activities, and being read to.

C. A good intervention for this student is to participate in learning center activities that are carefully planned by the teacher. Some learning centers that would benefit this student are writing centers, listening centers, computer centers, and independent reading.

D. This student could benefit from additional activities that support these skills. Some suggested intervention activities for this student are letter matching, cut-apart sentences, and oral reading activities.

## Strategies to Use

First, underline or circle key words. Next, review the information given carefully. Note that this question describes a classroom scenario in which students are gathered to listen to the teacher read a big book. This is a common activity in early primary classrooms. The task that the teacher is asking the student to perform is described. Additionally, it is noted that the student understands the task.

## Explanation

The best answer is **A.** This question deals with print concepts. Understanding word boundaries assists students in understanding that print conveys meaning (i.e., print concepts). The mastery of print concepts is a reliable predictor to reading success.

Some benchmarks in print concepts include identifying the front/back of the book, discriminating between a letter and a word, recognizing word and sentence boundaries, knowing where to begin reading on a page, and understanding that print goes from top to bottom and left to right. Choice B incorrectly states that framing a word will aid the understanding of phonics. The other activities in the answer are appropriate activities for early primary but would not be appropriate interventions for this student. In Choice C, the learning centers mentioned would not aid this student in mastering print concepts. Finally, Choice D suggests intervention activities that would not all be appropriate for helping this student in mastering print concepts.

## Content Specification 005: Understand important terminology and concepts involved in phonics instruction and recognize the role of phonics and sight words in reading development.

6. In a small group, a first-grade non-fluent reader is asked to read the following passage from the first-grade reader.

> Jack and Matt were friends. They had known each other for a very long time. They liked to play together. Sometimes they would play at Jack's house and sometimes they would play at Matt's house. They were good friends.

The words the student has the most difficulty decoding are *were, friends, known, very, they,* and *would.* The student attempts to sound out these words but is not successful and arrives at the completion of the text with limited understanding of what he has just read. What interventions should the teacher plan for this student?

A. If a child reads most words in the text correctly but misses some of the words, the teacher could provide opportunities for this student to practice reading fluently with support. Some activities that could help this student are choral reading, rereading, and listening to stories on tape.

B. If a child misses so many words that comprehension is affected, then the teacher could help this student by activating prior knowledge, encouraging predicting before the text is read, and using graphic organizers.

C. Additional phonics instruction could benefit this student and assist him in improving his decoding. Some activities that would help this student are instruction in word families, playing word games, and doing tongue twisters.

D. The words that seem to be most difficult for this student are sight words or high frequency words. The teacher should provide direct instruction in high frequency words and then practice reading high frequency words. Some activities that would help this reader include: using word walls, maintaining a personal dictionary, word study, and a concentration/matching game.

## Strategies to Use

The key words in this question are "interventions" and "teacher plan." Mark these key words. Note that the question mentions that this is a first-grade classroom and that the student is a non-fluent reader being asked to read a grade-level passage. The primary problem that this student is having is the inability to recognize the high frequency words within the text. Be careful that you are correctly diagnosing the problem in order to arrive at the correct answer.

## Explanation

The best answer is **D.** This student apparently is having difficulty in recognizing sight words or high frequency words. These are the errors mentioned in the information given. Readers need to build a repertoire of these words that occur most frequently in text (high frequency words). These are the words that can't be sounded out. It is helpful to try and connect these words to the student's experience to promote long-term memory. It's also beneficial to call students' attention to these words within and out of text. Some activities that help build high frequency word banks are word walls, personal dictionaries, word study after reading, and student writing. Therefore, D is the correct choice. Choice A doesn't correctly diagnose this student's problem, although the activities mentioned in the answer would promote fluency. Choice B correctly concludes that when a student makes many miscues when reading, comprehension is ultimately affected. This student's understanding of the text must be affected. The strategies mentioned in Choice B would help with comprehension. It's quite likely that if the student could correctly decode the high frequency words, he or she would understand the text, and so difficulty with comprehension would be a secondary problem. Choice C, additional phonics instruction, would not help this student decode the high frequency words that the student is decoding incorrectly and is, therefore, an incorrect answer.

## Content Specification 006: Understand how to develop students' phonics knowledge and skills and recognition of sight words to promote accurate word analysis that leads to automaticity in word recognition and contributes to spelling development.

7. In small group instruction, the teacher leads her group through the following activities:

   First, the teacher segments the following words:

   | chin | into | /ch/-/i/-/n/ |
   | reach | into | /r/-/ea/-/ch/ |
   | cherry | into | /ch/-/err/-/y/ |

   Then the students try to guess the word that the teacher is saying.

   The teacher then asks what sound was commonly heard in each of the words.

   Next, the teacher prints the letters *ch* on the board and shows the students a picture of some cherries. The teacher asks the students to think of some more words that have the /ch/ sound at either the beginning or the end. These words are written on the board and the students practice saying the words.

   Finally, the students practice this skill by reading selections on their own in which most of the words are decodable and include *ch* or high frequency words that have already been taught. The teacher carefully monitors each student's reading and makes corrections if necessary.

   What are the benefits of using the aforementioned strategies?

   A. These strategies reinforce concepts of print and the ability to recognize specific sounds.
   B. These strategies will help students recognize this digraph when decoding, spelling, and writing.
   C. These strategies will assist students achieve mastery in spelling.
   D. Students need to hear the way language sounds and see the print before them for extended periods of time to finally master the skill.

## Strategies to Use

First, underline or circle the key words. Note that the question very specifically asks what would be the "benefits" of the lesson. Which response specifically addresses the benefits of the lesson described? There could be other possible benefits to this lesson, but the choices might not provide appropriate answers, so you must eliminate them.

## Explanation

The best answer is **B.** This lesson would be a part of systematic, explicit phonics lesson within an organized program. The lesson describes instruction in letter clusters known as digraphs and begins with identifying them in words where they are heard, then seeing how they are written, and finally practicing reading them in connected text. These strategies play a critical role in decoding, in reading fluently, and ultimately in comprehending text. Therefore, the best answer to this question is B. These strategies do not constitute a phonemics awareness lesson as mentioned in Choice A, nor would it necessarily be a benefit to students to copy the words generated from the board. In Choice C, these strategies certainly would assist students in spelling words that contain the digraph *ch* but would not help students achieve mastery in spelling.

## Content Specification 007: Understand the role of syllabic and structural analysis and orthographic knowledge in reading development and how to develop students' knowledge and skills in these areas to promote accurate word analysis that leads to automaticity in word recognition and contributes to spelling development.

8. A fourth-grade classroom teacher is asked to submit student writing from his class to be published in a school newspaper. The students in the class are asked to interview a classmate, friend, or relative who immigrated to the United States. The students are to generate a list of questions to ask regarding the person's experience when arriving in a new country. One student submitted the following writing sample:

> My Mom
>
> When my mom came, she did not *speek* English because she was born in a *diffirent* country. No one could understand her because of her *axcent*. She was good in *swiming*. I think my mom is *amazzing*.

In analyzing the student's spelling errors, how does the teacher begin to interpret the student's spelling development and how might the teacher plan for further spelling instruction?

A. First of all, the teacher must identify the spelling errors in this student's paper. He can then return the paper to the student for correction. Then, the student can add the misspelled words to the student's weekly spelling list.

B. After identifying the students' spelling errors, the teacher can add these words to his class's weekly spelling list to enable his students to achieve mastery of these words. In future spelling lessons, the teacher can group his students according to the words they are having difficulty spelling and then provide activities to help them with these words.

C. The teacher should identify the misspelled words in this student's writing sample and should add this sample to other samples of this student's work. For further information about this student's spelling development, the teacher should administer a spelling inventory and analyze the results. This would provide him with more information on which to base word study lessons for his class.

D. The teacher notices in this sample that this student has made many errors with words that have doubled consonants, but he needs more information in order to determine this student's spelling development. Future lessons should include activities with the misspelled words of each student.

## Strategies to Use

Notice that the question states that this is a fourth-grade class. This student is making appropriate errors for a fourth grader. If the students made errors in other skills that should be mastered by the fourth grade such as beginning/ending consonants or short vowels, further assessments might be necessary. Importantly, the question asks about how the teacher "begins" to interpret her students' spelling development and how the teacher might "plan for further instruction."

## Explanation

The best answer is **C**. A good starting point for the instructor is to gain more information about his students' spelling stages by collecting samples of student writing from both formal inventories and from daily writing. Then the teacher can begin to compare the students' spelling abilities. Additionally, administering a spelling inventory to the class will assist the teacher in determining students' spelling stages of development. Although all students will pass through the same stages of development, they pass through at different rates. The inventory can provide the teacher with valuable information about each student's spelling developmental stage and subsequently help him in planning spelling instruction.

Additionally, presenting students with spelling words that are matched to their spelling developmental stage creates lessons in developing concepts rather than memorizing words. That's why Choice A is an incorrect answer.

Merely adding the misspelled words to a weekly list will not further this student's spelling development as would doing activities that promote the learning of the skill with which she is having difficulty. Similarly, the first sentence in Choice B is also incorrect although the next sentence suggests appropriate activities to do after spelling assessment to determine the students' developmental spelling levels. In Choice D, the teacher correctly notices the type of errors that the student has made on this particular sample but needs more than this one sample to determine his future spelling instructional plans for this student and the rest of the class.

# Domain 3

# Fluency

## Content Specification 008 and 009: Understand the role of fluency and factors that affect the development of fluency, and how to promote fluency.

9. During a small guided reading group assignment, a second-grade teacher notices that one student continues to struggle with oral reading fluency. What intervention strategies would best provide for the needs of this student?

A. The teacher should model reading with expression. In addition, the teacher should provide decodable text for this student and encourage the child to whisper read and reread passages to develop automaticity and appropriate phrasing.

B. The teacher needs to concentrate on using related workbook pages in prosody and word-recognition skills for this student to become an automatic reader.

C. The teacher should increase time for read-alouds, which would provide this student with more exposure to good literature. Doing this would also result in the added benefits of increasing the student's vocabulary and helping develop automaticity.

D. The teacher should give time for sustained, silent reading, which increases fluency and reading rate when the student is reading books at the student's reading level.

## Strategies to Use

First, underline or circle the key words. Note that the question very specifically asks about intervention strategies. Which response most specifically addresses strategies for this student's independent reading level? Notice that the question states that this student is in the second grade. Using your knowledge of reading, you may be able to quickly realize that this student is reading slowly to "figure out" or "decode" words. Therefore, one of the intervention strategies should include helping to decode text.

## Explanation

The best answer is **A**. This question is about fluency and the student's inability to orally read text effortlessly and with a full-range of expression. Reading should sound natural, as if the student is speaking. Students who have not yet developed reading fluency may exhibit slow, choppy, word-by-word spoken expressions. Teachers are good models of fluent reading, and by listening, students learn how a reader's voice can help written text make sense.

The teacher needs to provide systematic, direct instruction in prosody, including reading with expression, paying attention to punctuation, and variations in pitch and intonation. Direct instructional strategies help students to be more aware of the reading process. The goal of improving fluency is to increase reading comprehension so that the student will eventually be able to comprehend text with accuracy and ease.

Another method that is beneficial in improving reading fluency is for the teacher to offer opportunities for the student to repeat readings of the text. Repeated reading must be at the independent level, containing words the student can decode easily. A child's ability to make visual discriminations between words has a positive effect on his or her reading and confidence level.

# Domain 4

# Vocabulary, Academic Language, and Background Knowledge

**Content Specification 010: Understand the role of vocabulary, academic language, and background knowledge in reading development and factors that affect students' development of vocabulary, academic language, and background knowledge.**

**Content Specification 011: Understand how to promote students' development of vocabulary, academic language, and background knowledge.**

---

**Use the information below to answer the two questions that follow.**

The following diagram is provided for students in a third-grade classroom:

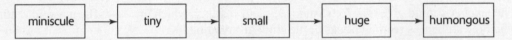

The students are told that one way to understand and remember new words is to think about how they are related. It is explained that one way to do this is to figure out how the word fits in a word hierarchy. This is a diagram in which the words are ranked. The teacher then leads a class discussion about each word, how it relates to the other words, and what the concept is about in each word. She then asks whether the students can add any words to the hierarchy. The students are then divided into small groups and given collections of other words to arrange into hierarchies. Finally, students are given general categories with which to develop word lists to arrange into hierarchies.

10. What would be the purpose of using the preceding strategy?

    **A.** Looking up words in a dictionary and using them in sentences is conducive to effective vocabulary instruction and constitutes purposeful learning at most grade levels.

    **B.** The purpose of this strategy is to increase students' word knowledge, although the knowledge of words doesn't directly determine how text is understood.

    **C.** The most important reason for using a similar strategy to teach vocabulary is for comprehending text and aiding students in acquiring new and varied vocabulary.

    **D.** This strategy will help students understand words with similar meanings and will increase student understanding of how words are related, including differences/similarities between words that have almost the same meaning.

11. The best way for the teacher to determine the words to use in future similar lessons is to use:

    **A.** recycled words selected from an old lesson including words from past weekly spelling tests.

    **B.** difficult words that the teacher selects in similar activities from the dictionary.

    **C.** words that the teacher selects from student writing or story selections read in class.

    **D.** words that the students select from daily or weekly reading activities.

---

## Strategies to Use

First, underline or circle the key words. Next, carefully analyze any chart or diagram included to help you to understand what information is being given. Remember to quickly eliminate answers that are not true or give false information.

## Explanation for 10

The best answer is **D.** Students need to have the ability to understand words that are similar in meaning. Oftentimes the inability to understand the shades of meaning of words contributes to poor comprehension of text. Good readers need to know a large number of words that can't only be acquired by wide reading, although encouraging student volume of reading can contribute to an increased vocabulary. This type of lesson can be extended to provide antonyms for the selected words.

Choice A, using the dictionary to look up words, does not contribute to effective vocabulary instruction. So you can eliminate Choice A. In Choice B, the first part of the statement is correct, but the second part is not true. Knowledge of words does directly determine how text is understood. In Choice C, increasing vocabulary contributes to better comprehension as does an increase in the volume of reading, but instruction in specific words and concepts is needed to produce in-depth vocabulary knowledge. This diagram shows how specific words are related.

## Explanation for 11

The best answer is **C.** Although the strategies in some of the other choices may be beneficial, it is probably more meaningful for these students to use words that the students use in writing or speech. The teacher should select these words to make sure the students get the most out of the lesson. In addition, the teacher may have students draw pictures of each word in their hierarchy. This task will assist the students' understanding.

# Domain 5

# Comprehension

## Content Specification 012: Understand literal, inferential, and evaluative comprehension and factors affecting reading comprehension.

12. A fifth-grade teacher puts the following chart on the board:

Story Title: _____

| Setting | |
|---|---|
| Characters | |
| Problem | |
| Solution | |

Students receive their own copy of this story map to complete. The students had received instruction and practice with this strategy beforehand, in addition the teacher modeled how to complete the chart while reading a previous story in a whole group setting. The teacher explains that the students are to use the story map to help them identify the key elements in the story they are about to read.

What might be the teacher's purpose for having students complete the story map, and what does this activity demonstrate about her understanding of developing reading comprehension in her students?

A. The teacher is demonstrating her understanding of the reading process by having her students complete this story map. By correctly completing this activity, the students demonstrate their understanding of cause-effect relationships and literal comprehension.

B. This teacher understands that reading comprehension is necessary learning for all students. By having her students complete this story map, she is providing effective instruction in reading comprehension and demonstrating her knowledge of what students need to comprehend the text.

**C.** The teacher is demonstrating her understanding that a story map assists students in clarifying text. By providing instruction in identifying story elements, this teacher has provided an activity that will help her students identify the important story elements and help her students identify and organize the relationship between them.

**D.** This teacher is showing how to explicitly demonstrate a comprehension technique. Additionally, she is demonstrating the importance of finding the main idea, something that these students will be able to do after completing this activity.

## Strategies to Use

First, review the chart that the question provides. Next, think about what responses might be appropriate and the purpose for this type of chart. Is it asking for cause-effect relationships? Or is it asking for important story elements? Now focus on the key words in the question. Be careful when answering questions that are asking about more than one item—in this case, *the teacher's purpose and what is demonstrated.* Be sure that the answer that you select adequately and specifically answers the complete question. Finally, notice that the question states that this is a fifth-grade classroom. The purposes for this chart might vary with the grade level.

## Explanation

The best answer is **C.** This type of activity facilitates student comprehension. Good readers are able to clarify text but need to be taught how to find the most important elements of a story. The teacher needs to create opportunities for students to learn and then independently practice comprehension techniques. Additionally, by having students write, before, during, or after reading, they are deepening their understanding of text. Choice A is incorrect because it makes a very general statement about the teacher demonstrating her understanding of the reading process and this activity does not demonstrate that. Additionally, the purpose of story mapping isn't to teach cause-effect relationships or literal comprehension. Choice B provides correct statements but it is not specific. Choice D might also be accurate, but does not address identifying the different story elements, which is a main purpose of this chart.

## Content Specification 013: Understand how to facilitate reading comprehension by providing instruction that prepares students for the reading task, scaffolds them as needed through the reading process, and prepares them to respond to what they have read.

13. After teaching a story in the text, a fifth-grade teacher uses upper grade student volunteers who are fluent readers to record the story on tapes. He plans to use the tapes with his English Language Learners (ELL) who can listen to the story another time at a listening station. What is an instructional advantage to using this strategy?

**A.** This strategy involves eliciting student prior knowledge as it relates to the content.

**B.** This approach helps the ELL student to build fluency and comprehension by hearing the story an additional time.

**C.** An advantage of using taped stories would be to enrich the language output of ELL students.

**D.** The advantage to this approach enables the ELL student to increase vocabulary enrichment.

## Strategies to Use

First, circle or underline the task to be completed. In this case, you are asked to identify an instructional advantage of using recorded tapes of upper grade fluent readers for English Language Learners to hear during "listening station" time. Think about what responses might be appropriate and the purpose of this question. It is asking to identify specific "reasons" this strategy might be effective. Even if you have no knowledge about explicit instructional strategies for "scaffolding" tasks, you might be able to make an educated guess about "hearing the story an additional time."

## Explanation

The best answer is **B.** Older peers are good models of fluent reading, and by listening to a story a second time at the student's reading level, English Language Learners can hear how a reader's voice can bring to life the meaning of the written text. Fluency is important because it builds a bridge between word recognition and comprehension, and as struggling students hear repeated stories of text, they are developing listening skills and greater opportunities for independent reading. Providing students with explicit instructional modeling strategies supports individualized instruction and helps students transfer comprehension from oral language to written language. This provides an instructional advantage in the classroom. Another strategy that the teacher might suggest is to record her lesson while she teaches and plays it for ELL students additional times. The students can listen to the lesson again, increasing their understanding and comprehension.

## Content Specification 014: Understand how to promote students' comprehension and analysis of narrative/literary texts and their development of literary response skills.

14. A fourth-grade teacher selects a core literature book for her students to read. After her students have completed reading the book, she asks them to go back through the text and find situations that the main character has experienced that remind the students of something in their own lives. The students are to use a response log to record their ideas. The teacher might choose this strategy as a follow-up to reading the book because:

   **A.** The teacher understands that helping her students connect real-life experiences to those of a character will deepen their understanding of a book, and she can analyze their responses to plan future appropriate instruction.

   **B.** The student responses can be used to evaluate the students' understanding of the text and will provide the teacher with information she can use to plan further assessments and testing.

   **C.** Writing in response logs provides good daily writing practice for students and are an appropriate strategy for fourth graders.

   **D.** Each teacher needs to be familiar with her district's core literature selections in order to provide appropriate material for her students.

## Strategies to Use

The teacher in the question provides a strategy for her students. You should consider the benefits that this strategy provides for students before reading the choices. Don't let the choices that state correct teaching practices distract you from the correct answer. Remember to find the *best* answer to this question.

## Explanation

The best answer is **A.** Encouraging students to connect text with personal experiences helps students relate what they're reading to their own lives. These types of connections might also be incorporated into students' writing. In addition to connecting what they are reading to their experiences, connections can be made to different story versions, to other books by the same author, and by connecting characters to people they know. Choice B is correct in that the teacher can gain information about her students' understanding of the text by reading their responses but it is not the *best* answer to this question. Choice C is also correct, but again, is not the *best* answer. Choice D focuses on *the teacher being familiar with the district's core literature selections to provide appropriate material*, which does not answer this question.

## Content Specification 015: Understand how to promote students' comprehension of expository/informational texts and their development of study skills and research skills.

15. An eighth-grade history teacher is beginning a unit on the history of the Civil Rights Movement in the United States. He begins by systematically collecting documents on the incident that involved a woman being asked to give up her bus seat in the Southern United States in 1955. Besides the school district provided history text, he collects artifacts to be contained within an archive bin that will give the students more information to read about the incident and that are correlated to the text. Some of the documents that the teacher includes regarding the incident are a newspaper article, an interview with the woman, photos, a letter to the woman, and an eyewitness account of the incident written by the woman involved. Next, the teacher involves the students in retrieving information about the incident from the various sources. The students will use the information provided for research, formulating ideas, preparing reports, and taking a test. Some important concepts to be taught about understanding information in this unit are to:

A. help students understand the organization of the text, notice the visual clues that will identify the important ideas, and understand the relationship between those ideas.

B. help the students understand the features of expository texts by including lessons regarding cause-effect relationships, how to compare/contrast, and how to summarize and identify the main idea.

C. have students, with the help of the teacher, complete a K-W-L chart to identify what the students already know about the subject, what they want to learn, and what they have learned when the unit is completed.

D. use graphic organizers to provide some important organizational skills for his students to process the information from the various sources.

## Strategies to Use

Notice that the question refers to an eighth-grade history class. All teachers are teachers of reading and they must possess the skills and knowledge to provide access for their students to the content areas. According to the question, all of the information that the students will need to read will be expository text. Also note that the question specifically asks about important concepts to be taught. Eliminate incorrect answers that do not answer this specific question, even if they contain true statements.

## Explanation

The best answer is **A.** The purpose of expository text is to provide facts and information. This type of text can often inform, explain, or persuade. As students progress through grade levels, more and more time is devoted to this type of text. Often, this type of text is more difficult for students because it involves more high-level thinking than does narrative text. These are the key concepts that students need to be taught to process this type of text. In addition to the items included in the archive bin mentioned in the question, the Internet could provide students with more information on the topic. According to research, student understanding about the text structure is strongly linked to their comprehension, so any instruction that includes expository text must help students understand how this type of text is organized. Often maps, charts, and diagrams are included in expository text. These items provide visual clues that provide information, and students need to be taught how to use these items to help understand the concepts.

Choice B describes some features that might occur in expository text, but one is not able to infer from the question that these skills must be taught. Choice C contains an effective strategy for processing expository text, the K-W-L chart (**K**now, **W**ant to know, **L**earned) but again, you cannot infer that the teaching of this strategy will help these students comprehend this specific text. In Choice D, the use of graphic organizers is a good strategy that will help students understand text, but this answer does not provide some key concepts and, therefore, is not as good as Choice A.

# Introduction to the Essay Questions

## The Focused Educational Problems and Instructional Tasks

The essay section is composed of four essay constructed-response questions from Domains 2, 3, 4, and 5. Assignments are labeled A, B, C, and D and show a reading problem related to an individual student, an entire class, a group of students, or a particular situation. The four essay domains are as follows:

| Question Number | Area Tested | Length | Estimated Total Value |
|---|---|---|---|
| Essay 1 (Assignment A) | Domain 2 | 150–300 words | 12 points |
| Essay 2 (Assignment B) | Domain 3 | 75–125 words | 6 points |
| Essay 3 (Assignment C) | Domain 4 | 75–125 words | 6 points |
| Essay 4 (Assignment D) | Domain 5 | 150–300 words | 12 points |

You should plan on spending approximately 15 minutes on each 75–125-word essay and 25–30 minutes on each 150–300 word essay. Your total time for the four essays should be about 90 minutes or 1½ hours.

## Understanding the Scoring

Let's take a careful look at the scoring system.

### Essay Scoring Guide

### Score 3

**You will receive a score of 3 if the response**

- ❑ reflects a thorough understanding of the relevant content and academic knowledge from the applicable RICA domain.
- ❑ responds fully to the given task(s), and identifies student's reading development need.
- ❑ describes specific instructional activities and/or strategies of individual learners.
- ❑ demonstrates an effective application of how strategies promote reading proficiency.
- ❑ provides strong supporting examples, evidence, and rationale based on the relevant content and academic knowledge from the applicable RICA domain.

### Score 2

**You will receive a score of 2 if the response**

- ❑ reflects an adequate understanding of the relevant content and academic knowledge from the applicable RICA domain.
- ❑ fulfills the purpose of the assignment adequately.
- ❑ responds adequately to the given task(s), and provides specific instructional strategies.
- ❑ is generally accurate, but may not provide accurate supporting evidence for all suggested instructional strategies.
- ❑ demonstrates a reasonably effective application of the relevant content but may lack depth of understanding a student's reading development needs.

## Score 1

**You will receive a score of 1 if the response**

- ❑ reflects limited or no understanding of the relevant content and academic knowledge from the applicable RICA domain.
- ❑ fails to fulfill or partially fulfills the purpose of the assignment.
- ❑ responds in a limited manner or inadequately to the given task(s).
- ❑ is inaccurate.
- ❑ demonstrates an ineffective application of the relevant specific content and academic knowledge from the applicable RICA domain.
- ❑ provides limited or no supporting examples, evidence, and rationale based on the relevant content and academic knowledge from the applicable RICA domain.

## U

**The response will receive a score of U for "unscorable" if it is**

- ❑ off task.
- ❑ unrelated to the assigned topic.
- ❑ illegible.
- ❑ not of sufficient length to score.
- ❑ written in a language other than English.

## B

**The response will receive a score of B if it is blank.**

# How to Respond to the Essay Questions

This section of the book will provide you with guidelines to help you understand the skills and strategies necessary to plan, develop, and execute your constructed response essays. Keep in mind that although this chapter discusses your written essay responses, most of the strategies discussed in this chapter will also help you with your written case study response assignment.

Each essay assignment is evaluated based upon your ability to: 1) address your instructional knowledge and understanding of the content specification areas, 2) effectively apply this knowledge to the content specification areas, and 3) provide details, examples, and evidence to support your knowledge.

These step-by-step guidelines include:

General Test-Taking Strategies for Essay Writing

The Essay Approach Checklist

Specific Guidelines for RICA Essay Writing

Strategies to Plan and Pre-Write Essays

## General Test-Taking Strategies for Essay Writing

First, briefly scan the four essay questions. Do not attempt to answer an individual question at this point. Simply scan for general content to decide which question you will work on first. Select the one with which you feel the most comfortable. If you take the questions out of order, **be sure to write your answer on the appropriate essay sheets** and be careful not to skip any questions.

The following steps will help you get started:

1. **Read and mark the question.** That is, circle or underline what the question is asking. For example, does the question ask you to describe what a teacher should do? Does it ask you to explain why a strategy or activity would be effective? Does it ask you for a series of steps or a number of examples?

2. **Focus on what is stated.** Refer back to the question to make sure that your answer is focused on what is stated in the question. Marking the question will help to maintain your focus.

3. **Restate the question to yourself before attempting to answer the item.** It is essential that you clearly understand what the question is asking.

4. **Quickly jot down, in the area provided in the test booklet, pertinent facts and information needed to answer the question.** You can make a list of individual words or jot down phrases. Do not attempt to make a complete formal outline of your answer. Time constraints limit the effectiveness of detailed formal outlines.

5. **Answer each question.** Before skipping a question, read it a few times to see whether you can gain insight concerning the question. The questions are generally designed so that you can receive partial credit if you have some knowledge of the subject. Partial answers will get partial credit. An answer that receives only one point will be added to your total points. If you are completely unfamiliar with a question prompt, try a common-sense answer or an educated guess. *Do not get stuck!* Skip the question as the last resort if you cannot make an educated guess. By recognizing that you can skip a question you know nothing about will allow you to gain time for other questions.

6. **Answer the entire question.** It's easy to forget part of the question under the time pressure, so be sure to answer all parts of an individual question. For example, if you are asked to list two causes for something and address their results in your response, do not forget to list the two results.

## The Essay Writing Approach Checklist

Keep the following points in mind before approaching your essay response.

❑ Keep track of your time. Pace yourself. Save time to briefly review your responses to make sure that you've answered the question. Look for major errors in focus.

❑ Don't be overly concerned with minor spelling or grammar errors.

❑ Complete each essay in the proper booklet. Then, if time permits, review or reread your responses.

❑ Make sure that you write a response to each of the four essay questions.

## The Approach

1. **Gather Information**—circle or underline the key words in the information to help you focus your understanding of

   ❑ The problem, situation, or task that is presented.

   ❑ The student's grade level.

   ❑ The student's history.

2. **Prewrite.**

   ❑ Organize your thoughts and ideas by keeping simple notes in the area provided or by making simple lists.

   ❑ Jot down your topic sentence idea.

3. **Write the essay.**

   ❑ Begin the essay by revising your topic sentence idea into a complete sentence.

   ❑ Be clear, concise, and stay focused on the problem that you are asked to address.

   ❑ Show what you know by providing supporting specific examples.

   ❑ Remember you can use bullet points, drawings, etc.

4. **Essay writing reminders.**
   ❏ Identify the specific need for the individual student.
   ❏ Recommend explicit and systematic instructional strategies and student activities.
   ❏ Differentiate instruction to meet the needs of individual learners.
   ❏ Explain your choice of intervention strategies (your rationale).

## Specific Guidelines for RICA Essay Writing

Follow these guidelines in writing your RICA essay responses.

1. **Specificity.**   When you write your essay answer, be as specific as possible while answering the question or tasks given. Your answers will be easier to write if you use specific examples. *Specificity in research and pedagogy will help you provide a clear, concise response.* For example, if you are asked to give the benefits of reading a variety of books aloud to a class, it might be much easier to base your answer on a few specific books or types of books, rather than discussing a variety of books in general.

2. **Demonstrate your knowledge.**   Many questions ask you to identify a problem or need, recommend a strategy or activity, and explain why this strategy would be effective. Be sure to use specific assessments, activities, materials, and key words ("buzzwords") to help illustrate your expertise in the field of reading instruction. Review "Strategies to Plan and Pre-Write Essays" in this chapter for further ideas about planning specific strategies.

3. **Essay answers vary in length.**   Do not write more than you need to write. That is, keep in mind that two of the essays require 75–125 word answers and two require 150–300 word answers. Since the 150–300 word essays have more value than the 75–125 word essays, budget your time accordingly. Spend about 15 minutes on each short essay and about 30 minutes on each longer essay. Remember, if you spend too much time on one question, you might not have time to adequately complete your other essays.

4. **Use your time wisely.**   Do not spend an inordinate amount of time on any individual factor in a question that asks for multiple factors. Your overall score will be based on your ability to answer all parts of the question, not simply one part.

5. **Constructed responses are *not* formal essays.**   Remember, your responses are not formal three-, four-, or five-paragraph essays. You are trying to show the readers that you know the content specifications and can apply your knowledge and practice in a classroom. The RICA is not a test of your writing ability; rather, it is a test of your knowledge and practice of reading instruction. You may show steps and use bullet points, drawings, and so on. Unless specifically asked, do not write a conclusion or summary for any question. The question format does not normally require this type of response.

## Strategies to Plan and Pre-Write Essays

The RICA test is comprised of standards from a comprehensive and balanced language arts program (California English-Language Arts Standards). According to these standards, curriculum and instruction are *differentiated* according to the assessed needs of students. Based upon these standards, it is helpful to keep the following questions in mind as reference points before you plan and write your essay responses.

1. Based on individualized assessments, what is the best intervention strategy for this particular individual student?

2. How can I use data to differentiate instruction to meet the needs of individual learners?

3. Ask yourself—Am I incorporating my knowledge of explicit and systematic instructional strategies in my essay answers? Note that it is helpful to develop a list of at least *three strategies* for reading instruction in the following areas:

   Phonemic awareness

   Phonics

Decoding

Word-attack skills

Spelling

Vocabulary

Fluency

Comprehension skills

Writing skills

Listening and speaking skills

If you can develop a list of instructional strategies *before* the exam, you will be well-prepared on the day of the exam to describe intervention strategies based upon your planned responses. Some test-takers find it helpful to make flash cards listing each of the instructional areas above on one side of the card, and on the opposite side of the card listing at least three instructional strategies (methods) for remediating the problem.

**Now let's take a closer look at examples of Educational Problems and Instructional Tasks.**

# Domain 2

# Word Analysis

---

**Use the following information to complete the given exercise.**

The role of phonemic awareness in beginning reading has been well researched. Phonemic awareness is related to reading achievement. Study the following example of a phonemic awareness task.

---

**Sample Phonemic Awareness Task**

Students listen to a sequence of separately spoken phonemes. They then combine the phonemes to form a word. They then say the word.

Teacher:    What word is /c/-/a/-/t/?

Students:   /c/-/a/-/t/ is cat.

Teacher:    Good. Now try this word—/s/-/oa/-/p/.

Students:   /s/-/oa/-/p/ is soap.

Teacher:    Very good. Let's try one more—/f/-/l/-/igh/-/t/.

Students    /f/-/l/-/igh/-/t/ is flight.

---

<u>Examinee Task</u>

Based on the information given above, write a response in which you:

(1) describe how phonemic awareness is related to beginning reading achievement; (2) identify the phonemic awareness task being taught in the example; and (3) explain why the identified task is essential in developing phonemic awareness.

---

Your essay should be approximately 150–300 words in length.

## The Approach

**Understand the situation given.**

- ❏ First, circle or underline the key words in the information.
- ❏ Note the students' *phonemic awareness skill addressed.*
- ❏ Review the example. *What is the teacher asking of the students? What do the students reply?*
- ❏ Focus on the problem or situation.

**Carefully read and examine the task.**

- ❏ Underline the key words. Your underlining might have looked like this:

  *Based on the information given above, write a response in which you:*

  (1) *describe* how *phonemic awareness* is related to *reading achievement;*

  (2) *identify* the phonemic awareness *task in the example;* and

  (3) *explain* why this *task* is *essential* in the *development* of phonemic awareness.

- ❏ Now focus on the tasks of (1) **describing**, (2) **identifying**, and (3) **explaining**.

**Prewrite—make some notes.**

Your notes might have looked like this:

*P.A. strongly related to reading*

*Stanovich, Adams research*

*Example—oral blending*

*Blend individual phonemes spoken word p/i/g*

*Blend sounds and then identify words*

*Segment sounds*

*Fully manipulate sounds*

*Firm foundation*

**Write the essay.**

## Sample Essay

**Note:** This sample essay is intended to provide the reader with ideas and concepts about the content area response. It may not reflect the actual length of a 150–300 word essay.

Phonemic awareness is strongly related to reading achievement. Keith Stanovich's research shows that phonemic awareness is the core causal factor separating normal from disabled readers. Phonemic awareness, as noted in Marilyn Adams' research, is one of the three predictors of success in early reading. Adams notes that if a student does not attain mastery of phonemic awareness, he or she will probably never be able to read on grade level.

The phonemic awareness task being performed in the example is oral blending. Oral blending is an essential skill in phonemic awareness development. Blending is one of the final areas in phonemic awareness tasks. Students learn to blend individual phonemes into spoken words such as p/i/g. It is essential that students perform this task with mastery. Then they can blend sounds and identify words. When this skill is attained, students then learn to segment the sounds in words rather than blending the sounds. With these skills, putting sounds in words together (blending) and pulling sounds in words apart (segmenting), students are then able to fully manipulate sounds. They have a firm foundation in the auditory skills of phoneme manipulation, and phonemic awareness, an essential element in reading achievement, is mastered.

## Evaluating the Essay

The essay clearly informs the reader that phonemic awareness is directly related to reading achievement. The author then notes two specific researchers who support this statement. Next, the author fulfills the second part of the task with the answer that oral blending is the phonemic awareness task used in the example.

The third part of the examinee tasks asks for a rationale. Why is the identified task essential? The essay clearly explains that oral blending is essential in hearing and identifying sounds put together to form words. Putting sounds together, blending, and identifying words forms the necessary foundation in the alphabetic code for putting sounds and symbols together to identify words and, thus, begin reading.

# Domain 3

# Fluency

---

**Use the following information to complete the given exercise.**

Ms. Grayson has noticed that several of her third-grade students who are having difficulty with reading comprehension are slow readers.

**Examinee Task**

Write a response in which you describe an effective method for Ms. Grayson to help improve the students' comprehension.

---

Your essay should be approximately 75–125 words in length.

## The Approach

**Understand the situation given.**

- ❑ First, circle or underline the key words in the prompt.
- ❑ Note the students' grade—*third grade*. This should indicate that the students are in a grade level at which they should be focusing on comprehension.
- ❑ Also, notice the students' history—*difficulty with comprehension*.
- ❑ Next, focus on the problem or situation—*slow readers*.

**Carefully read and examine the task.**

- ❑ Underline the key words. Your underlining might have looked like this:

  *Ms. Grayson has noticed that several of her <u>third-grade</u> students who are having <u>difficulty with</u> reading <u>comprehension</u> are <u>slow readers</u>.*

  *Write a response in which you <u>describe an effective method</u> for Ms. Grayson to help <u>improve the students' comprehension.</u>*

- ❑ Now focus on the tasks. You need to (1) **identify** that if students are slow readers, they have a problem with fluency that needs to be addressed; (2) **explain** the importance of fluency and its connection to comprehension; and (3) **describe** strategies and/or activities for working on fluency.

Because the writer is asked to describe how he or she will proceed, he or she should describe the process of teaching fluency, which would include assessing, modeling, guided practice, independent practice and application, and monitoring or re-assessment (in this case self-assessment).

**Prewrite—make some notes.**

Your notes might have looked like this:

> *Fluency = building block of comprehension*
> *Assess fluency—one-minute timed reading*
> *Without fluency, comprehension won't be good*
> *Modeling—read aloud at fluent rate*
> > *Listen to taped readings*
> ✓ *Practice—repeated readings*
> > *Readers' Theatre*
> ✓ *partner reading*
> > *reading to others*
> ✓ *choral reading*
> > *tape themselves*
> > *neurological impress*
> > *decodable books*
> > *phrase-cued reading*
> > *familiar material*
> > *make it sound like talking*
> > *read the punctuation*
> *Evaluation—self-assessment/reassessment—one-minute timed readings*
> > *graphing the results for motivation*

The writer has used the pre-writing technique of brainstorming to help form possible ideas about different methods of teaching fluency. Because this is a short essay, 75–125 words, notice that the writer has placed check marks next to only a few the ideas. It is not necessary, or relevant, to include all of the ideas in the essay response, nor is it likely that the writer will have time to do so.

**Write the essay.**

## Sample Essay

Fluency is a building block of comprehension competency. Ms. Grayson must begin with assessing whether the fluency rates are affecting students' comprehension abilities. This can be done by calculating the students' reading rate on a one-minute timed oral reading assignment to see how many words are correctly read.

If students are reading slowly, they may be spending too much time decoding words, which would affect their ability to comprehend. The teacher should consider increasing fluency instruction before concentrating on comprehension. She should model fluent reading by reading aloud, by using tape-assisted reading, and by having students listen to a fluent reader while reading along silently.

Fluency instruction can include repeated readings using choral and partner reading. Ongoing progress can be self-monitored by reading silently for one minute, counting the number of words read, and graphing the number on paper.

## Evaluating the Essay

This essay fulfills the assignment by identifying that the issue to be addressed is fluency. It correctly explains why a good fluency rate needs to be in place before comprehension can be addressed.

It follows a logical sequence of first calculating the students' rate of words correct per minute. Next, it describes how this particular skill—fluency—can be modeled. Then, it gives two strategies for practicing fluency. It ends by explaining how the students can evaluate their own progress.

There are many ways to increase fluency. Because this is a short essay, the writer selected just two: repeated readings and Readers' Theatre. Some other methods of working on fluency are:

- reading to someone else
- listening to themselves reading fluently and nonfluently and comparing the two
- reading familiar material
- reading material at their independent reading level
- reading phrase-cued material
- reading songs or poems with a rhythm
- instructing directly by asking students to make what they're reading sound like talking, or reading the punctuation
- reading widely
- offering support during reading, such as neurological impress

# Domain 4

# Vocabulary, Academic Language, and Background Knowledge

**Use the following information to complete the given exercise.**

Mr. North has been teaching vocabulary to his fifth-grade students by having them look up the words in a dictionary and copy the definitions. He noticed that although the students do well on the weekly vocabulary tests, after a week the students no longer remember what the words mean.

**Examinee Task**

Describe effective strategies the teacher might use to enhance the students' ability to learn the meanings of vocabulary words.

Your essay should be approximately 75–125 words in length.

## The Approach

**Understand the situation given.**

- ❑ First, circle or underline the key words in the prompt.
- ❑ Note the students' grade—*fifth grade.*
- ❑ Also, notice the students' history—*teacher teaches vocabulary by having students look up words in the dictionary and copying definitions.*
- ❑ Next, focus on the problem or situation—*students don't remember vocabulary words long-term after learning them for a vocabulary test.*

**Carefully read and examine the task.**

- ❑ Underline the key words. Your underlining might have looked like this:

  *Mr. North has been teaching <u>vocabulary</u> to his <u>fifth-grade</u> students by having them <u>look up the words in the dictionary</u> and <u>copying the definitions</u>. He noticed that although the students do well on the weekly vocabulary tests, after a week the students <u>no longer remember what the words mean</u>.*

  *<u>Describe effective strategies</u> the teacher might use to <u>enhance the students' ability to learn the meanings of vocabulary words.</u>*

- ❑ Now focus on the tasks. You need to (1) **identify** the problem of trying to teach vocabulary by merely having students look up and copying the definitions; (2) **explain** why is this an ineffective method for teaching vocabulary; and (3) **describe** effective strategies and/or activities for teaching vocabulary.

❑ Address all concepts of the prompt in your response—in this prompt the writer has to 1) understand and describe how vocabulary is learned and remembered; (2) understand and describe what is wrong with the teacher's current teaching methods; (3) describe effective methods for teaching vocabulary; and (4) understand and describe why these strategies will lead to better progress in learning vocabulary.

**Prewrite—make some notes.**

Your notes might have looked like this:

> *Looking up words in the dictionary and copying the definitions ≠ learning. It is memorization*
> *Vocabulary learning = deep structure*
> *Direct instruction*
> ✓ *Morphology*
>     *Affixes*
>     *Roots*
>     *Base words*
>         ✓ *Combining stems*
>         ✓ *Etymology*
>     *Greek*
> ✓ *Latin*
>     *Anglo Saxon*
> ✓ *Graphic organizers*
> ✓ *Webs*
> ✓ *Matrix*
> ✓ *Frayer model*
>     *Word squares*
>     *Semantic map*
>     *Cognates*
>     *Synonyms, antonyms*
> ✓ *Context*
>     *Degree line*
>     *Word study*
>         *Word bank*
>         *Word sorts*
>     *Word games*
>         *Jeopardy*
>     *Wide reading*

The writer has used a brainstorming technique to create a list of all of the different methods of teaching vocabulary that he/she knows. Because this is a short essay, 75–125 words, he or she has selected only some of the methods to discuss in the essay. Notice that there is a check mark next to those he or she considers important to include in the essay response.

**Write the essay.**

## Sample Essay

Students will often memorize vocabulary word definitions for tests, but neglect to learn the deep structures of word meanings. Since our brain structures seek patterns for learning, vocabulary should be taught in a manner that enables students to form connections.

Fifth graders should learn words through morphology—learning meanings of roots, base words, stems, and affixes—and then combine them to form many related words with the same word parts. It is helpful to use a semantic web for this process. Students can start with known words and then add new words. Morphology can also include word origins (i.e., Latin). Other strategies can include:

- Using graphic organizers (i.e., Frayer Model and word-meaning matrices) to make connections.
- Practice seeing and using words in context. Seeing a word in many contexts will build a schema of that word in the brain.

## Evaluating the Essay

This essay fulfills the assignment because it begins by explaining what is ineffective about Mr. North's methods. It then correctly gives grade-appropriate methods for teaching vocabulary and explains why those methods are effective and what needs to be in place for deep learning to occur.

The writer listed three methods for learning vocabulary: morphology, graphic organizers, and practice in context. She gave specific examples, which is one of the requirements of the rubric. Examples of morphemes given were roots, base words, stems, and affixes. An example of a word origin is Latin. Examples of graphic organizers are Frayer Model, matrix, and semantic web.

Because this is a short essay, the writer chose some vocabulary methods from a list of many. Some other methods for teaching vocabulary are cognates for English Learners, synonyms and antonyms, word sorts, and meaning degree line.

# Domain 5

# Comprehension

---

**Use the following information to complete the given exercise.**

Understanding what we read or reading comprehension is the reason for reading. It is not enough to first read the words; we must understand the meaning. Therefore, capable seventh-grade readers, as they read, are both purposeful and active readers. They are purposeful for a number of reasons, depending on the content of the text. Good readers are engaged in actively thinking about what they read. They use their prior knowledge and reading comprehension strategies to make sense of text.

**Comprehension Strategy Examples**

1.  The reader thinks to herself:

    "I don't understand that paragraph."

    "I don't get what the author means."

    "Oh, yes, the author means that . . ."

    "The author talked about the characters in the previous chapter. I think I will reread that chapter to understand the character better."

---

2. The reader is reading a chapter comparing mammals and reptiles. To help himself understand the likenesses and differences he might create a visual such as this:

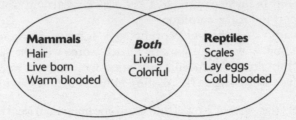

<u>Examinee Task</u>

Based on the information given and using your knowledge of reading comprehension, write a response in which you (1) identify each comprehension strategy in the example; (2) describe the strategy; and (3) clearly state how the strategy helps the reader in comprehension or understanding.

Your essay should be approximately 150–300 words in length.

## The Approach

**Understand the situation given.**

- ❑ First, circle or underline the key words in the information.
- ❑ Note the grade level—*seventh grade*.
- ❑ Note each *comprehension strategy in the example*.
- ❑ Also, identify *each comprehension strategy*.
- ❑ Next, focus on the problem: *Explain how each strategy helps the reader to comprehend*.

**Carefully read and examine the task**.

- ❑ Underline the key words. Your underlining might have looked like this:

    *Based on the information given and using your knowledge of reading comprehension, write a response in which you (1) <u>identify each comprehension strategy</u> in the example; (2) <u>describe</u> the <u>strategy</u>; and (3) clearly <u>explain how the strategy helps</u> the reader in <u>comprehension</u> or understanding.*

- ❑ Now focus on the tasks of (1) **identifying**; (2) **describing**; and (3) **explaining.**

**Prewrite—make some notes.**

Your notes might have looked like this:

*#1 comprehension monitoring*
*aware of understanding*
*use fix-up strategies*
*reader questions, adjusts*
*problem solves*

*strategy helps understanding*
*aware of what they understand*
*identify what they don't get*

*#2 graphic organizer*
*visuals, illustrate concepts and relationships*
*list types of organizers*
*help students see how ideas are related*
*help students remember and focus*
*tools for understanding text, summarizing*

## Sample Essay

**Note:** This sample essay is intended to provide the reader with ideas and concepts about the content area responses. It may not reflect the actual length of a 150–300 word essay.

The first example is comprehension monitoring. It involves the reader being aware of her understanding of the text and using specific fix-up strategies when needed. Comprehension monitoring is a form of thinking about one's thinking or metacognition. The reader questions, adjusts, modifies, and clarifies as she is reading to "get" (comprehend) the meaning in the text.

This strategy helps readers in understanding or comprehension because they are consistently aware of what they do understand. In addition, they can identify what they do not get or understand, and they are able to use fix-up strategies to solve problems in understanding. Fix-up strategies appropriate for the example are identifying that there is a difficulty, identifying what the difficulty is, restating what the author means, and re-reading for meaning.

The second example uses a graphic organizer. Graphic organizers are visuals that illustrate concepts and relationships among concepts in a text. There are many types of graphic organizers such as: semantic maps, webs, charts, graphs, and the type used in the example: Venn diagrams. Graphic organizers help students to organize ideas and concepts and to see how ideas are interrelated. They also help the reader to remember the information. Graphic organizers provide visual tools for students to use in understanding and representing text. In addition, they help students in "putting it all together," understanding, and summarizing text.

## Evaluating the Essay

The essay fulfills the task by addressing each comprehension strategy in the example separately. First, the comprehension strategy is identified or named. Next, the author tells what it is or describes the strategy. The descriptions are very clear—almost definitions. The explanations with the descriptions tell the reader that the author understands the strategy in depth. After the description, the author explains how this strategy helps the reader to understand or gain meaning from the text. It is important that the author demonstrates knowledge of how each strategy assists students in understanding. They are tools. How does each help? In comprehension monitoring, the key ideas of "I get it, don't get it, or I know how to solve the problem" are addressed. The author carefully discusses how graphic organizers assist the reader in seeing relationships and summarizing.

# Extra Practice

## Domain 2

### Practice Essay Topic 1

> **Use the following information to complete the given exercise.**
>
> A kindergarten student writes, "I luv my kitee" underneath his drawing of child and a pet.
>
> **Examinee Task**
>
> Write a response in which you explain what this tells the teacher about the student's understanding of print and his readiness to read. Explain how the teacher should follow up.

Your essay should be approximately 150–300 words in length.

**You may use the space below to make notes. The notes will not be scored. Use two sheets of college-ruled paper to write your practice essay.**

# RICA Practice Essay Evaluation Form

**Use this checklist to evaluate your essay:**

1. To what extent does this response reflect an **understanding of the relevant content** and academic knowledge from the applicable RICA domain?

| **thorough** | **adequate** | **limited or no** |
| understanding | understanding | understanding |

2. To what extent does this response **fulfill the purpose of the assignment?**

| **completely** | **adequately** | **partially** |
| fulfills | fulfills | fulfills or fails to |

3. To what extent does this essay **respond to the given task(s)?**

| **fully** | **adequately** | **limited or inadequately** |
| responds | responds | responds |

4. How **accurate** is the response?

| **very** | **generally** | **inaccurate** |
| accurate | accurate | |

5. Does the response **demonstrate an effective application** of the relevant content and academic knowledge from the applicable RICA domain?

| **yes** | **reasonably** | **no** |
| effective | effective | ineffective and inaccurate |

6. To what extent does the response **provide supporting examples, evidence, and rationale** based on the relevant content and academic knowledge from the applicable RICA domain?

| **strong** | **adequate** | **limited or no** |
| support | support | support |

## Important Points

Some of the points your essay could have covered for Practice Topic 1 (Domain 2) were as follows:

- ❑ The student is connecting print to meaning and is progressing through the stages of writing development.
- ❑ Writing and reading are closely connected, and the student's ability to connect his print to his picture most likely predicts his readiness for reading. It is important that the teacher asks him to read his story to her and that she praises him.
- ❑ Often, this situation presents a teachable moment for writing and spelling instruction.
- ❑ The teacher needs to give numerous opportunities for meaningful writing experiences for her students (that is, writing on self-selected topics, practicing invented/temporary spelling, and reading story aloud to audience).
- ❑ The student is an emergent reader, and appears to be a beginning reader.
- ❑ The teacher should provide further assessment to determine the student's independent reading level and then provide books for the student to read on that level.

# Domain 2

## Practice Essay Topic 2

**Use the following information to complete the given exercise.**

A fifth-grade teacher uses an essay assignment to survey student writing and spelling ability. In reading the essays he can see that more than half of his class seems to be having difficulty with spelling.

**Examinee Task**

Write a response that describes some steps the teacher should take to assist his students as a result of the data from this assessment.

Your essay should be approximately 150–300 words in length.

**You may use the space below to make notes. The notes will not be scored. Use two sheets of college-ruled paper to write your practice essay.**

# RICA Practice Essay Evaluation Form

**Use this checklist to evaluate your essay:**

1. To what extent does this response reflect an **understanding of the relevant content** and academic knowledge from the applicable RICA domain?

| **thorough** | **adequate** | **limited or no** |
|---|---|---|
| understanding | understanding | understanding |

2. To what extent does this response **fulfill the purpose of the assignment?**

| **completely** | **adequately** | **partially** |
|---|---|---|
| fulfills | fulfills | fulfills or fails to |

3. To what extent does this essay **respond to the given task(s)?**

| **fully** | **adequately** | **limited or inadequately** |
|---|---|---|
| responds | responds | responds |

4. How **accurate** is the response?

| **very** | **generally** | **inaccurate** |
|---|---|---|
| accurate | accurate | |

5. Does the response **demonstrate an effective application** of the relevant content and academic knowledge from the applicable RICA domain?

| **yes** | **reasonably** | **no** |
|---|---|---|
| effective | effective | ineffective and inaccurate |

6. To what extent does the response **provide supporting examples, evidence, and rationale** based on the relevant content and academic knowledge from the applicable RICA domain?

| **strong** | **adequate** | **limited or no** |
|---|---|---|
| support | support | support |

## Important Points

Some of the steps your essay could have described for Practice Topic 2 (Domain 2) were as follows:

1. Forming flexible skills groups for universal access.
2. Use a developmental model to assess students' spelling level. *The Synchrony of Reading, Writing, and Spelling Development* by Bear is an excellent tool to pinpoint spelling levels as linked with reading and writing levels.
3. Use informal, diagnostic teaching tools such as Bear's *Qualitative Spelling Checklist*, collect spelling samples, and analyze for the stages of spelling development. Hendersen (1974) noted the following stages of spelling development.
   - Pre-Literate
   - Early Letter Name
   - Middle and Late Letter Name
   - Within Word Pattern
   - Syllable Juncture
   - Derivational Constancy
4. Plan instruction and monitor growth. Questions to ask in monitoring include what does the student know? Use but confuse? What developmental stage? Where in the stage (beginning/middle/end)?
5. Plan direct instruction lessons in spelling patterns, root words, and common word endings.

# Domain 2

## Practice Essay Topic 3

---

**Use the following information to complete the given exercise.**

An eighth-grade English teacher is concerned that the students entering her class do not possess strong enough spelling/reading skills, so she gives her students the "Upper Level Qualitative Spelling Inventory" at the beginning of each school year.

**Examinee Task**

Using your knowledge of reading, write a response in which you explain some instructional strategies the teacher could use to further spelling and reading development.

---

Your essay should be approximately 150–300 words in length.

**You may use the space below to make notes. The notes will not be scored. Use two sheets of college-ruled paper to write your practice essay.**

# RICA Practice Essay Evaluation Form

**Use this checklist to evaluate your essay:**

1. To what extent does this response **reflect an understanding of the relevant content** and academic knowledge from the applicable RICA domain?

   | **thorough** | **adequate** | **limited or no** |
   |---|---|---|
   | understanding | understanding | understanding |

2. To what extent does this response **fulfill the purpose of the assignment?**

   | **completely** | **adequately** | **partially** |
   |---|---|---|
   | fulfills | fulfills | fulfills or fails to |

3. To what extent does this essay **respond to the given task(s)?**

   | **fully** | **adequately** | **limited or inadequately** |
   |---|---|---|
   | responds | responds | responds |

4. How **accurate** is the response?

   | **very** | **generally** | **inaccurate** |
   |---|---|---|
   | accurate | accurate | |

5. Does the response **demonstrate an effective application** of the relevant content and academic knowledge from the applicable RICA domain?

   | **yes** | **reasonably** | **no** |
   |---|---|---|
   | effective | effective | ineffective and inaccurate |

6. To what extent does the response **provide supporting examples, evidence, and rationale** based on the relevant content and academic knowledge from the applicable RICA domain?

   | **strong** | **adequate** | **limited or no** |
   |---|---|---|
   | support | support | support |

## Important Points

Some of the points your essay could have covered for Practice Topic 3 (Domain 2) were as follows:

❑ Assessing students at the beginning of the school year provides data for the teacher to begin planning and targeting instruction for the students.

❑ There is a strong relationship between students' orthographic knowledge and reading achievement. When students have strong orthographic knowledge, their reading is easier and more fluent.

❑ Using the Error Guide for the Inventory, the teacher can identify the student's spelling level. Direction can then be planned, which is specific to the student's need.

❑ We know from Adams' research that success in one component of the reading process predicts success in the other components. The teacher can use assessment, instruction, and practice to help students to achieve success in spelling. This should, in turn, assist in students' attaining further success in reading.

❑ Instructional strategies such as webbing, word clusters, and graphic organizers may be used with flexible skill groups to provide practice, help students make connections, and, thus, build spelling ability.

# Domain 4

## Practice Essay Topic 4

---

**Use the following information to complete the given exercise.**

Vocabulary knowledge is integral to the development of word recognition and fluency.

**<u>Examinee Task</u>**

Using your knowledge of reading, discuss the important issues related to the development of vocabulary.

---

Your essay should be approximately 75–125 words in length.

**You may use the space below to make notes. The notes will not be scored. Use two sheets of college-ruled paper to write your practice essay.**

# RICA Practice Essay Evaluation Form

**Use this checklist to evaluate your essay:**

1. To what extent does this response reflect an **understanding of the relevant content** and academic knowledge from the applicable RICA domain?

   | **thorough** | **adequate** | **limited or no** |
   |---|---|---|
   | understanding | understanding | understanding |

2. To what extent does this response **fulfill the purpose of the assignment?**

   | **completely** | **adequately** | **partially** |
   |---|---|---|
   | fulfills | fulfills | fulfills or fails to |

3. To what extent does this essay **respond to the given task(s)?**

   | **fully** | **adequately** | **limited or inadequately** |
   |---|---|---|
   | responds | responds | responds |

4. How **accurate** is the response?

   | **very** | **generally** | **inaccurate** |
   |---|---|---|
   | accurate | accurate | |

5. Does the response **demonstrate an effective application** of the relevant content and academic knowledge from the applicable RICA domain?

   | **yes** | **reasonably** | **no** |
   |---|---|---|
   | effective | effective | ineffective and inaccurate |

6. To what extent does the response **provide supporting examples, evidence, and rationale** based on the relevant content and academic knowledge from the applicable RICA domain?

   | **strong** | **adequate** | **limited or no** |
   |---|---|---|
   | support | support | support |

## Important Points

Some of the points your essay could have covered for Practice Topic 4 (Domain 4) were as follows:

❑ Early vocabulary development (prekindergarten to second grade) is critical in students' later achievement in vocabulary and reading.

❑ The gap addressed in the Matthew Effect has a strong impact on students' growth in vocabulary.

❑ Vocabulary knowledge and concept development are interrelated. Vocabulary acquisition involves concept learning.

❑ Vocabulary learning is incremental. Therefore, the more examples in context that are understood by students, the greater will be their depth of understanding and vocabulary development.

❑ In vocabulary instruction it is important to use strategies that promote knowledge of a larger set of words than the target words.

❑ Recognize the critical role of independent reading in the development of vocabulary.

❑ Recognize the different tiers of general academic vocabulary.

❑ Know that an effective, explicit vocabulary program includes direct teaching of specific words, development of word learning strategies, promoting word consciousness, and promoting wide reading.

# Domain 5

## Practice Essay Topic 5

---

**Use the following information to complete the given exercise.**

A second-grade teacher is concerned about his students' understanding and appreciation of literature. He decides to select a different story each day to read to his class. The teacher also considers rereading some of the stories.

**<u>Examinee Task</u>**

Using your knowledge of reading, write a response in which you (1) discuss the benefits of reading a new story each day and (2) explain the benefits of rereading a story.

---

Your essay should be approximately 150–300 words in length.

**You may use the space below to make notes. The notes will not be scored. Use two sheets of college-ruled paper to write your practice essay.**

# RICA Practice Essay Evaluation Form

**Use this checklist to evaluate your essay:**

1. To what extent does this response reflect an **understanding of the relevant content** and academic knowledge from the applicable RICA domain?

   | **thorough** | **adequate** | **limited or no** |
   | --- | --- | --- |
   | understanding | understanding | understanding |

2. To what extent does this response **fulfill the purpose of the assignment?**

   | **completely** | **adequately** | **partially** |
   | --- | --- | --- |
   | fulfills | fulfills | fulfills or fails to |

3. To what extent does this essay **respond to the given task(s)?**

   | **fully** | **adequately** | **limited or inadequately** |
   | --- | --- | --- |
   | responds | responds | responds |

4. How **accurate** is the response?

   | **very** | **generally** | **inaccurate** |
   | --- | --- | --- |
   | accurate | accurate | |

5. Does the response **demonstrate an effective application** of the relevant content and academic knowledge from the applicable RICA domain?

   | **yes** | **reasonably** | **no** |
   | --- | --- | --- |
   | effective | effective | ineffective and inaccurate |

6. To what extent does the response **provide supporting examples, evidence, and rationale** based on the relevant content and academic knowledge from the applicable RICA domain?

   | **strong** | **adequate** | **limited or no** |
   | --- | --- | --- |
   | support | support | support |

## Important Points

Some of the points your essay could have covered for Practice Topic 5 (Domain 5) were as follows:

- ❑ Increases exposure to good literature.
- ❑ Promotes story enjoyment and literature appreciation.
- ❑ Good for noting what the author does in the writing process so students may make similar choices for themselves.
- ❑ There are good reasons to reread a familiar story. Rereading is often used in shared reading, when the teacher is using the text to teach concepts.
- ❑ Rereading enhances student understanding of prosody, vocabulary development, and the love of reading.

# Domain 5

## Practice Essay Topic 6

**Use the following information to complete the given exercise.**

Each week a second-grade teacher reads a different story aloud to her class. Before she gets to the end of the story, she asks students to tell her how they think the story will end.

**Examinee Task**

Using your knowledge of reading, write a response in which you (1) identify some of the benefits of her technique and (2) explain how this technique works.

Your essay should be approximately 150–300 words in length.

**You may use the space below to make notes. The notes will not be scored. Use two sheets of college-ruled paper to write your practice essay.**

# RICA Practice Essay Evaluation Form

**Use this checklist to evaluate your essay:**

1. To what extent does this response reflect an **understanding of the relevant content** and academic knowledge from the applicable RICA domain?

   | **thorough** | **adequate** | **limited or no** |
   |---|---|---|
   | understanding | understanding | understanding |

2. To what extent does this response **fulfill the purpose of the assignment?**

   | **completely** | **adequately** | **partially** |
   |---|---|---|
   | fulfills | fulfills | fulfills or fails to |

3. To what extent does this essay **respond to the given task(s)?**

   | **fully** | **adequately** | **limited or inadequately** |
   |---|---|---|
   | responds | responds | responds |

4. How **accurate** is the response?

   | **very** | **generally** | **inaccurate** |
   |---|---|---|
   | accurate | accurate | |

5. Does the response **demonstrate an effective application** of the relevant content and academic knowledge from the applicable RICA domain?

   | **yes** | **reasonably** | **no** |
   |---|---|---|
   | effective | effective | ineffective and inaccurate |

6. To what extent does the response **provide supporting examples, evidence, and rationale** based on the relevant content and academic knowledge from the applicable RICA domain?

   | **strong** | **adequate** | **limited or no** |
   |---|---|---|
   | support | support | support |

## Important Points

Some of the points your essay could have covered for Practice Topic 6 (Domain 5) were as follows:

- ❑ The teacher is utilizing **prediction** questions, among the best kind of open-ended questions.
- ❑ Readers describe what they think will happen in a story or predict an ending before they read it.
- ❑ They confirm, adjust, or disprove their predictions.
- ❑ Children use prior knowledge, past experiences, and what they see in the pictures.
- ❑ Older children use these factors in addition to what they already know about authors and literature.
- ❑ Prediction questions work equally well with nonfiction and sometimes stimulate children's interest in a topic.
- ❑ The higher order thinking skill prediction is similar to forming a hypothesis, and students must analyze data and make a reasonable prediction.
- ❑ The teacher is having the class practice a comprehension strategy as a group. This will provide a firm foundation for the students to independently use the strategy.
- ❑ Prediction is a comprehension strategy that can be used in other content areas such as science and social studies.

# Introduction to the Case Study

## Based on Student Profile

The case study portion of the RICA is designed to measure your ability to evaluate and assess an individual student's reading performance (grades K through 8), while suggesting reading intervention strategies, and providing an explanation as to why these intervention strategies might be effective. Examinees will be given six to eight pages of a substantial body of evidence and information about a student including:

- background information
- samples and assessments of reading performances
- worksheets
- teacher and parent comments and evaluations

You will be given four pages and asked to write an essay of approximately 300–600 words to

- assess the reading performance.
- prescribe instructional strategies and/or activities.
- explain "why" strategies would be effective.

Each case-study essay is scored on a 1–4 scoring scale by two readers, so the actual combined scores range from 2 to 8. Since the case study is weighted by a factor of three (score is multiplied by 3), the estimated total points possible for the case study are 24. Although the case study section can be time-consuming, you can earn a lot of points, so make sure to leave **at least 1 hour** to read the information and to write the essay.

## Understanding the Scoring

Now let's take a careful look at the scoring system.

### Case Study Scoring Guide

## Score 4

**You will receive a score of 4 if your response**

- reflects a thorough understanding of the relevant content and academic knowledge from the applicable RICA domains.
- responds fully to the given task(s).
- differentiates the specific need for individual learners.
- describes explicit and systematic instruction strategies.
- provides strong supporting examples, evidence, and rationale based on the relevant content and academic knowledge from the applicable RICA domains.

## Score 3

**You will receive a score of 3 if your response**

- reflects an adequate understanding of the relevant content and academic knowledge from the applicable RICA domains.

❑ identifies general reading development instrumental strategies.

❑ responds adequately to the given task(s).

❑ is generally accurate about explicit instructional activities.

❑ demonstrates a reasonably effective application of how strategies promote reading development.

❑ provides adequate supporting examples, evidence, and rationale based on the relevant content and academic knowledge from the applicable RICA domains.

# Score 2

**You will receive a score of 2 if your response**

❑ reflects a limited understanding of the relevant content and academic knowledge from the applicable RICA domains.

❑ fulfills the purpose of the assignment only partially, and fails to identify differential instruction.

❑ responds in a limited way to the given task(s).

❑ is partially accurate, but may contain significant inaccuracies in promoting reading development.

❑ demonstrates a limited or generally ineffective application of the relevant content and academic knowledge in explicit and systematic instruction.

❑ provides limited supporting examples, evidence, and rationale based on the relevant content and academic knowledge from the applicable RICA domains.

# Score 1

**You will receive a score of 1 if your response**

❑ reflects little or no understanding of the relevant content and academic knowledge from the applicable RICA domains.

❑ fails to fulfill the purpose of the assignment.

❑ responds inadequately to the given task(s).

❑ is inaccurate.

❑ demonstrates an ineffective application of the relevant content and academic knowledge from the applicable RICA domains.

❑ provides little or no supporting examples, evidence, and rationale based on the relevant content and academic knowledge from the applicable RICA domains.

# U

**Your response will receive a score of U for "unscorable" if it is**

❑ off task.

❑ unrelated to the assigned topic.

❑ illegible.

❑ not of sufficient length to score.

❑ written in a language other than English.

# B

**The response will receive a score of B if it is blank.**

# How to Respond to a Case Study

## Some General Strategies

The following steps will get you started. Keep in mind that the strategies presented in the Essay Writing section starting on page 10 will also help you in planning and developing your case study response.

1. Read and mark the tasks given. That is, circle or underline what you are being asked to do. Remember, typically you will be asked to identify strengths and/or weaknesses, to describe or recommend a strategy and/or activity, and to explain how this strategy/activity will be effective.

2. Quickly jot down, in the area provided in the test booklet, pertinent facts and information needed to answer the question. You can make a list of individual words or jot down phrases. Do not attempt to make a complete formal outline of your answer. Time constraints limit the effectiveness of detailed formal outlines.

## Some General Guidelines for Writing

Follow these guidelines in writing your case-study essay.

❑ Write in a clear, concise style.

❑ Identify the strengths, weaknesses, or needs; recommend a strategy or activity; and explain why this strategy would be effective.

❑ Answer all of the tasks given. It's easy to skip a part under the time pressure—for example, identifying three weaknesses, describing activities, but forgetting to explain why they will be effective.

❑ Refer back to the tasks to make sure that your answer is focused. Marking the tasks will help in maintaining your focus.

❑ Your use of specific assessments, activities, materials, and key words ("buzzwords") that are used in the field will often help demonstrate your knowledge of a subject.

## Some Points for Checking Your Essay

Keep the following points in mind.

❑ Keep track of your time. Pace yourself. Allow time to briefly scan your essay to make sure that you've answered the given tasks.

❑ Watch out for major errors in focus. Don't be overly concerned with minor spelling or grammar errors.

❑ Complete the case-study essay in the proper booklet.

## The Approach

Plan to spend 1 hour working on the case study—analyzing and writing.

## The Analysis

1. Divide the area provided for scratch work into three columns. Label one column **"strengths,"** one column **"weaknesses,"** and one column **"instructional strategies and activities."**

2. Read each piece of data in the case study. While reading each document, when you notice a strength, write it in the strength column. When you see a weakness, write it in the weakness column. If you see the same strength or weakness in other documents as you read, put a check mark next to where you wrote it on your notes page.

3. After reviewing all the data given to you in the case study, look at your notes page for the strengths and weaknesses that appear the most. Those should be the ones to focus on in your write up of the case study. You should also focus on skills that are more elementary or basic before you focus on skills that are more advanced. For example, if a student has trouble with short vowel sounds in single-syllable words and suffixes in multi-syllabic words, you should recommend working on the short vowels before working on multi-syllabic words. Put a star or check mark next to the strengths and weaknesses on which you will focus.

4. Next to the strengths you will be building on and the weaknesses you will be remediating, list in the last column specific strategies and activities for the strengths and weaknesses you identified.

| *strengths* | *weaknesses* | *instructional strategies and activities* |
| --- | --- | --- |
| | | |

## The Writing

1. When you write your analysis of the case study, first describe the student's strengths and cite the piece or pieces of data from the case study that led you to the conclusion that those were strengths.

2. Next, do the same for the weaknesses: Explain what the weaknesses are and cite the specific data showing that they were weaknesses.

3. Finally, write your recommendations for instructional strategies and activities to meet the student's strengths and needs (weaknesses). Describe what each strategy and/or activity is and how it works. Give your rationale for why you selected that specific strategy or activity for this individual student. You want to answer the questions, "What would you do about it?" and "How would you do it?"

**Important Note:** The more specific you can be, the higher you will score. If you can include names of specific programs or assessments that address the student's strengths or weaknesses, you should do so. It is also helpful to include names of specific researchers, types of materials, or titles of books to use in your examples. If you are not sure that a specific program or assessment actually addresses the specific need, then don't mention it. In that case it is better to be more general than to risk being inaccurate.

# A Sample Case Study

## Case Study 1: Danny

This case study focuses on a student named Danny, who is in the seventh grade. The documents on the following pages describe Danny's performance during the middle of the school year. Using these materials, write a response in which you apply your knowledge of language arts assessment and instruction to analyze this case study. Your response should include three parts:

1. identify three of Danny's important reading strengths and/or needs at this point in the school year, citing evidence from the documents to support your observations;

2. describe two specific instructional strategies and/or activities designed to enhance Danny's literacy development by addressing the needs and/or building on the strengths you identified; and

3. explain how each strategy/activity you describe would promote Danny's reading proficiency.

Your response should be approximately 300–600 words in length.

**You may use the space below to make notes. These notes will not be scored.**

## Word Recognition Assessment

Danny's reading teacher gave him a test to measure the recognition of words out of context. The test consists of graded word lists to get an idea of what grade level further testing should be done. Mispronunciations are written down next to the word. The teacher noted that Danny read the words slowly, sounding them out. The results of this assessment are on the following page.

# San Diego Quick Assessment - Record Form

Name __Danny__          Grade __7__          Date __Feb. 4__

Directions: Begin with a list that is at least two or three sets below the student's grade level. Have the student read each word aloud in that list. Continue until the student makes three or more errors in a list.

Reading Levels: One error, independent level; two errors, instructional level; three errors, frustration level. When testing is completed, record the highest grade level in each of these categories in the spaces below.

Independent __3__          Instructional __3__          Frustration __4__

*sound out words*

| Preprimer | Primer | Grade 1 | Grade 2 | Grade 3 |
|---|---|---|---|---|
| see | you | road | our | city |
| play | come *can* | live | please | middle |
| me | not | thank | myself | moment |
| at | with | when | town | frightened |
| run | jump | bigger | earl | exclaimed |
| go | help | how | send | several |
| and | is | always | wide | lonely |
| look | work | night | believe | drew |
| can | are | spring | quietly | since |
| here | this | today | carefully | straight *start* |

| Grade 4 | Grade 5 | Grade 6 | Grade 7 |
|---|---|---|---|
| decided *decide* | scanty | bridge | amber |
| served *serve* | business | commercial | dominion |
| amazed | develop | abolish | sundry |
| silent | considered *consider* | trucker | capillary |
| wrecked *wreck* | discussed *discuss* | apparatus | impetuous |
| improved | behaved *behave* | elementary | blight |
| certainly *certain* | splendid | comment | wrest |
| entered *enter* | acquainted *account* | necessity | enumerate |
| realized | escaped | gallery | daunted |
| intercepted *interpt* | grim | relatively | condescend |

| Grade 8 | Grade 9 | Grade 10 | Grade 11 |
|---|---|---|---|
| capacious | conscientious | zany | galore |
| limitation | isolation | jerkin | rotunda |
| pretext | molecule | nausea | capitalism |
| intrigue | ritual | gratuitous | prevaricate |
| delusion | momentous | linear | visible |
| immaculate | vulnerable | inept | exonerate |
| ascent | kinship | legality | superannvate |
| acrid | conservatism | aspen | luxuriate |
| binocular | jaunty | amnesty | piebald |
| embankment | inventive | barometer | crunch |

## Informal Reading Assessment

Danny's reading teacher gave him an informal assessment of reading performance to assess the rate and accuracy with which a student reads aloud. For this assessment, Danny read aloud short, graded passages, and the teacher made notes about his performance. Following are the results of some of the passages he read. The teacher put a line through words that he misread, writing what he said above the printed word. After reading each passage, Danny was asked to retell what the paragraph was about, and he was able to do so with reasonable accuracy.

## Tool I
## ORAL READING TEST

|  |  | 1st Testing | 2nd Testing | 3rd Testing |
|---|---|---|---|---|

**No.4**

*cowboy*

Three more cowboys tried their best to rope and
tie a calf as quickly *r* as Red, but none of them
came within ten seconds of his time. Then came
the long, thin cowboy. He was the last one to
enter the contest.

| Errors | Level | 1st | 2nd | 3rd |
|---|---|---|---|---|
| 1 (0-2) | (Indep) | X | ☐ | ☐ |
| 3-4 | Instr. | ☐ | ☐ | ☐ |
| 5-6 | Frust. | ☐ | ☐ | ☐ |
| **Speed:** | Fast | ☐ | ☐ | ☐ |
|  | Avg. | ☐ | ☐ | ☐ |
|  | (Slow) | X | ☐ | ☐ |
|  | V. Slow | ☐ | ☐ | ☐ |

**No.5**

*hill*

High in the hills they came to a wide ledge
*sc* *rock r*
where trees grew among the rocks. Grass grew
in patches and the ground was covered with bits
of wood from trees blown over a long time ago
and dried by the sun. Down in the valley it was
already beginning to get dark.

| Errors | Level | 1st | 2nd | 3rd |
|---|---|---|---|---|
| 2 (0-2) | (Indep) | X | ☐ | ☐ |
| 3-4 | Instr. | ☐ | ☐ | ☐ |
| 5-6 | Frust. | ☐ | ☐ | ☐ |
| **Speed:** | Fast | ☐ | ☐ | ☐ |
|  | Avg. | ☐ | ☐ | ☐ |
|  | (Slow) | X | ☐ | ☐ |
|  | V. Slow | ☐ | ☐ | ☐ |

**No.6**

*subropan*

Businessmen from suburban areas may travel to
*helicopter a*
work in helicopters, land on the roof of an office
building, and thus avoid city traffic jams. Families
can spend more time at summer homes and
*cabin r*
mountain cabins through the use of this
*sc*
marvelous craft. People on farms can reach city
*shop*
center quickly for medical service, shopping,
*sales*
entertainment, or sale of products.

| Errors | Level | 1st | 2nd | 3rd |
|---|---|---|---|---|
| 0-2 | Indep. | ☐ | ☐ | ☐ |
| 3-4 | Instr. | ☐ | ☐ | ☐ |
| 6 (5-6) | (Frust) | X | ☐ | ☐ |
| **Speed:** | Fast | ☐ | ☐ | ☐ |
|  | Avg. | ☐ | ☐ | ☐ |
|  | Slow | ☐ | ☐ | ☐ |
|  | V. Slow | X | ☐ | ☐ |

| Errors | Level | 1st | 2nd | 3rd |
|---|---|---|---|---|
| 0-2 | Indep. | ☐ | ☐ | ☐ |
| 3-4 | Instr. | ☐ | ☐ | ☐ |
| 5-6 | Frust. | ☐ | ☐ | ☐ |
| **Speed:** | Fast | ☐ | ☐ | ☐ |
|  | Avg. | ☐ | ☐ | ☐ |
|  | Slow | ☐ | ☐ | ☐ |
|  | V. Slow | ☐ | ☐ | ☐ |

Key   sc = self correct
      r = repeated a word
      ⌢ = repeated a phrase

**65**

## Fluency Assessment

Danny was timed on a fifth-grade level reading passage. He read aloud for 1 minute. The teacher recorded his performance on the following page. She put a line through the words he misread and wrote what he said above the printed words. He read a total of 111 words in 1 minute with 12 errors, so that he read 99 words correctly per minute.

## Grade 5 Probe 3

            **horizone**                        **use**

Where the horizon is hilly and uneven, it can be used as a sun calendar.     15

                       **sc**              **horazone**

A Native American group, the Hopi, use such a horizon calendar.     26

**observe**

Observing from the same place each day, the Hopi take note of where the     40

   **rise**            **impatent**            **impatent**     **a**

sun rises and sets on important days. Each important day has the peak of     54

a hill or notch of a valley named after it—the peak or notch where the     71

   **rise**                   **watch**

sun rises or sets on that day. The sun-watcher looks for the first glimpse     85

                                                    **r**

of the sun in the morning, and the sun's last gleam in the evening. He     100

                 **notch**                   **warn**

numbers the days with notches on a wooden stick, and warns the people     113

when an important day is coming. The time for planting corn or beans,     126

the time for the flute dance, the main harvest, and the winter-solstice     139

ceremony—all are marked on the distant horizon.     147

 Halfway around the world, Russian peasants track the sun in the same     159

way as the Hopi. In the Caucasus Mountains, village chiefs choose an     171

old man to watch for sunset each day. He sits on a bench and watches     186

the sun disappear behind the jagged mountain peaks. Using landmarks     196

on the horizon to keep track of the year is a very old practice used by     212

people everywhere.     214

 This method could be used in early times because it was so simple.     227

Nothing had to be built. All that was needed was a good view of the     241

horizon, with natural landmarks and a place to stand while watching     253

the sunrise and sunset.     257

Key    sc = self correct

        r = repeated a word

     ⌢ = repeated a phrase

## Phonics Test

Danny's reading teacher gave him a phonics assessment in which he read multisyllabic words containing the most common phonograms and spelling patterns. The purpose was to determine which phonics elements he could read, and on which ones he needed to work. The results of the assessment are on the following two pages. When Danny misread a word, the teacher wrote what he said on the line next to it. The page after that contains the scoring matrix for the assessment.

*California Reading & Literature Project: Focusing on Results, Pre K - 3*

## CALIFORNIA READING, PROFESSIONAL DEVELOPMENT INSTITUTE

*California Language Arts Content Standards 1.1, 1.2*

| | |
|---|---|
| *Reading* | |
| CUNNINGHAM NAMES TEST | |
| BEGINNING-OF-YEAR    NAME: **Danny**    DATE: **1-31**    CORRECT: **19** /25 | |

| | | | |
|---|---|---|---|
| 1. Jay Conway | _____ | 14. Wendy Swain | _____ |
| 2. Tim Cornell | ✓ **Carnell** | 15. Glen Spencer | _____ |
| 3. Chuck Hoke | ✓ **Hawk** | 16. Fred Sherwood | _____ |
| 4. Yolanda Clark | _____ | 17. Flo Thornton | ✓ **Trenton** |
| 5. Kimberly Blake | _____ | 18. Dee Skidmore | _____ |
| 6. Roberta Slade | **Robetta Slad** | 19. Grace Brewster | _____ |
| 7. Homer Preston | _____ | 20. Ned Westmoreland | _____ |
| 8. Gus Quincy | _____ | 21. Ron Smitherman | _____ |
| 9. Cindy Sampson | _____ | 22. Troy Whitlock | ✓ **Whitelock** |
| 10. Chester Wright | _____ | 23. Vance Middleton | _____ |
| 11. Ginger Yale | _____ | 24. Zane Anderson | _____ |
| 12. Patrick Tweed | _____ | 25. Bernard Pendergraph | **Bernerd** ✓ |
| 13. Stanley Shaw | _____ | | |

*California Reading & Literature Project: Focusing on Results, Pre K - 3*

## CALIFORNIA READING, PROFESSIONAL DEVELOPMENT INSTITUTE

## SCORING MATRIX FOR THE NAMES TEST          Name: **Danny**          Date: **Feb. 5**

| NAME | CONSONANTS | CONSONANTS BLENDS | CONSONANTS DIGRAPHS | SHORT VOWELS | LONG VOWELS | VOWEL DIAGRAPHS | CONTROLLED VOWELS | SCHWA |
|---|---|---|---|---|---|---|---|---|
| Jay Conway | J, C, w | | | o, on | | | (or) | |
| Tim Cornell | T, C, n | | | i, im, e, ell | | ay | | |
| Chuck Hoke | H | ck | Ch | u, uck | (o)oke | | ar, ark | o, a |
| Yolanda Clark | Y | Cl | | a, and | y, a, ake | | er | o, a |
| Kimberly Blake | K, b, l | Bl | | i, im | (a)ade | | (er)ert | o |
| Roberta Slade | R | Sl | e, est | o, ome | | | er | o |
| Homer Preston | H, n | Pr, st | | u, us, u, i, in | y | | er | |
| Gus Quincey | G, Qu, c | | | i, ind, a, amp | y | | | |
| Cindy Sampson | C, S, n | mp | Ch, Wr | e, est | i, ight | | er | |
| Chester Wright | | | | i, in | a, ale | | er | |
| Ginger Yale | G, Y | | | a, at, i, ick | e, eed | | | |
| Patrick Tweed | P, r | tr, ck, Tw | | a, an | ey | | | |
| Stanley Shaw | | St, Sh | | e, end | ai, ain, y | aw | | |
| Wendy Swain | W, d | Sw | | e, en | | | | |
| Glen Spencer | c | Gl, Sp | | e, ed | | oo, ood | er | |
| Fred Sherwood | W | Fr, Sh | | i, id | o | | er | |
| Flo Thornton | t | Fl, Th | | | ee, o, ore | | (or)orn | o, on |
| Dee Skidmore | D, m | Sk | | e, ed, est, a, and | a, ace | | er, ter | |
| Grace Brewster | | Gr, Br, st | | o, on, i, ith, a, an | o, ore | ew | er | |
| Ned Westmoreland | N, W, m, l | | | (i,it) o, ock | | | er | |
| Ron Smitherman | R | Sm | th | a, ance, i, id, iddle | | | er | |
| Troy Whitlock | l | Tr | Wh | A, And | a, ane | oy | o, on | |
| Vance Middleton | V, M | | | e, end, a, aph | | | er | o, on |
| Zane Anderson | Z, s | | | | | | er, err, ar, ard | |
| Bernard Pendergraph | B, n, P | gr | ph | | | | | |
| | 44/44 | 35/36 | 6/6 | 65/67 | 27/31 | 6/6 | 14/21 | 12/12 |

## Qualitative Spelling Inventory

Danny's language arts teacher gave the class a qualitative spelling inventory of 25 words to examine the types of errors they made in spelling. The teacher then classified the students into particular developmental stages of spelling. Danny's spelling test and analysis of his errors on the Feature Guide are on the following two pages.

## Spelling Test

Name **Danny**

1. speck
2. switch
3. throat
4. nirse ✓
5. scrap ✓
6. charge
7. phone
8. smugg ✓
9. point
10. squoret ✓
11. drawing
12. trapt ✓
13. waving
14. powerful
15. battle
16. fever
17. lesson
18. penies ✓
19. fraction
20. salier ✓
21. diestins ✓
22. confusion
23. discovery
24. resadint ✓
25. visable ✓

# Feature Guide for Upper Elementary Spelling Inventory

Student's Name **Danny**  Teacher _____  Grade **7**  Date **02/04**  Total Points **44/58**

| Word | Short Vowels | Digraphs and Blends | Long Vowel Patterns | Other Vowel Patterns | Syllable Junctures, Consonant Doubling, Inflected Endings, Prefixes, Suffixes | Bases and Roots | Points |
|------|------|------|------|------|------|------|------|
| 1 speck | e | sp, ck | | | | | |
| 2 switch | i | sw, tch | | | | | |
| 3 throat | | thr | o-a | | | | |
| 4 nurse | | | | u̶r | | | |
| 5 scrape | | scr | a̶-e̶ | | | | |
| 6 charge | | ch | | ar | | | |
| 7 phone | | ph | o-e | | | | |
| 8 smudge | u | sm, dge | | | | | |
| 9 point | | nt | | oi | | | |
| 10 squirt | | squ | | i̶r | | | |
| 11 drawing | | dr | | aw | ing | | |
| 12 trapped | a | | | | pp, ed | | |
| 13 waving | | | | | ing | | |
| 14 powerful | | | | ow | er, ful | | |
| 15 battle | a | | | | tt, le | | |
| 16 fever | | | | | ev, er | | |
| 17 lesson | | | | | ss, on | | |
| 18 pennies | e | | | | n̶n̶, ies | | |
| 19 fraction | | | | | tion | frac | |
| 20 sailor | | | a̶i̶ | | or | | |
| 21 distance | | | | | an̶ce | d̶i̶s̶ | |
| 22 confusion | | | | | con, sion | fus | |
| 23 discovery | | | | | dis, ery | cov | |
| 24 resident | | | | | e̶ht | re̶sid | |
| 25 visible | | | | | ble | vi̶si | |
| feature totals | 6/6 | 12/13 | 2/4 | 4/6 | 19/23 | 3/6 | |

Words 15/25

## Interest Survey

Danny's language arts teacher created an interest survey for her students to complete at the beginning of the year. Printed on the following page are Danny's responses to this survey.

## Interest Survey

1. What do you like to do at home? <u>listen to rap music, draw, surf the internet,</u>
   <u>play video games</u>

2. What do you like to do with your friends? <u>Skateboard, play basketball, sports, have fun</u>

3. What is your favorite subject in school? <u>Art</u>

4. Do you like school? Why? Or Why not? <u>Sometimes, I get to be with my friends.</u>
   <u>I don't like when I get in trouble or have to do hard work.</u>

5. What would you like to do better? <u>Get better grades</u>

6. Do you like to read? Why? Or Why not? <u>Not much. It's boring</u>

7. Do you read at home? <u>When I'm bored</u>

8. What kinds of things do you like to read? <u>Sci fi and adventure books</u>

## Case Study 1: Danny

Your three columns of notes from Danny's profile might have looked something like this

| _strengths_ | _weaknesses_ | _instructional strategies and activities_ |
|---|---|---|
| comprehension strong | lacks fluency | repeated readings of familiar text |
| retells well | reads slowly | easy sci fiction, advent books |
| monitors for meaning | sounds out words | freq. 1-min. silent reading assessments |
| self corrects | comprehension will suffer | chart no. of words read, helps motivation |
| motivated to do better | confused long vowels (e ending) | work in groups, Readers' Theatre |
| lots of interests | R-controlled vowels | word sorts for long vowels |
| likes drawing | | making words activities |
| video games | | word walls, spelling lists, word hunts |
| | | encourage to keep on self-monitoring |

## Sample Essay

Although Danny, a seventh grader, is performing below grade level—as evidenced by a third-grade level Word Recognition Assessment and a fifth-grade level Oral Reading Test—his overall abilities show some reading strengths. For example, his text comprehension is relatively strong. After reading a passage at his reading level, he was able to retell the passage reasonably well, and he was able to monitor his reading to check his understanding and meaning. On his Oral Reading and Fluency Assessments, he self-corrected when his reading didn't make sense, and he repeated words to check for meaning. His motivation to improve his skills is illustrated in his written response on the Interest Survey. When asked "What would you like to do better," he responded by writing, "Get better grades."

Danny lacks fluency in his reading. His Fluency Test indicated that he correctly read 99 words in 1 minute while reading a passage at a fifth-grade level. On his Oral Reading Test, the teacher marked that he read at a slow rate. On the Word Recognition Test, Danny sounded out the words instead of reading them as a whole. Although Danny's text comprehension is fairly good, without developing good fluency skills, his ability to read more demanding material will suffer. If he does not improve his ability to recognize words automatically, he may spend too much time struggling to decode words, and little of his attention will be left for comprehension.

Another area of weakness for Danny is that he was confusing long vowels, especially ones with the silent _e_ ending, on the Phonics Test and Fluency Assessment. He had trouble spelling long vowel words on the upper elementary qualitative spelling inventory. This weakness puts him in the within-word stage of reading.

An instructional strategy for fluency would be repeated readings of familiar text at Danny's independent reading level, which is material that he can read with an accuracy rate of 95 percent or greater. The teacher may choose to provide him with some easy-level reading science fiction and adventure books. Selecting material that Danny takes pleasure in will make his practice enjoyable, fun, and rewarding. It is suggested that the teacher use frequent one-minute silent reading assessments and then graph the number of words read on a chart. By practicing this regularly, Danny may become more motivated because he wants to get better grades and he can visually see his progress. He can also benefit from Readers' Theatre scripts, which are easier to read than original text, and it is done in a group. Danny's Interest Survey indicated that he likes to work in groups, to "spend time with his friends in school," and to "listen to rap music." With this in mind, he may benefit from reading selections that provides rhythm and meaning, such as poetry or reading lyrics to songs to improve his fluency. He could also read along with lyrics while listening to the rhythms of music on a CD at a classroom listening center.

Danny's reading development can also benefit from a better understanding of long vowels with word sorts, which involves sorting words with different long vowel spelling patterns, or sorting words with the same vowel that contains short vowel sounds and long vowel sounds ending with a silent *e,* such as *mat* and *mate,* or *rip* and *ripe.* With repeated exposure to this method, he will learn long-vowel spelling patterns. He may also be helped by "Making Words" activities, which involve constructing smaller words from the letters of a larger word. In this assignment, he would be asked to build words that have different long vowel spelling patterns.

Danny should be encouraged to self-monitor his reading to help track his comprehension. If he misreads a word, the teacher can inform him and then ask that he go back and reread in order to make sense of the text. The teacher can also prompt Danny to repeat what he read orally, and then ask, "Did that make sense?" Doing this will help direct his focus to the meaning.

# Case Study 1: Danny

## Evaluating the Essay

This is a strong case-study analysis because it addresses all parts of the prompt. Some of Danny's strengths were listed first, followed by some of his weaknesses. The strengths and weaknesses described were taken from a list of several possibilities. The person who did this analysis chose what she thought were the most salient strengths and weaknesses. In an analysis of this length not every possible strength and weakness needs to be listed. Danny's strengths were comprehension and retelling, using meaning cues, self-correcting, and motivation to read better. After mentioning each strength, the writer gave evidence from the data in the case study that led her to her conclusions. She listed which piece or pieces of data demonstrated every strength. An analysis that did not include the evidence to back up the writer's conclusions would not be as strong.

The same excellent job was done identifying Danny's weaknesses. The weaknesses listed were fluency and long vowels. Again, these weaknesses were determined to be the most salient from a list of possible weaknesses. A strong essay includes at least two strengths and two weaknesses. The writer probably wouldn't be able to discuss more than that in the space given. A different analysis that isn't as strong might just list one strength and one weakness. A poor analysis might be missing either strengths or weaknesses. In this essay, the writer followed each weakness with evidence from the data that proved that these were weaknesses. For fluency, she cited the fluency test, oral reading test, and word recognition test. This demonstrates that the writer can take data from several sources and extrapolate a conclusion. She is able to use multiple measures. An analysis that is acceptable, but not as strong, might just cite one piece of data. For long vowels, this writer used three pieces of data: the phonics assessment, the fluency test, and the qualitative spelling inventory. Keep in mind that every piece of data in the case study is there to provide information for your analysis and should be used in some way to earn a strong score. The writer even included a rationale for why fluency is important. This shows that she truly understands the components of reading.

After listing Danny's strengths and weaknesses, this writer described instructional strategies for working on fluency, the instructional strategies for working on long vowels, and then strategies to build on Danny's strengths. In this way, she addressed both how to improve his weaknesses and how to capitalize on his strengths. An acceptable, but not strong, essay might only list instructional strategies for weaknesses.

The prompt asked for at least two methods or strategies that would assist the student's reading development. This analysis is strong because it included four strategies for fluency and the rationale behind selecting them. The writer told why Danny, specifically, would benefit from them. Those strategies were repeated readings of familiar and interesting text, 1-minute fluency assessment practices, graphing the words read in 1 minute, and Readers' Theatre. These four methods are all successful ways to work on fluency and were selected from many possible fluency strategies because the writer determined that they would be suitable for Danny's needs. The connection about why these strategies would be compatible with Danny's interests and learning styles was taken from the information given in the case study. Three strategies were also listed for working on long vowels. They were word sorts; repeated exposure to words, presumably through reading; and making words. One strategy was listed for building on one of Danny's strengths: self-monitoring. An acceptable essay might have included just one strategy for working on fluency, one for working on long vowels, and one method for continuing to build on a strength. A poor essay might only describe a single strategy in total, or might list two or three but not go into sufficient detail about how any of them would work or how any would benefit the student. It would merely be a list. This analysis is strong because it describes several possible strategies that would work and doesn't simply list them. However, all the methods and strategies you list should actually be proven to be effective with the specific reading component being addressed. It is more important to be accurate than to have a long list.

# A Thorough Analysis of Case Study 1: Danny

The following is a very thorough analysis of the case study. This thorough analysis is designed to show you many of the possible items that you could have mentioned in the case-study essay. It is also designed to help you understand some of the items to look for as you do your analysis. **Note: The following analysis is intended to assist you in understanding the task at hand. You will not have time for completing such a detailed analysis in your case study on the day of your test.**

## The Analysis

Overall, Danny is a poor reader. He is reading below grade level. He scored at third-grade level on the word recognition assessment, and his independent and instructional levels were at the fifth-grade level on the oral reading test. Weak readers recognize words in context more easily than out of context because they overrely on context in reading as a result of not having become proficient in word recognition strategies. Hence, Danny scored worse on the test in which he read words out of context than on the one in which he read leveled passages. On the upper elementary qualitative spelling inventory, Danny scored at the within word developmental stage of spelling.

### Strengths

Some of the following strengths may be pointed out:

- Danny is motivated to do better as he indicated on his Interest Survey when he wrote that he would like to get better grades.
- Danny likes working in groups. On his Interest Survey, he listed several activities he likes to do with his friends, and he wrote that what he likes best about school is being with his friends.
- Danny has lots of interests that he noted on the Interest Survey. He likes rap music, skateboarding, drawing, the Internet, video games, and sports.
- Danny wrote on his Interest Survey that he likes reading science fiction and adventure books.
- He is relatively strong in comprehension. On the oral reading test his teacher noted that he was able to retell what he read reasonably well.
- Danny self-corrected and repeated words on his oral reading test and fluency assessment. This indicates that he is reading for meaning, and he is trying to make sense out of what he is reading.

### Recommendations Based on Strengths

Some of the following recommendations for activities and assignments can be made to build on Danny's strengths, so that he can start from where he is strong and move to his areas of need.

- Danny can work in groups on projects because he likes being with other students. He could be the illustrator of the group because he likes drawing.
- Danny can read books about rap music, skateboarding, video games, and sports because he is interested in those topics. Have books about those topics in your classroom library, along with science fiction and adventure books, because those are his favorite types of books to read.
- Since Danny likes to surf the Internet, give him assignments to locate and read information on the Internet. Have him do a research project on rap music, skateboarding, video games, or sports in which he finds information on the Internet. Since he likes to skateboard, play basketball, and engage in sports with his friends, he could complete a group project on those topics. Danny could be given the text of songs to read. Since he already knows the songs, he will be getting practice reading material that is familiar to him.
- Danny could draw pictures about what he has read because he likes drawing. This will build on his comprehension strengths because he is transferring the meaning of what he has read into a visual representation. This is using the comprehension strategy of visualization.
- Danny could write science fiction and adventure stories to practice his spelling skills and then illustrate them.
- Praise Danny when he self-corrects or rereads for meaning. When he misreads a word, prompt him by asking, "Did that make sense?" Or tell him "Go back and look at that again and make sure that it makes sense."

## Weaknesses

Danny's assessments indicated four major weaknesses:

- Fluency
- Long vowels
- Word endings—suffixes and inflectional endings, especially *ed* for past tense and *s* for plurals
- R-controlled vowels

## Fluency

Comprehension of the material read is the goal of reading. Reading instruction should focus on comprehension strategies. Fluency is one of the two building blocks of comprehension. Fluency is the ability to read with ease and automaticity. It is a combination of reading speed and accuracy. Although fluent reading is not an end in itself, it leads to better comprehension. Fluent readers are able to focus their attention on understanding the text. When students read fluently, they are not struggling to decode the words, so that their efforts can be concentrated on comprehension and making meaning. Nonfluent readers must focus their attention on decoding, thus leaving little attention free for comprehension. Although Danny's comprehension is adequate for what he is reading, he is reading at least two years below grade level. A student who reads haltingly and makes several reading errors is unlikely to have good comprehension of high demand text.

On his fluency test, Danny read 99 words correct per minute (WCPM). He made 12 errors on his reading passage. At the minimum, a seventh grader should be reading more than 120 WCPM with less than 6 errors. A person needs to read more than 140 WCPM in order to handle all of the cognitive demands of the text and to maximize comprehension. An average adult reads 200 WCPM.

On the oral reading test, the teacher marked that Danny read the fourth and fifth grade passages at a slow rate, and the sixth-grade passage at a very slow rate. Oral reading gives a good indication of the fluency with which a child is able to read.

On the word recognition test, the teacher noted that Danny sounded out the words instead of reading them fluently and rapidly.

For students who read more slowly than average, more practice is needed at their independent level so that they can gain fluency.

## Recommendations for Working on Fluency

There are several strategies for working on fluency. Following are some of the ones that might be helpful to Danny.

- Repeated readings—Reading a familiar text many times for a variety of purposes. The material read should be at his independent reading level, which is text that he can read with an accuracy rate of 95 percent or greater. He should not have to struggle with the decoding so that he can concentrate his efforts on the fluency practice. His teacher should have books in the classroom library that are at Danny's independent reading level, which the oral reading test showed to be at fifth-grade level. On the Interest Survey, Danny wrote that he doesn't like school when the work is hard or when he gets in trouble. Therefore, if the reading material is too difficult, Danny will become frustrated and perhaps misbehave because he is "turned off" to the task.

  The forms of repeated readings that might be especially effective for Danny would be choral reading, Readers' Theatre, partner reading, and reading to someone else because these are group activities, and Danny likes working in a group. Readers' Theatre would make the reading task appealing to Danny because it promotes cooperative interaction with his classmates, and the scripts appear less daunting than whole books, so reading wouldn't seem like hard work. In partner reading, Danny would be reading with a stronger reader who would read first to model fluent reading. Then Danny would read the same text aloud.

- Modeling—Read aloud to Danny so that he can hear examples of fluent reading.

- Tape assisted reading—Danny could get support by listening to the text read by a fluent reader on an audiotape or CD and follow along. He could record himself reading text that he knows well and reading unfamiliar text. He could then listen to his rate and be made aware of what fluent reading sounds like in contrast to nonfluent reading.

- Timed readings—Give Danny and other students 1 minute to read silently and have them count how many words they read in 1 minute. Once again, the material read should be familiar text at his independent level. It can be text about his interests such as music, skateboarding, sports, adventure, and science fiction. It would be effective for Danny to keep a running graph and chart the number of WCPM after each timed reading so that he can see his progress. This would be motivating to him because on his interest survey he wrote that he would like to get better grades. On the graph he would be able to see his ongoing progress toward improvement. After the first 1-minute timing, Danny could be timed on the same passage again to immediately see his progress between the first and second readings.

- Phrase reading—The text could be segmented into phrases by drawing a pencil line at the end of each phrase. Danny could be told to read all the words between two pencil lines together in one breath.

  Practice phrasing and intonation by reading works with rhythm such as songs or poems. Since Danny likes rap music, he could read the lyrics to rap songs. That would work especially well because rap music is like talking to a beat with a very definite rhythm.

- Direct instruction—Ask Danny to read it quickly, make it sound like talking, or read the punctuation.

- Wide reading—Danny needs to read a lot in order to get enough practice to improve his fluency. He should do silent sustained reading and/or independent reading every day in school, and he should read at home every night. He could keep a reading log of what he reads and the number of pages read every day in school, and he could also have a home reading log.

## Word Endings

Often nonnative English speakers leave the endings off words because they don't have suffixes in their first languages that mark tenses, so they don't notice the *ed* endings. They are not familiar enough with the structure of English to realize that when they leave an *s* off the ending of a plural, it doesn't sound right.

Danny needs to work on learning the structure of language. He needs to get lots of practice hearing the endings of the words and distinguishing between words with suffixes and inflections and words without them both orally and in print.

On the qualitative spelling test, Danny did not write *ed* at the end of *trapped.* He wrote *trapt.* This shows that he needs to work on the structure of past tenses because he wrote what he heard and not what he should know about past tense.

On the word recognition test, every error that Danny made in the fourth- and fifth-grade tests was the omission of an ending.

On the oral reading test, Danny left the *s* off many plural nouns. In fact, that type of error comprised the majority of all his errors. Some examples of these errors were that he read *cowboy* instead of *cowboys, hill* instead of *hills,* and *cabin* instead of *cabins.*

On the fluency assessment, Danny left off *ed* and *s.* He read *use* instead of *used* and *notch* instead of *notches.*

## Recommendations for Working on Word Endings

- Direct instruction on suffixes and their meanings will be beneficial. Danny could practice putting suffixes onto base words. Give him definitions of the words to create, and he has to find the base and syllable that would make the words with the given meanings.

- Practice reading words with suffixes and breaking down words by syllables in reading and writing.

- Direct instruction on singulars and plurals is also recommended.

- Tell Danny to look at the whole word. Uncover a word slowly, one part at a time, until he reads the whole word.

- Leave blanks in a selection in which Danny has to figure out which word goes in the blank (**cloze activities**). He needs to use the context of the other words in the sentences to figure out which structure of the word would make sense. The words that fit meaningfully in the blanks would be words with suffixes.

- Have Danny sort words into the categories of those that have suffixes and those that don't (**word sorts**). For example, one column would be words without a suffix and words with *ed,* or one column could be for singular words, and one could be for plurals. Then Danny could sort for several suffixes at a time. For example, one column could be for words that end with *ed,* another column would be words that end with *ly,* and a third column could be words that end with *ing.*

- Have Danny record words with a specific suffix in a word study notebook (**word hunts**). When he finds more words with the targeted suffix in his reading, he will add them to the word study notebook.

- Have the teacher post words with a specific suffix on a word bank on the wall, and Danny will add to it (**word walls**).

- Have Danny build smaller words from the letters in a longer word (**making words**). The words that he builds will have some *ed* or *s* endings. Then he will sort the words he built by the endings.

- Have Danny play concentration games for practice. Danny will uncover two cards with words written on them from among an array of cards. If the cards consist of a base word on one card, and the same base word plus a suffix on the other card, then he has a match. If he reads the words on the cards correctly, he gets to keep them.

### Confusion with Long Vowels

Danny's teacher gave the phonics test after she gave the word recognition test and oral reading test to find out the cause of his poor oral reading performance. She wanted to see whether it was due to a phonics problem and with which specific phonics elements he was having difficulty, so that she could target instruction to those needs. On the phonics test, he said "slad" instead of "Slade" and "hawk" instead of "Hoke."

On the spelling inventory, Danny wrote *scrap* instead of *scrape.* This places him at the mid within word stage of spelling where students "use but confuse" long vowel patterns. On the fluency assessment, Danny read *horizone* with an /ō/ sound instead of *horizon* with a schwa sound.

The vowel pattern with which he is having the most difficulty is the long vowel with a silent *e* at the end, which puts him in the mid within word developmental stage of spelling.

### Recommendations for Working on Long Vowel Patterns

- Put Danny in a small flexible group with other students working on the same patterns or who are in the mid within word stage because he likes working with others.

- Give Danny and/or his group spelling activities and games for practice from the mid within word stage using resources such as *Words Their Way.*

- Have Danny sort words into the columns of words with a short vowel sound and words of the long vowel sound for the same vowel, such as short *a* words and long *a* words (**word sorts**). Then he can sort all long vowel words together for words that have the same spelling pattern. So there would be a column for /ā/, /ē/, /ī/, /ō/, /ū/, and all the words in the /ā/ column would have the silent *e* at the end, and all the words in the columns for the other long vowels would have silent *e* at the end. He could also sort for different spelling patterns of the same vowel sound; for /ō/ he could have a column for the spelling with silent *e* at the end, for *oa,* for *o,* and so on.

- Have Danny record words with a specific long vowel in a word study notebook (**word hunts**). When he finds more words with the targeted spelling pattern in his reading, he will add them to the word study notebook.

- The teacher will post words with a specific long vowel spelling pattern on a word bank on the wall and Danny will add to it (**word walls**).

- Have Danny build smaller words from the letters in a longer word (**making words**). The words that he builds will have different spelling patterns for long vowels. Then he will sort the words he built by the spelling patterns.

### R-Controlled Vowels

On the phonics tests, Danny misread the *er* in *Roberta,* the *ar* in *Bernard,* and the *or* in *Cornell* and *Thornton.*

On the qualitative spelling test, Danny misspelled the *or* in *sailor,* the *ur* in *nurse,* and the *ir* in *squirt.* He spelled all the *er* patterns correctly.

On the fluency test, Danny misread the *or* in *important.*

On the oral reading test, Danny misread the *ur* in *suburban.*

It appears that Danny is not having much trouble with the *er* pattern, but he is having some trouble with the other r-controlled vowels.

On the basic phonics skills tests, qualitative spelling inventory, and phonics names test, r-controlled vowels is a more difficult skill to master than long vowel spelling patterns. The developmental spelling level for r-controlled vowels is more advanced than the one for long vowel spelling patterns. On the phonics tests, long vowel spelling patterns come before r-controlled vowels in the hierarchy of phonic elements to learn.

### Recommendations for Working on R-Controlled Vowels

- Wait until Danny has learned long vowel patterns.
- When starting to work with Danny on r-controlled short vowels, have him distinguish between two at a time. He could start with *or* and *ar* because those are the two with which he is having the most difficulty. Since he does pretty well with *er,* he does not need to work with that pattern until he is distinguishing among all five.
- Have Danny sort words into categories of different r-controlled vowels **(word sorts)**. He would start with two vowels. For example one column would be *or* words and one column would be *ar* words. Then he could do one for *ur* words and *ir* words, and he could follow with other combinations of two. Next Danny could sort for three r-controlled vowels, then four, and finally all five.
- Have Danny record words containing the various r-controlled vowels in a word study notebook **(word hunts)**. When he finds more words with the targeted r-controlled vowels in his reading, he will add them to the word study notebook.
- Post words on the word wall with r-controlled vowels. Danny can add to it **(word walls)**.
- Give Danny lists of words for spelling tests that are made up of words with r-controlled vowels **(spelling lists)**. At first the list could have only two r-controlled vowels and then combinations of three, four, and all five.

# A Case Study for Practice

Now try analyzing the following case study and writing an essay. Use the four lined pages on pages 96–99 to write your essay. Limit your time to **1 hour** to complete this case study practice.

## Case Study 2: Sam

This case study focuses on a first-grade student named Sam. The documents and information on the following pages describe Sam's reading performance during the middle of the school year. After reviewing the information and materials, write a response in which you demonstrate your knowledge of language arts assessment and instruction in the analysis of this case study. Your response should include three parts:

1.  identify strengths and weaknesses in Sam's reading ability at this point in the school year, citing evidence from the documents to support your observations;
2.  describe at least two methods or instructional strategies and/or activities designed to assist Sam's reading development by addressing the strengths and weaknesses you identified; and
3.  explain how each method, strategy, and/or activity you describe would work in promoting Sam's reading proficiency.

Your response should be approximately 300–600 words in length.

**You may use the space below to make notes. These notes will not be scored.**

## Home Survey

Sam's teacher sent home a survey to be completed by the parents prior to parent-teacher conferences during the school year's first grading period. The survey was brought to the conference and discussed.

**Home Survey**

**My Child as a Reader and Writer**

Child's Name __Sam__          Date __11/2010__

Please take a few minutes to answer the following questions about your child's reading and writing. Because you are your child's first teacher, we appreciate your insight into how your child learns.

Does your child like going to school? Why or why not? __Yes.__

What are your child's strengths? __He knows a lot about animals and tries hard.__

What goals do you have this school year for your child? __He learns how to read.__

Does your child enjoy reading? __No. He likes me to read to him.__

What does your child like to read at home? __Science books.__

What types of books do you read at home? __Anything - school or library books.__

How often do you read at home? __We try each night.__

For how long? __15 minutes__

How well do you think your child is reading? __He struggles.__

How does your child feel about his/her own reading? __He thinks it is hard.__

What does your child like to write at home? __He likes to draw.__

Does your child use his/her own or developmental spelling? __Yes.__

Does your child share his/her writing with anyone in the family? __sometimes.__

How well do you think your child is writing? __It's hard for him to get started.__

How does your child feel about his/her own writing? __It's not his favorite.__

What activities do you do together as a family? __Sports, movies, pets.__

What are your child's interests? __sports and animals.__

How do you think your child learns best? __with praise and a chance to be active.__

What else would you like me to know about your child? __His parents are divorced and there is shared custody.__

Signature __Sam's mom__

## Student Survey

Four months into the school year Sam's teacher sat down and asked Sam the questions on this survey. The teacher was attempting to learn more about Sam's attitude toward reading.

## Myself as a Reader

Child's Name __Sam__

Do you enjoy reading? Why or why not? __No, It is hard.__

Are you a good reader? How do you know? __No, I am really slow and sound out words.__

What are your favorite books at school? __Animal books.__

What are your favorite books at home? __snake books.__

Who reads to you at home? __mom and sometimes dad.__

Where is your favorite place to read? __In bed.__

Do you enjoy talking about books you have read? __No.__

How have you improved as a reader? __I try hard.__

What do you do when you come to a word you don't know? __Ask the teacher.__

What is one thing you would like to do better in reading? __Sound out words and read hard books.__

## Running Record

For this running record the teacher was assessing which level book Sam could read at an instructional level. The running record was completed in the fifth month of first grade. The benchmark level for first graders at the end of the year is level 16.

The teacher listened as Sam read the book to her. The teacher made marks for each word the student read on the running record form that follows. The teacher analyzed the running record and noted the cueing systems the student used while decoding words.

Notes were also taken as the student retold the story. See the last part of the running record form for information about the student's retelling of the story.

## BOOK EVALUATION

Name: **Sam**

Date: **1-15-2010**

Recorder: _____

| LEVEL | ACC. | %SC rate |
|-------|------|----------|
| 6 | 93% | 1:56 |

Title: **The Busy Mosquito**

Phrasing and Fluency: **X** word by word ____ in short phrases
____ in longer phrases ____ punctuation

| Page # | Sentence | Word Count 112 | 7 E | 2 SC | Cues Used E MSV | Cues Used SC MSV |
|--------|----------|-----------|-----|------|-------|-------|
| 2 | ✓ musquit ✓ ✓ ✓<br>The mosquito buzzed the cow. | 5 | 1 | | MSⓋ | |
| | ✓ ✓ ✓<br>"Buzz, buzz, buzz." | 3 | | | MSⓋ | |
| | ✓ oway _____ /A ✓ ✓ ✓<br>"Go away, mosquito," said the cow, | 6 | 2 | | MSV | |
| | ✓ ✓ ✓ fell oway<br>and the mosquito flew away. | 5 | 2 | | MSⓋ | |
| 4 | ✓ ✓ ✓ ✓ her<br>The mosquito buzzed the horse. | 5 | 1 | | MSⓋ | |
| | ✓ ✓ ✓<br>"Buzz, buzz, buzz." | 3 | | | | |
| | ✓ cut ✓ ✓ ✓ h-or-s ✓<br>"Go away, mosquito," said the horse, | 6 | 1 | | ⓂSV | |
| | ✓ ✓ ✓ fell /SC<br>and the mosquito flew/away. | 5 | | 1 | MSⓋ | ⓂSⓋ |
| 6 | ✓ ✓ ✓ ✓ ✓<br>The mosquito buzzed the dog. | 5 | | | | |
| | ✓ ✓ ✓<br>"Buzz, buzz, buzz." | 3 | | | | |
| | ✓ ✓ ✓ ✓ ✓<br>"Go away, mosquito," said the dog, | 6 | | | | |
| | ✓ ✓ ✓<br>and the mosquito flew away. | 5 | | | | |
| 8 | ✓ ✓ ✓<br>The mosquito buzzed the cat. | 5 | | | | |
| | ✓ ✓ ✓<br>"Buzz, buzz, buzz." | 3 | | | | |

page 1

| | | | | | | |
|---|---|---|---|---|---|---|
| | ✓ ✓ ✓ ✓ ✓ ✓<br>"Go away, mosquito," said the cat, | 6 | | | | |
| | ✓ ✓ ✓ ✓ ✓<br>and the mosquito flew away. | 5 | | | | |
| 10 | ✓ ✓ ✓ ✓<br>The mosquito buzzed me. | 4 | | | | |
| | ✓ ✓ ✓<br>"Buzz, buzz, buzz." | 3 | | | | |
| | ✓ ✓ ✓ ✓✓<br>"Go away, mosquito," I said. | 5 | | | | |
| | ✓ ✓ ✓✓ ✓ ✓<br>The mosquito did not go away. | 6 | | | | |
| 12 | ✓ ✓✓✓ ✓<br>I got a fly swatter. SC | 5 | | 1 | M⊗V | ⊛SV |
| | ✓ ✓ ✓ ✓<br>"Go away, mosquito," I said. | 5 | | | | |
| | ✓ ✓ ✓<br>and the mosquito flew away. | 5 | | | | |
| | ✓ ✓ ✓<br>"Buzz, buzz, buzz." | 3 | | | | |

| RETELLING | NOTES |
|---|---|
| T: *"Tell me in your own words what happened in the story"*<br><br>Initial retelling included:___characters___important details<br><br>___vocabulary/special phrases from the story___setting<br><br>___events in sequence ✓events out of sequence___ending<br><br>T: *If initial retelling is incomplete, prompt: "Tell me more."*<br><br>Added information about: : ✓characters___important details<br><br>✓vocabulary/special phrases from the story ✓setting<br><br>___events in sequence___events out of sequence ✓ending | Needed<br>to be prompted<br>to retell.<br><br>✓ |

## High Frequency Words

During the fifth month of first grade, the teacher assessed Sam's automatic reading of the 100 most frequently used words. By the end of the school year, first graders are expected to know the first 100 words automatically.

# Fry's Sight Word Recording Sheet

Student: **Sam**          Fall **(Winter)** Spring

| List 1 | | Pre | Post |
|---|---|---|---|
| 1 | the | ✔ | |
| 2 | of | ✔ | |
| 3 | and | ✔ | |
| 4 | a | ✔ | |
| 5 | to | ✔ | |
| 6 | in | ✔ | |
| 7 | is | ✔ | |
| 8 | you | — | |
| 9 | that | ✔ | |
| 10 | it | ✔ | |
| 11 | he | ✔ | |
| 12 | was | **saw** | |
| 13 | for | ✔ | |
| 14 | on | ✔ | |
| 15 | are | ✔ | |
| 16 | as | ✔ | |
| 17 | with | ✔ | |
| 18 | his | ✔ | |
| 19 | they | ✔ | |
| 20 | I | ✔ | |
| 21 | at | ✔ | |
| 22 | be | ✔ | |
| 23 | this | ✔ | |
| 24 | have | ✔ | |
| 25 | from | ✔ | |
| | | **23**/25 | /25 |

| List 2 | | Pre | Post |
|---|---|---|---|
| 26 | or | ✔ | |
| 27 | one | **on** | |
| 28 | had | ✔ | |
| 29 | by | ✔ | |
| 30 | word | — | |
| 31 | but | ✔ | |
| 32 | not | ✔ | |
| 33 | what | **wait** | |
| 34 | all | ✔ | |
| 35 | were | — | |
| 36 | we | ✔ | |
| 37 | when | ✔ | |
| 38 | your | — | |
| 39 | can | ✔ | |
| 40 | said | **sad** | |
| 41 | there | ✔ | |
| 42 | use | **us** | |
| 43 | an | ✔ | |
| 44 | each | — | |
| 45 | which | — | |
| 46 | she | ✔ | |
| 47 | do | ✔ | |
| 48 | how | ✔ | |
| 49 | their | — | |
| 50 | if | ✔ | |
| | | **15**/25 | /25 |

| List 3 | | Pre | Post |
|---|---|---|---|
| 51 | will | ✔ | |
| 52 | up | ✔ | |
| 53 | other | — | |
| 54 | about | — | |
| 55 | out | ✔ | |
| 56 | many | ✔ | |
| 57 | then | ✔ | |
| 58 | them | ✔ | |
| 59 | these | — | |
| 60 | so | ✔ | |
| 61 | some | **som** | |
| 62 | her | ✔ | |
| 63 | would | — | |
| 64 | make | **mack** | |
| 65 | like | ✔ | |
| 66 | him | — | |
| 67 | into | ✔ | |
| 68 | time | **tim** | |
| 69 | has | ✔ | |
| 70 | look | **lock** | |
| 71 | two | — | |
| 72 | more | — | |
| 73 | write | — | |
| 74 | go | ✔ | |
| 75 | see | ✔ | |
| | | **13**/25 | /25 |

| List 4 | | Pre | Post |
|---|---|---|---|
| 76 | number | — | |
| 77 | no | **on** | |
| 78 | way | — | |
| 79 | could | — | |
| 80 | people | — | |
| 81 | my | ✔ | |
| 82 | than | ✔ | |
| 83 | first | **fist** | |
| 84 | water | — | |
| 85 | been | **bean** | |
| 86 | call | ✔ | |
| 87 | who | — | |
| 88 | oil | — | |
| 89 | mow | — | |
| 90 | find | **fand** | |
| 91 | long | — | |
| 92 | down | — | |
| 93 | day | ✔ | |
| 94 | did | ✔ | |
| 95 | get | ✔ | |
| 96 | come | **com** | |
| 97 | made | **mad** | |
| 98 | may | ✔ | |
| 99 | part | — | |
| 100 | over | — | |
| | | **7**/25 | /25 |

## Writing Sample

This is a writing sample taken from Sam's journal. In his guided reading lesson, after reading a book about making breakfast, Sam was to write a question and answer using words he had read in the book.

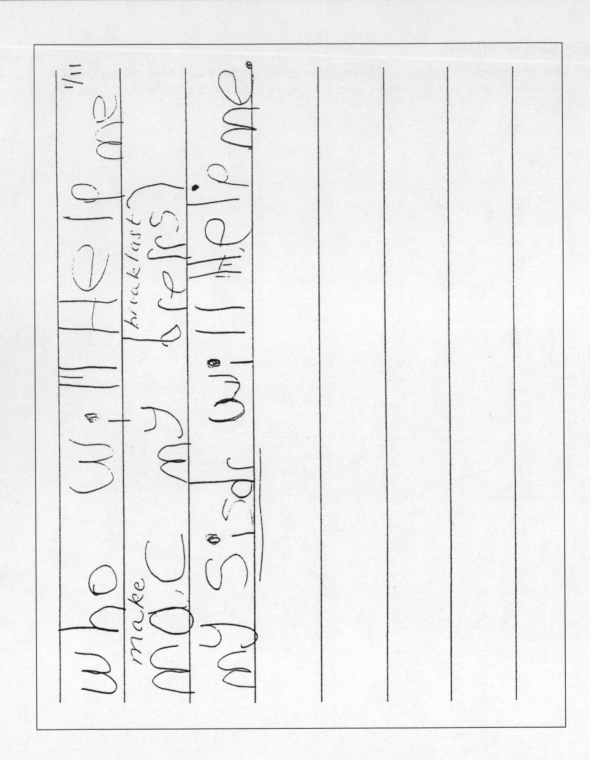

## Teacher's Comments

Sam's teacher also made the following comments about his classroom work and behavior.

Sam is easily frustrated, especially when reading or writing.

Sam has a difficult time starting to write independently.

Sam loves science and animals.

Sam often loses things and forgets materials.

Sam responds best to praise and rewards.

Sam loves sports.

Write your case study essay on the following four pages. After you complete your case-study essay, use the Evaluation Form to evaluate your response.

_____
_____
_____
_____
_____
_____
_____
_____
_____
_____
_____
_____
_____
_____
_____
_____
_____
_____
_____
_____
_____
_____
_____
_____
_____

# RICA Practice Case Study Evaluation Form

**Use this checklist to evaluate your essay:**

1.  To what extent does this response reflect an **understanding of the relevant content** and academic knowledge from the applicable RICA domain?

    | **thorough** | **adequate** | **limited or no** |
    |---|---|---|
    | understanding | understanding | understanding |

2.  To what extent does this response **fulfill the purpose of the assignment**?

    | **completely** | **adequately** | **partially** |
    |---|---|---|
    | fulfills | fulfills | fulfills or fails to |

3.  To what extent does this essay **respond to the given task(s)?**

    | **fully** | **adequately** | **limited or inadequately** |
    |---|---|---|
    | responds | responds | responds |

4.  How **accurate** is the response?

    | **very** | **generally** | **inaccurate** |
    |---|---|---|
    | accurate | accurate | |

5.  Does the response **demonstrate an effective application** of the relevant content and academic knowledge from the applicable RICA domain?

    | **yes** | **reasonably** | **no** |
    |---|---|---|
    | effective | effective | ineffective and inaccurate |

6.  To what extent does the response **provide supporting examples, evidence, and rationale** based on the relevant content and academic knowledge from the applicable RICA domain?

    | **strong** | **adequate** | **limited or no** |
    |---|---|---|
    | support | support | support |

**Following is a sample essay for this case study followed by an evaluation of the essay.**

# Case Study 2: Sam

## Sample Essay

Sam is a struggling reader, but he has some reading strengths. The student survey indicates that he is motivated to be a better reader. He indicated that he tries hard and would like to learn how to sound out words and read hard books. He likes to be read to, and his mother reads to him regularly. He is interested in sports, animals, science, and drawing, as noted in his home survey, student survey, and teacher comments.

Sam has little confidence in his reading ability. Both Sam and his mother noted in their respective surveys that he does not like reading, and he thinks it is hard. He also struggles with writing. His mother indicated that it is hard for him to get started, and he does not like writing. His writing sample contained many errors, and his teacher wrote that he has a difficult time getting started.

In his survey, Sam wrote that he asks the teacher when he comes to a word he does not know, and he would like to sound out words better. He needs to learn more sight words because he read only 58 out of 100 words correctly on the Sight Word Test. On his running record, he read word by word, further indicating that he is not recognizing words by sight. Sam would benefit from increasing his sight word vocabulary by quickly reading words on flashcards. For practice, his teacher could give him a word ring with words written on cards. He can play sight word identification games such as Concentration and My Pile, Your Pile, which can help him quickly identify the words on the cards.

Additionally, sight words are learned by multiple exposures to those words, so Sam should read widely in order to see the words in print many times. Decodable books would be appropriate because they would provide him with the multiple exposures to the sight words that he needs. He could also read books at his independent level about science, sports, and animals. Since those are his interests, books about those topics would be very motivating for him.

On his running record, Sam read a level 6 selection with 93 percent accuracy, so level 6 is his instructional level. He should continue reading books at level 6 while working to overcome his weaknesses. If the books are about science, sports, and animals, they will be more motivating, thereby capitalizing on his strengths. The teacher should supply the classroom library with books on these topics. Reading books about his favorite subjects will also help boost his confidence because he will understand what he is reading.

Sam relied on visual cues on his running record. He especially had trouble with vowel sounds. He could do word sorts with different vowel sounds to learn to distinguish among them. Sam should be encouraged to check for meaning, so that when he misreads a word, he can be prompted with a question such as "Did that make sense?"

Since he has a difficult time getting motivated to write, Sam should write about sports, animals, and science. Because he is interested in these topics, he will have an easier time getting started. He likes to draw, so if he draws an illustration first and then writes a story about it, he will also be more motivated to write. His mother should continue reading to him since that was listed as a strength, and because he reads word by word, listening to fluent reading will be a good model to try to emulate.

## Evaluating the Essay

This is a strong case-study analysis because it addresses all parts of the prompt. It listed Sam's reading strengths and weaknesses and described at least two methods or strategies that would assist in his reading development. Some of Sam's strengths were listed and then some of his weaknesses. Sam did not exhibit many reading strengths, so the writer took them from his interests. The strengths highlighted were that he is motivated to read better; his mother reads to him; and he is interested in sports, animals, science, and drawing. After each strength, the writer gave evidence from the data in the case study that led him to the conclusions that he made about it. He listed which specific piece or pieces of data demonstrated each strength. An analysis that failed to include the evidence to back the writer's conclusions would not score as highly.

The writer also did an excellent job analyzing Sam's weaknesses. The weaknesses described were taken from a list of several possibilities. The writer of this analysis chose what he thought were the most prominent weaknesses. That is, they were the ones that showed up in several pieces of data and/or are the most necessary to be mastered first in order to ensure future reading progress. The weaknesses listed were lack of confidence, writing, small sight word vocabulary, and decoding vowel sounds. A strong essay lists at least two strengths and two weaknesses. In this analysis, the writer described three strengths and four weaknesses. An analysis that isn't as strong may just list one strength and weakness. A poor analysis might be missing either the strengths or the weaknesses. After each weakness, the writer gave evidence from the data that demonstrated that these were weaknesses. For lack of confidence, he cited the parent and student surveys. For writing, he cited the parent survey, writing sample, and teacher comments. For sight word vocabulary he used the student survey, sight word test, and running record. For decoding vowel sounds he cited the running record. The writer clearly demonstrated that he is able to use multiple measures to draw conclusions. An acceptable, but not as strong, analysis might just cite one piece of data. Keep in mind that every piece of data in the case study is there to provide information for the analysis and should be used in some way to achieve a high score. The writer even showed that he knows about instructional levels, which proves that he understands about reading instruction.

The writer described instructional strategies for working on sight words, next instructional strategies for working on Sam's confidence, then strategies to work on vowels, and finally strategies to improve Sam's writing. In his descriptions of these strategies, this writer addressed both how to improve on Sam's weaknesses and how to build on his strengths. An acceptable, but not as strong, essay might only list instructional strategies for overcoming the weaknesses without building on the strengths.

The prompt asked for at least two methods or strategies that would assist the student's reading development. This analysis is strong because it described four strategies for sight word vocabulary. Those strategies were flashcards, word rings, word identification games, and reading books about topics in which he is interested at his instructional level. These four methods are all successful ways to build sight word vocabulary. Strategies for boosting Sam's confidence were to read and write about topics in which he is interested. His interests were determined from the parent and student surveys. The writer also made a connection between reading and writing about the topics of interest to Sam and motivation, which is one of his strengths. In doing this, the writer has shown how to work on a weakness by building on a strength, thereby, using strategies that address both strengths **and** weaknesses. Two strategies were also listed for working on decoding vowel sounds. They were word sorts and checking for meaning.

This writer concluded his analysis with the suggestion that Sam's mother should continue reading to him. This is an attempt to build upon a strength. The writer could have made this point more strongly by explaining why he is recommending that Sam's mother should continue reading to him. An acceptable essay might have one strategy for working on one weakness and one for working on another. A poor essay might only describe one strategy in total or might list two or three but not go into detail about how any of them would work or how any would benefit the student. It would merely be a list. This analysis was strong because it described several possible strategies that would work, and it did not simply list them. However, all the methods and strategies listed should be understood to be effective with the specific reading component being addressed. It is more important to be accurate than to have a long list.

**PART II**

# REVIEW OF EXAM AREAS

The following section is designed to **give you a review of the important basic concepts** of reading instruction as it applies to the RICA test. It includes a review of the five domains and a glossary of important terms and concepts.

**Read this section carefully.** Make notes in the margins to help you understand the terms or concepts.

# RICA Content Specifications Review

## Reading Domains

The purpose of the RICA written and video assessment is to determine a teacher's knowledge and skills necessary for effective reading instruction. Teachers must demonstrate competency in the content for effective reading instruction. These competencies are described in the RICA Content Specifications in the RICA bulletin.

The goal of reading instruction as stated in the RICA bulletin is to "develop competent, thoughtful readers who are able to use, interpret, and appreciate all types of text."

### Effective Reading Instruction as Noted in the RICA Information Bulletin

- is based on the results of ongoing assessment.
- reflects knowledge of state and local reading standards for different grade levels.
- represents a balanced, comprehensive reading curriculum.
- is sensitive to the needs of all students.

The knowledge and abilities necessary for teachers to deliver this effective instruction are organized into five domains in the RICA.

**Domain 1: Planning, Organizing, and Managing Reading Instruction Based on Ongoing Assessment**

**Domain 2: Word Analysis**

**Domain 3: Fluency**

**Domain 4: Vocabulary, Academic Language, and Background Knowledge**

**Domain 5: Comprehension**

# Questions to Focus Your Review

The following questions will be discussed in the domain review that follows. You should use the questions in each domain as a diagnostic test of your knowledge of the content areas. These questions can also be used as a review test and to reinforce your learning after completing the domain review.

## Domain 1

## Planning, Organizing, and Managing Reading Instruction Based on Ongoing Assessment

**Competency 1:**

1. What are some factors to consider in planning reading instruction?
2. What factors may be used in long-term and weekly/daily lesson plans?
3. What are some factors to consider when setting up your classroom to manage, organize, and differentiate instruction in reading?
4. How can a teacher motivate students to engage in purposeful, independent reading?

**Competency 2:**

1. What are some of the tests to use for ongoing assessment to plan reading instruction?
2. What criteria are used to select the test or assessment to use?
3. How do you use the data from tests?
4. What are some ways you would use test results in relation to the Reading/Language Arts Standards?

## Domain 2

## Word Analysis

**Competency 3:**

1. What is the difference between phonological awareness and phonemic awareness?
2. What part does phonemic awareness play in learning to read?
3. What do teachers need to know concerning phonemic awareness?
4. What is the role of phonemic awareness in learning to read?
5. What instruction can be presented to assist in the development of phonemic awareness?
6. How can a teacher plan direct systematic, explicit, and implicit instruction in phonemic awareness?
7. How can a teacher address the full range of learners in the classroom with respect to their development of phonological development, including phonemic awareness?

**Competency 4:**

1. What role do concepts about print and an understanding of how the letters, words, and sentences are represented in written language play in students' learning to read?

**Competency 5:**

1. What are systematic, explicit phonics and other word-identification strategies?
2. What tasks must the teacher address to implement a systematic, explicit phonics program?
3. How are phonics development and spelling development related?

**Competency 6:**

1. What skills need to be taught at the beginning decoding stage?
2. What steps in the instructional process should a teacher consider when planning instruction in decoding?
3. What should a teacher consider when planning instruction in sight words?

**Competency 7:**

1. What should a teacher include when providing instruction in structural and syllabic analysis?
2. What are some ways a teacher might provide students with frequent opportunities to develop their syllabic analysis skills, structural analysis skills, and orthographic knowledge in their reading and writing?
3. How can a teacher differentiate instruction in word analysis for struggling readers, students with special needs, English Learners, and advanced learners?

# Domain 3

# Fluency

**Competency 8:**

1. What are the key indicators of fluency?
2. What are some of the strategies a teacher might use to help develop fluency?
3. What are some of the factors that can disrupt fluency?

**Competency 9:**

1. How can a teacher differentiate instruction in fluency for various populations, such as struggling readers, students with special needs, English Learners, and advanced learners?

# Domain 4

# Vocabulary, Academic Language, and Background Knowledge

**Competency 10:**

1. What are some of the important issues related to the development of vocabulary, academic language, and background knowledge that a teacher needs to consider?

**Competency 11:**

1. What steps are included in direct instruction of vocabulary words?
2. How can a teacher use explicit instruction to build on students' prior knowledge, improve listening and speaking vocabulary, and enhance vocabulary development?
3. How can a teacher differentiate instruction in vocabulary, academic language, and background knowledge for struggling readers, students with special needs, English Learners, and advanced learners?

# Domain 5

## Comprehension

**Competency 12:**

1. What are the levels of comprehension? How should these levels be taught?
2. How can a teacher facilitate student attainment of comprehension?

**Competency 13:**

1. What are comprehension strategies? How should these strategies be taught?

**Competency 14:**

1. How can a teacher teach elements of literary analysis and criticism?
2. How can a teacher assist students in making connections and responding to literature?

**Competency 15:**

1. How can the teacher teach reading strategies for students to gain meaning from text in a variety of ways?
2. What does a teacher need to know to teach content-area literacy/comprehension?
3. How does a teacher teach study and research skills?
4. How can a teacher differentiate instruction in reading comprehension for struggling readers, students with special needs, English Learners, and advanced learners?

# Some Important Notes from the RICA Information Bulletin

1. Two or more content areas are included in each Domain.
2. The order of the content areas and the order of the competency statements within each content area do not indicate relative importance or value.
3. Examples are included with many of the competencies. These examples are provided to help clarify the knowledge and abilities described in the particular competency.
4. The examples given with the competencies should be helpful but are not comprehensive.
5. The competencies pertain to the teaching of reading in English, even though many of the competencies may also be relevant to the teaching of reading in other languages.
6. Each competency refers to the provision of instruction to all students, including English Learners, speakers of nonmainstream English, struggling readers, students with special needs, and advanced learners. The term "advanced learners" refers to students who are advanced with respect to relevant state standards addressed by the competency, and is not meant to imply that the learners are necessarily advanced in all areas of reading.
7. Instruction should be characterized by a sensitivity to and respect for the culture and language of the students and should be based on students' developmental, linguistic, functional, and age-appropriate needs; that is, instruction should be provided in ways that meet the needs of the individual student.
8. The RICA is not designed to assess the candidate's writing ability. It is designed to assess the knowledge of the reading research and skills necessary for competent readers.
9. Candidates must communicate a clear understanding and knowledge of the necessary pedagogy and skills. The candidate should know the reading research and how to apply the findings from the research in a classroom situation.
10. Candidates can obtain further information regarding the RICA through the RICA Registration Bulletin or by checking the website at www.rica.nesinc.com.

# The RICA Domains—A Closer Look

## Domain 1

## Planning, Organizing, and Managing Reading Instruction Based on Ongoing Assessment

### Competency 1: Understand how to plan, organize, and manage standards-based reading instruction.

Including:

(1) Demonstrate knowledge of fundamental principles involved in planning, organizing, and managing reading instruction in a research-based, standards-based reading program.

*For example:*

a. basing instruction on the standards/curriculum outlined in the English Language Arts (ELA) Content Standards through the primary use of California State Board of Education (SBE)–adopted materials for both instruction and intervention

b. ensuring that instruction provides a balanced, comprehensive reading program as described in the California Reading/Language Arts (RLA) Framework (2007)

c. making instructional decisions based on ongoing assessment results

d. ensuring that instruction is systematic and explicit and promotes prevention of reading difficulties before they occur

e. recognizing that systematic reading instruction is based on the assumption that students master particular skills and knowledge at designated points in time and that earlier skills are foundational and requisite for later, more complex, higher-order skills and knowledge

f. ensuring that daily instruction is differentiated to address the full range of learners in the classroom and conveys high expectations to all learners

g. ensuring that planning includes both short- and long-term goals that lead to daily evidence-based learning objectives

(2) Demonstrate knowledge of key factors to consider in planning differentiated reading instruction.

*For example:*

a. students' assessed knowledge and skills in the specific area(s) of reading

b. prerequisite knowledge and skills (i.e., the knowledge and skills required for students to be able to benefit from instruction)

c. pacing of instruction

d. complexity of the content/skills to be presented

e. scaffolds to ensure that all students have access to higher-level knowledge and skills

(3) Demonstrate knowledge of how to organize and manage differentiated reading instruction and interventions to meet the needs of all students.

*For example:*

    **a.** using flexible grouping, individualized instruction, and whole-class instruction as needed

    **b.** using all components of core California SBE–adopted materials to make grade-level content accessible to all students

    **c.** recognizing that students should be grouped for interventions according to the severity of their difficulties (i.e., benchmark, strategic, and intensive groups)

**(4)** Demonstrate knowledge of components of effective instructional delivery in reading as described in the California RLA Framework (2007).

*For example:*

    **a.** orientation (e.g., engagement, teacher demonstration)

    **b.** presentation (e.g., explicit instruction, modeling, pacing)

    **c.** structured and guided practice (e.g., reinforcement, questioning, feedback, corrections, peer-mediated instruction)

    **d.** independent practice and application

**(5)** Demonstrate knowledge of strategies for engaging students in reading instruction and motivating them to progress in their reading development.

*For example:*

    **a.** providing instruction that enables students to develop the skills necessary for successful reading

    **b.** creating a stimulating learning environment

    **c.** providing appropriate reading materials (e.g., readable, interesting)

    **d.** reading aloud to students

    **e.** encouraging parents/guardians to read to their children and to model the value of reading at home for pleasure and information

**(6)** Demonstrate knowledge of a variety of strategies for promoting purposeful independent reading of a wide variety of narrative/literary and expository/informational texts (e.g., teaching students how to select books at appropriate reading levels, using students' personal interests to help motivate and increase independent reading, providing structured independent-reading opportunities in class, supporting at-home reading) and methods for monitoring students' independent reading (e.g., student-maintained reading logs, book reports, formal and informal oral presentations, class discussions, book talks).

**(7)** Demonstrate knowledge of factors involved in creating a literacy-rich environment and strategies for promoting students' lifelong appreciation for reading for pleasure and for information (e.g., encouraging book clubs, literature circles, author studies, and other reading discussion groups; helping students use reading to set and pursue their own research goals).

**(8)** Demonstrate knowledge of support systems that can be used to promote the skillful teaching of reading (e.g., reading coach, grade-level team meetings, and professional development that are focused on instruction and California SBE–adopted materials).

## Questions for Review

**1.1. What are some factors to consider in planning reading instruction?**

Your answers might include reference to some of the following:

- Assessment data, analysis, and findings
- Instructional plan, including assessment data, standards, components of literacy, grouping, time/pacing, instructional strategies/possible interventions, student activities, individual student needs, text, and materials

- Resources, technology, and other curriculum variables
- Instruction, including direct instruction and other instructional strategies
- Strategies to meet the needs of special populations, such as struggling readers, students with special needs, English Learners, and advanced learners
- Meaningful practice
- Assessment

**1.2. What factors may be used in long-term and weekly/daily lesson plans?**

Your answers might include:

| Long-Term Planning | Weekly/Daily Plan |
|---|---|
| California State Standards | Results of ongoing assessment |
| District Standards | Developmental level of students |
| Text guidelines | Individual student needs |
| Grade-level expectations | Text guidelines |
| District Pacing Guide | Site timeline/pacing |

**1.3. What are some of the factors to consider when setting up your classroom to manage, organize, and differentiate instruction in reading?**

Your answers might include:

- State and District Standards
- Instructional materials, technology, and other resources available
- Groupings, such as flexible, individualized, skill-specific, and whole groups
- Planning and implementing timely interventions
- Learning environment, print rich to support literacy, areas noted for specific literacy activities, centers, hands-on activities, and small-group collaboration
- Providing differentiated or individualized instruction

**1.4. How can a teacher motivate students to engage in purposeful independent reading?**

Your answers might include:

- Provide a print-rich room environment by labeling areas of the room, displaying word charts, and setting out a variety of reading materials for students to view
- Provide a wide variety of books at a range of reading levels in a classroom library
- Plan book clubs, book talks, and book-sharing opportunities
- Organize a system wherein students take home books to read nightly

# Competency 2: Understand the purposes of reading assessment and best practices related to standards-based, entry-level assessment; monitoring of student progress; and summative assessment.

Including:

(1) Demonstrate knowledge of the three primary purposes of reading assessment:

    **a.** performing entry-level assessment (e.g., using standards/curriculum-based assessments to determine the extent to which students possess crucial prerequisite skills and knowledge expected at their grade level and to determine students' current skills and knowledge in a specific area of reading prior to planning instruction and/or intervention in that area)

**b.** monitoring of student progress—for example:

- Conducting curriculum-based assessment on an ongoing basis to determine whether students are progressing adequately toward achieving standards
- Analyzing whether instruction has been effective or requires adjustment to meet the needs of students
- As needed, using formal and informal diagnostic assessments in word analysis, fluency, vocabulary, academic language, background knowledge, and comprehension to determine students' specific instructional needs

**c.** summative assessment (e.g., using standards-based assessments to determine whether students have achieved the goals defined by the standards or a group of standards)

**(2)** Recognize that students with an Individualized Education Program (IEP) may require alternative assessments.

**(3)** Demonstrate knowledge of quality indicators (e.g., reliability, validity) that apply to standardized assessments.

**(4)** Demonstrate ability to interpret results of assessments and to use evidence from assessments to determine whether a student is performing below, at, or above expected levels of performance with respect to grade-level content standards and benchmarks, and demonstrate knowledge of strategies for collecting, organizing, and documenting these results to support effective instructional planning.

**(5)** Demonstrate knowledge of assessments used to determine students' independent, instructional, and frustration reading levels; how to interpret results of these assessments; and how to use this information to plan interventions for individuals and small groups.

**(6)** Demonstrate knowledge of strategies for communicating assessment results and reading progress to students, parents/guardians, and relevant school and district personnel.

## Questions for Review

**2.1. What are some of the tests to use for ongoing assessment to plan reading instruction?**

Your answers might include:

- Phonemic Awareness Survey, such as the Yopp-Singer or the Rosner Phonemic Awareness Survey
- Alphabet Recognition Test, Letter Identification, Alphabetic Principle
- Phonics Survey, such as Shefelbine's Beginning Phonics Skills Test (BPST)
- Concepts of Print Survey, such as Marie Clay's Concepts of Print Survey
- Sight/High-Frequency Words, such as the Dolch List or First Grade 100 Words
- Reading Comprehension, such as text comprehension, retellings, or cloze test
- Running Records
- Spelling tests, such as Donald Bear's Qualitative Spelling Inventory
- Vocabulary tests

These are some of the available assessments; there are many more from which to choose. The California Reading/Language Arts Framework is another source of assessment ideas.

**2.2. What criteria are used to select the test or assessment to use?**

Your answers might include:

- State and district Language Arts standards
- Developmental level of students
- Skill level of students; identified skill needs
- District guidelines/assessments
- Grade-level expectations

**2.3. How do you use the data from tests?**

Some uses of data might include:

- Target instruction to meet individual needs.
- Communicate; grade-level peers, parents, students, and administrators.
- Determine student reading level; independent, instructional, and frustration.
- Form flexible skill groups.
- Plan instruction, including intervention, to meet student needs.
- List materials, resources needed.

The California State Reading/Language Arts Standards can be viewed as the bar for determining whether a student's performance is at, below, or above grade level.

**2.4. What are some ways you would use test results in relation to the Reading/Language Arts Standards?**

Your answers might include:

- Record individual student progress toward mastery of standards.
- Plan reading groups to meet identified needs.
- Communicate with parents.
- Plan interventions for students who need additional help.
- Communicate specific performance information based on standards to students, parents, and school personnel.

Your answers should include a rationale for selecting data, description on how to use the data, and the context for collecting, analyzing, and presenting.

# Domain 2

# Word Analysis

## Competency 3: Understand the role of phonological and phonemic awareness in reading development and how to develop students' phonological and phonemic awareness skills.

Including:

(1) Demonstrate knowledge of the role of phonological and phonemic awareness in reading development.

(2) Recognize the distinction between phonological awareness (i.e., the awareness that oral language is composed of smaller units, such as spoken words and syllables) and phonemic awareness (i.e., a specific type of phonological awareness involving the ability to distinguish the separate phonemes in a spoken word).

(3) Demonstrate knowledge of the continuum of research-based, systematic, explicit instruction in phonological awareness (e.g., detecting and identifying word boundaries, syllables, rhyming words, onset/rime), including phonemic awareness (e.g., recognizing that words are made up of separate phonemes; distinguishing initial, medial, and final phonemes; blending, segmenting, deleting, and substituting phonemes).

(4) Recognize the relationship between phonemic awareness and the development of phonics knowledge and skills (e.g., letter-sound correspondence, blending), and demonstrate knowledge of strategies for helping students make explicit connections between their phonemic awareness and letters (e.g., teaching phonemic awareness both preceding instruction in letter knowledge and in concert with instruction in the alphabetic principle and letter-sound correspondence).

(5) Demonstrate knowledge of how to address the full range of learners in the classroom with respect to their development of phonological awareness, including phonemic awareness (i.e., Universal Access as described in chapter 7 and relevant ELA Content Standards in the California RLA Framework [2007]).

*For example:*

**a.** providing differentiated instruction in phonological awareness, including phonemic awareness, to address the needs of struggling readers and students with reading difficulties or disabilities (e.g., focusing on key skills, especially blending and segmenting; reteaching skills that are lacking; using a variety of concrete examples to explain a concept or task; providing additional practice)

**b.** providing differentiated instruction in phonological awareness, including phonemic awareness, to support students with special needs (e.g., using a variety of concrete examples to explain a concept or task, including using visual, auditory, kinesthetic, and tactile techniques; reteaching skills that are lacking; providing additional practice)

**c.** providing differentiated instruction in phonological awareness, including phonemic awareness, to address the needs of English Learners and speakers of nonstandard English (e.g., capitalizing on transfer of relevant knowledge and skills from the primary language, explicitly teaching nontransferable phonemes and phoneme sequences)

**d.** providing differentiated instruction in phonological awareness, including phonemic awareness, to address the needs of advanced learners (e.g., increasing the pace of instruction, building on and extending current skills)

(6) Demonstrate knowledge and ability in assessment (i.e., entry-level assessment, monitoring of progress, and summative assessment) with respect to phonological awareness, including phonemic awareness.

*For example:*

**a.** demonstrating ability to describe and use appropriate formal and informal assessments in phonological awareness, including phonemic awareness, for different assessment purposes (i.e., entry-level assessment, monitoring of progress, and summative assessment)

**b.** demonstrating ability to analyze and interpret results from these assessments

**c.** demonstrating ability to use the results of assessments to plan effective instruction and interventions in phonological awareness, including phonemic awareness; adjust instruction and interventions to meet the identified needs of students; and ultimately determine whether relevant standards have been met

## Questions for Review

**3.1. What is the difference between phonological awareness and phonemic awareness?**

- Phonological awareness is the awareness that oral language is composed of smaller units, such as spoken words and syllables.
- Phonemic awareness is a specific type of phonological awareness involving the ability to distinguish the separate phonemes in a spoken word.

**3.2. What part does phonemic awareness play in learning to read?**

Answers to the question should address some of the following:

- Phonemic awareness is the awareness of the sounds (phonemes) that make up spoken words.
- Phonemic awareness is the ability to hear, identify, and manipulate individual sounds.
- Phonemic awareness is more highly related to learning to read than general intelligence, reading readiness, or listening comprehension (Stanovich).
- Phonemic awareness can be directly taught so that a beginning or poor reader can learn that words are composed of phonemics or speech sounds (Adams).

- Students must be able to perceive and produce the specific sounds of the English language and understand how the system works.

- Phonemic awareness can improve students' word reading and reading comprehension.

- Phonemic awareness helps students learn to spell. (See "Put Reading First" by the National Institute for Literacy for elaboration and further ideas.)

**3.3. What do teachers need to know concerning phonemic awareness?**

1. The English sound system, including the consonant and vowel phonemes of English

2. How to assess student needs in auditory awareness, and discrimination of sounds and spoken language (e.g., Phonemic Awareness Survey, Yopp-Singer)

3. How to plan systematic, explicit instruction

4. How to choose materials and activities to assist in the understanding and the manipulation of sounds (phonological awareness)

5. A system for comparing speech sounds in other languages with the speech sounds in English—thus, contrasts can be made explicit for English Learners when appropriate

**3.4. What is the role of phonemic awareness in learning to read?**

A few possible answers are as follows:

- It is a predictor of success in learning to read (Adams).

- Phonemes, the smallest units in spoken language are identified, practiced, and manipulated. The phonemic awareness instructional progression includes words, syllables, onsets and rimes, and phonemes.

**3.5. What instruction can be presented to assist in the development of phonemic awareness?**

- Awareness that words are made up of sounds

- Awareness of the English sounds system, consonant and vowel phonemics in English

- Auditory awareness and discrimination of sounds, identifying and categorizing phonemes

- Word awareness (recognize word boundaries), syllable awareness

- Instruction and practice in phoneme awareness (e.g., rhymes, blending sounds, substituting sounds, segmenting sounds in a word, deleting sounds)

- Selection of appropriate materials and activities for teaching phonemic awareness skills

**3.6. How can a teacher plan direct systematic, explicit, and implicit instruction in phonemic awareness?**

- Instruction should be structured and planned using assessment data of student need in phonemic awareness developmental progression.

- Plan should address assessment data, academic standards, individual student needs, grouping, time, technology, text, materials and resources, district standards and pacing guide, and other curriculum variables.

- Present direct, explicit instruction in phonemic awareness. Include a variety of lessons in phonemic awareness skills, such as sound manipulation and identification, comparison blending, substitution and segmentation, and onsets and rimes.

- Focus instruction on only one or two types of phoneme manipulation at a time.

- Select activities and materials to make the connection between oral language and print (e.g., Big Books, songs, alliteration, word play).

- Knowledge of instructional strategies for teaching phonemic awareness both before and during beginning reading.

- Provide meaningful practice in phonemic awareness skills.

- Plan ongoing assessment to demonstrate student progress toward mastery of state standards.

**3.7  How can a teacher address the full range of learners in the classroom with respect to their development of phonological awareness, including phonemic awareness?**

- Review assessment data to determine in which skills the student is lacking awareness (segmenting, blending, rhyming, etc.)
- Group students according to their awareness
- Modify pacing
- Modify complexity but ensure the content remains rigorous
- Include a variety of oral language games and activities that manipulate beginning, medial, and ending sounds

## Competency 4: Understand the role of concepts about print, letter recognition, and the alphabetic principle in reading development and how to develop students' knowledge and skills in these areas.

Including:

(1) Recognize the role of print awareness in early reading development and identify explicit, research-based strategies for teaching various concepts about print (e.g., developing an awareness of the relationship between spoken and written language and an understanding that print carries meaning; recognizing letter, word, and sentence representation; recognizing the directionality of print; developing the ability to track print in connected text; developing book-handling skills).

(2) Recognize the importance of accurate and rapid uppercase and lowercase letter recognition in reading development and demonstrate knowledge of research-based, systematic, explicit instruction in letter recognition, letter naming, and letter formation, including factors to consider when planning instruction in these areas (e.g., how to systematically introduce visually and auditorily similar letters, the importance of providing practice in writing letters and words).

(3) Recognize the role of the alphabetic principle in reading development, in particular the interrelationships among letter-sound (i.e., grapheme-phoneme) correspondence, phonemic awareness, and beginning decoding (e.g., sounding out and blending letter sounds), and demonstrate knowledge of research-based, systematic, explicit instruction in the alphabetic principle.

(4) Recognize the role of writing (i.e., students' use of phonetic spelling) in promoting and reinforcing students' understanding of the alphabetic principle and letter-sound correspondence.

(5) Demonstrate knowledge of how to address the full range of learners in the classroom with respect to their development of concepts about print, letter recognition, and the alphabetic principle (i.e., Universal Access).

*For example:*

   a. providing differentiated instruction in these areas of reading to address the needs of struggling readers and students with reading difficulties or disabilities (e.g., focusing on key concepts and skills; reteaching concepts, letters, and skills that are lacking; using a variety of concrete examples to explain a concept or task; providing additional practice)

   b. providing differentiated instruction in these areas of reading to support students with special needs (e.g., focusing on key concepts; using a variety of concrete examples to explain a concept or task; reteaching concepts, letters, and skills that are lacking using visual, auditory, kinesthetic, and tactile techniques; providing additional practice)

   c. providing differentiated instruction in these areas of reading to address the needs of English Learners and speakers of nonstandard English (e.g., capitalizing on transfer of relevant knowledge and skills from the primary language; recognizing that not all languages are alphabetic and that key features of alphabets vary, including letters, directionality, and phonetic regularity)

   d. providing differentiated instruction in these areas of reading to address the needs of advanced learners (e.g., increasing the pace of instruction, building on and extending current knowledge and skills)

(6) Demonstrate knowledge and ability in assessment (i.e., entry-level assessment, monitoring of progress, and summative assessment) with respect to concepts about print, letter recognition, and the alphabetic principle.

*For example:*

a. demonstrating ability to describe and use appropriate formal and informal assessments in concepts about print, letter recognition, and the alphabetic principle for different assessment purposes (i.e., entry-level assessment, monitoring of progress, and summative assessment)

b. demonstrating ability to analyze and interpret results from these assessments

c. demonstrating ability to use the results of assessments to plan effective instruction and interventions in concepts about print, letter recognition, and the alphabetic principle; adjust instruction and interventions to meet the identified needs of students; and ultimately determine whether relevant standards have been met

## Questions for Review

**4.1. What role do concepts about print and an understanding of how the letters, words, and sentences are represented in written language play in students' learning to read?**

Answers to this question might include:

- An understanding that knowing concepts of print is an essential element in learning to read. It is a predictor of success in reading (Adams).

- The role of concepts about print, such as left to right sequence and word identity, conveys the critical knowledge that print represents language.

- Print is oral language or talking put on paper.

Therefore, concepts about print must be explicitly taught to students who demonstrate a need. To do this, teachers must perform some of the following:

- Assess student understanding of concepts about print and design instruction to meet any identified need. Several surveys and observation tools are available to assess understanding and plan appropriate instruction.

- Plan instruction and select appropriate materials and activities in alignment with the instructional progression of concepts about print, such as letter, word, state standards, sentence representation, directionality, tracking of print, and understanding that print carries meaning.

- Plan instruction and select appropriate materials in recognition of letters in print, accompanied by practice both in and out of context. Recognition should include uppercase and lowercase letters, shapes, and letter names.

- Select and design engaging materials and activities, including multisensory techniques (visual, auditory, kinesthetic, and tactile).

- Provide meaningful practice in concept of print skills. Use multisensory techniques—for example, visual, auditory, kinesthetic, and tactile.

- Use ongoing assessment to demonstrate progress toward mastery of standards.

## Competency 5: Understand important terminology and concepts involved in phonics instruction and recognize the role of phonics and sight words in reading development.

Including:

(1) Recognize the role of phonics and sight words in accurate, automatic word identification, including how word identification contributes to word recognition (i.e., the process by which readers connect a decoded word to an existing word in their oral vocabulary) and how automaticity in word recognition supports development of reading fluency and comprehension.

(2) Recognize the importance of sequencing phonics and sight-word instruction according to the increasing complexity of linguistic units and demonstrate knowledge of terminology and concepts related to these units.

*For example:*

    **a.** types of consonant sounds (e.g., continuous sounds, stop sounds)

    **b.** common, regular letter combinations (e.g., consonant digraphs, consonant blends, vowel digraphs, diphthongs, r- and l-controlled vowels)

    **c.** common inflected morphological units that are taught as part of phonics instruction (e.g., the suffixes *–ed, –er, –est, –ing,* and *–s*)

    **d.** common word patterns of increasing difficulty (e.g., VC, CVC, CVCC, CCVC, CVVC, CVCe)

    **e.** common syllable patterns and syllabication as applied to decoding multisyllabic words

    **f.** why some words are phonetically irregular and never decodable (e.g., *of, the, was*)

    **g.** how and when irregular words fit into the continuum of phonics instruction

    **h.** why some decodable words must be taught as sight words until their phonetic pattern has been taught (e.g., *park* is decodable but is taught as a sight word until r-controlled *a* is introduced)

(3) Recognize that decoding and encoding are reciprocal skills and demonstrate knowledge of the interrelationships between phonics development and stages of spelling development (i.e., precommunicative writing, semiphonetic, phonetic, transitional, and conventional).

*For example:*

    **a.** how phonics knowledge supports both reading and spelling/orthographic development

    **b.** how development of spelling/orthographic knowledge supports development of decoding skills

    **c.** how research-based, systematic, sequential spelling instruction reinforces phonics and vocabulary development

    **d.** how writing activities provide opportunities for applying phonics knowledge in context

    **e.** how a student's stage of spelling development has implications for both spelling and phonics instruction

## Questions for Review

**5.1. What are systematic, explicit phonics and other word-identification strategies?**

Answers might include the following:

- Organized program in which letter-sound correspondences both for letters and letter clusters are directly taught in a manner that builds from simple to complex in a gradual manner.
- Organization of instruction, which includes sound-symbol relationship, decoding skills, and word attack skills.
- Students being taught information sequenced according to organizational patterns that are intrinsic to the English language. These include concepts about print, letter recognition, sound-symbol association, rapid fluent recognition of sounds, sight vocabulary, syllable patterns, and meaningful parts, and fluent application of these skills to text.

**5.2. What tasks must the teacher address to implement a systematic, explicit phonics program?**

    **1.** Assess phonics and other word-identification strategies. Select and use formal and informal tools, such as decoding tests, fluency tests, and sight word checks, to collect data and analyze to plan instruction.

    **2.** Plan instruction that is systematic, explicit, and sequenced according to the increasing complexity of linguistic units, including sounds, phonemes, onsets and rimes, letters, letter combinations, syllables, and morphemes.

3. Select or design resource materials and strategies for assessment and instruction. Resources include materials for teaching decoding, word-identification strategies, and sight word mastery in multiple and varied reading and writing experiences.

4. Explicitly teach and model phonics, decoding, and other word identification strategies in reading for meaning. Positive explicit feedback for word identification errors is an essential strategy in this process.

5. Provide fluency practice in a variety of ways.

- Practice decoding and word attack skills so they become automatic in reading text.
- Provide application and practice decoding skills to fluency in decodable (controlled vocabulary) text and word recognition skills taught out of context.
- Continue to develop fluency through the use of decodable texts and other texts written at the student's instructional level.

6. Ongoing assessment to demonstrate student progress toward mastery of state standards.

To implement this systematic, explicit program, the teacher must possess the following:

- Knowledge of the terminology and concepts of phonics decoding and word attack skills (blends, digraphs, diphthongs, syllables, prefixes, and so on) is necessary for all teachers.
- Knowledge of instructional strategies and knowledge that the purpose of learning phonics is to recognize words fluently and to read for meaning (comprehension). Creating independent readers, who are motivated and comprehend what they read, is the goal of reading instruction.

**5.3. How are phonics development and spelling development interrelated?**

A knowledge of phonics supports spelling development. A knowledge of spelling supports decoding skills. Spelling also reinforces phonics.

## Competency 6: Understand how to develop students' phonics knowledge and skills and recognition of sight words to promote accurate word analysis that leads to automaticity in word recognition and contributes to spelling development.

Including:

(1) Demonstrate knowledge of the continuum of research-based, systematic, explicit instruction in phonics and sight words appropriate for students at the beginning-reading stage (i.e., as students progress from sounding out letter by letter to recognizing words as units of letters).

*For example:*

a. teaching sounding out and blending of regular VC and CVC words

b. teaching whole-word reading focused on single-syllable regular words and some high-frequency irregular sight words

c. using decodable text to ensure that students have abundant practice with phonics elements and sight words already taught

d. teaching students to use phonics knowledge to spell VC and CVC words

(2) Demonstrate knowledge of the continuum of research-based, systematic, explicit instruction in phonics and sight words appropriate for students at more advanced stages of decoding development (i.e., as students progress in word reading involving words with increasing linguistic complexity).

*For example:*

    **a.** teaching CVCC, CCVC, and CVVC words containing common, regular letter combinations

    **b.** teaching regular CVCe words

    **c.** teaching words containing phonics elements that are less common (e.g., *kn, ph*)

    **d.** continuing use of decodable text to ensure that students have abundant practice with phonics elements and sight words already taught

    **e.** teaching words formed by adding a common inflected ending (e.g., *–ed, –er, –est, –ing, –s*) to a base word

    **f.** teaching students to use phonics knowledge to spell more complex orthographic patterns in single-syllable words and in words formed by adding a common inflected ending to a single-syllable word

**(3)** Demonstrate knowledge of research-based, systematic, explicit instruction in sight words, including:

    **a.** identifying high-frequency words that do and do not conform to regular phonics/spelling patterns

    **b.** recognizing factors that affect the sequence of instruction for specific sight words (e.g., the frequency with which a word occurs in students' reading materials, how visually similar or dissimilar a word is to other sight words)

    **c.** identifying explicit strategies for helping students master the spelling of high-frequency sight words

**(4)** Demonstrate knowledge of how to address the full range of learners in the classroom with respect to their development of phonics skills, sight-word knowledge, and spelling of single-syllable words (i.e., Universal Access).

*For example:*

    **a.** providing differentiated instruction in phonics, sight words, and spelling of single-syllable words to address the needs of struggling readers and students with reading difficulties or disabilities (e.g., focusing on key phonics skills and high-frequency sight words, reteaching phonics skills and sight words that are lacking, using a variety of concrete examples to explain a concept or task, providing additional practice)

    **b.** providing differentiated instruction in phonics, sight words, and spelling of single-syllable words to support students with special needs (e.g., using systematic and explicit synthetic phonics instruction; focusing on key concepts and skills, such as key phonics elements and sight words; using a variety of concrete examples to explain a concept or task; using visual, auditory, kinesthetic, and tactile techniques to teach spelling and to promote mastery of new sight words; reteaching content and skills that are lacking; providing additional practice)

    **c.** providing differentiated instruction in phonics, sight words, and spelling of single-syllable words to address the needs of English Learners and speakers of nonstandard English (e.g., capitalizing on transfer of relevant knowledge and skills from the primary language; explicitly teaching sounds that do not transfer; explicitly teaching the meaning of sight words, if needed)

    **d.** providing differentiated instruction in phonics, sight words, and spelling of single-syllable words to address the needs of advanced learners (e.g., increasing the pace or complexity of instruction, building on and extending current knowledge and skills)

**(5)** Demonstrate knowledge and ability in assessment (i.e., entry-level assessment, monitoring of progress, and summative assessment) with respect to phonics, sight words, and spelling of single-syllable words.

*For example:*

    **a.** demonstrating ability to describe and use appropriate formal and informal assessments in phonics, sight words, and spelling of single-syllable words for different assessment purposes (i.e., entry-level assessment, monitoring of progress, and summative assessment)

    **b.** demonstrating ability to analyze and interpret results from these assessments

    **c.** demonstrating ability to use the results of assessments to plan effective instruction and interventions in phonics, sight words, and spelling of single-syllable words; adjust instruction and interventions to meet the identified needs of students; and ultimately determine whether relevant standards have been met

## Questions for Review

**6.1. What skills need to be taught at the beginning decoding stage?**

1. To read simple, new regular words from left to right
2. To generate sounds from all the letters
3. To blend sounds into a recognizable word

**6.2. What steps in the instructional process should a teacher consider when planning instruction in decoding?**

Answers might include:

- Progress systematically from simple words and word length to more complex words
- Model (letter-sound correspondence, blending, reading whole words)
- Sequence words strategically
- Provide initial practice in controlled text
- Provide repeated opportunities for students to read words
- Use decodable text based on specific phonics lessons
- Teach necessary sight words

**6.3. What should a teacher consider when planning instruction in sight words?**

- High-frequency words that do and do not conform to phonics and spelling patterns
- The frequency with which a word occurs in students' reading materials
- How visually similar or dissimilar a word is to other words
- Strategies to help students master the spelling of sight words

## Competency 7: Understand the role of syllabic and structural analysis and orthographic knowledge in reading development and how to develop students' knowledge and skills in these areas to promote accurate word analysis that leads to automaticity in word recognition and contributes to spelling development.

Including:

(1) Recognize how phonics skills, sight-word knowledge, and knowledge and skills in syllabic and structural analysis and orthography all work in concert to support students' development of accurate word analysis, which leads to automaticity in word recognition.

(2) Recognize the role of structural analysis (e.g., decoding multisyllabic words formed by adding a prefix and/or suffix to a base word or base morpheme) and syllabic analysis (e.g., decoding multisyllabic words composed of common syllable patterns, such as open and closed syllables) in accurate word analysis and spelling of multisyllabic words.

(3) Demonstrate knowledge of systematic, explicit instruction in structural and syllabic analysis and spelling of multisyllabic words.

*For example:*

a. teaching multisyllabic words formed by adding a common prefix or suffix to a base word
b. teaching multisyllabic words that follow common syllable patterns
c. teaching students to use knowledge of structural analysis and syllable patterns to spell multisyllabic words

**(4)** Recognize the strong relationship between orthographic knowledge and word analysis and demonstrate knowledge of systematic, explicit instruction in spelling/orthography.

*For example:*

    **a.** teaching students to spell larger, more complex chunks of letters (phonograms), such as *–ight*

    **b.** teaching students to apply common orthographic generalizations (rules) (e.g., changing the ending of a word from *–y* to *–ies* when forming the plural)

    **c.** teaching students to accurately recognize and use common homophones (e.g., *to, two,* and *too; hair* and *hare*)

**(5)** Recognize the importance of providing students with frequent opportunities to develop and extend their syllabic analysis skills, structural analysis skills, and orthographic knowledge in their reading and writing.

*For example:*

    **a.** frequently reading texts that contain words using affixes, syllable patterns, and orthographic patterns and rules already taught

    **b.** frequently engaging in writing activities that include opportunities to apply knowledge of more complex orthographic patterns and spelling of multisyllabic words

**(6)** Demonstrate knowledge of how to address the full range of learners in the classroom with respect to their development of syllabic and structural analysis and orthographic knowledge to support decoding and spelling of multisyllabic words and spelling of words that follow more complex orthographic patterns or rules (i.e., Universal Access).

*For example:*

    **a.** providing differentiated instruction in these areas to address the needs of struggling readers and students with reading difficulties or disabilities (e.g., focusing on key skills and knowledge, such as frequently occurring syllable patterns and affixes and related orthographic patterns; reteaching concepts and skills that are lacking; using a variety of concrete examples to explain a concept or task; providing additional practice)

    **b.** providing differentiated instruction in these areas to support students with special needs (e.g., focusing on key skills and knowledge, such as frequently occurring syllable patterns and affixes and related orthographic patterns; using a variety of concrete examples to explain a concept or task; using visual, auditory, kinesthetic, and tactile techniques; reteaching concepts and skills that are lacking; providing additional oral practice with new words)

    **c.** providing differentiated instruction in these areas to address the needs of English Learners and speakers of nonstandard English (e.g., explicitly teaching common English roots and affixes)

    **d.** providing differentiated instruction in these areas to address the needs of advanced learners (e.g., increasing the pace and/or complexity of instruction, building on and extending current knowledge and skills)

**(7)** Demonstrate knowledge and ability in assessment (i.e., entry-level assessment, monitoring of progress, and summative assessment) with respect to development of syllabic analysis, structural analysis, orthographic knowledge, spelling of multisyllabic words, and spelling of words that follow more complex orthographic patterns or rules.

*For example:*

    **a.** demonstrating ability to describe and use appropriate formal and informal assessments in these areas for different assessment purposes (i.e., entry-level assessment, monitoring of progress, and summative assessment)

    **b.** demonstrating ability to analyze and interpret results from these assessments

    **c.** demonstrating ability to use the results of assessments to plan effective instruction and interventions in these areas, adjust instruction and interventions to meet the identified needs of students, and ultimately determine whether relevant standards have been met

## Questions for Review

**7.1. What should a teacher include when providing instruction in structural and syllabic analysis?**

Answers might include:

- adding a common prefix or suffix to a base word
- words that follow common syllable patterns

**7.2. What are some ways a teacher might provide students with frequent opportunities to develop their syllabic analysis skills, structural analysis skills, and orthographic knowledge in their reading and writing?**

- frequently reading texts that contain words using affixes, syllable patterns, and orthographic patterns and rules already taught
- frequently engaging in writing activities that include opportunities to apply knowledge of more complex orthographic patterns and spelling of multisyllabic words

**7.3. How can a teacher differentiate instruction in word analysis for struggling readers, students with special needs, English Learners, and advanced learners?**

- **a.** for struggling readers and students with disabilities, focus on key skills and knowledge, such as frequently occurring syllable patterns and affixes and related orthographic patterns; reteaching concepts and skills that are lacking; using a variety of concrete examples to explain a concept or task; providing additional practice
- **b.** for students with special needs, focus on key skills and knowledge, such as frequently occurring syllable patterns and affixes and related orthographic patterns; use a variety of concrete examples to explain a concept or task; use visual, auditory, kinesthetic, and tactile techniques; reteach concepts and skills that are lacking; provide additional oral practice with new words
- **c.** for English Learners and speakers of nonstandard English, explicitly teach common English roots and affixes
- **d.** for advanced learners, increase the pace and/or complexity of instruction, build on and extend current knowledge and skills

# Domain 3

# Fluency

## Competency 8: Understand the role of fluency in reading development and factors that affect students' development of fluency.

Including:

(1) Demonstrate knowledge of the role of fluency in all stages of reading development (e.g., the progression from letter naming to word reading to connected text).

(2) Demonstrate knowledge of key indicators of reading fluency and their interrelationships:

- **a.** accuracy (i.e., accurate decoding and word recognition)
- **b.** rate
- **c.** prosody (i.e., reading with expression, including using appropriate stress or emphasis, variation in pitch and intonation, and pausing in a manner that reflects meaningful phrasing and knowledge of syntax and mechanics)

(3) Demonstrate knowledge of the interrelationships among word analysis skills, fluency, vocabulary, academic language, background knowledge, and comprehension.

*For example:*

    **a.** the role of fluency as a bridge between word analysis skills and comprehension (i.e., fluency includes the ability to decode automatically and thereby have the capacity to comprehend text at the same time)

    **b.** why fluency supports reading comprehension (e.g., automaticity theory)

    **c.** the reciprocity between prosody and comprehension

**(4)** Demonstrate knowledge of factors that can disrupt fluency (e.g., weak word analysis skills, stopping frequently to decode unrecognized or unfamiliar words, lack of familiarity with content vocabulary, lack of background knowledge, texts that contain a large number of one-use and multisyllabic content words, lack of familiarity with more complex syntactic structures).

**(5)** Recognize the role of decodable text in promoting fluent reading in students who are acquiring basic phonics skills and the importance of transitioning students to a broader range of appropriate texts as they progress in their word analysis skills.

**(6)** Recognize the critical role of systematic, explicit instruction in promoting fluency development.

**(7)** Recognize the limitations of using independent silent reading to increase automaticity (i.e., students who do not have automaticity need to practice reading aloud, primarily to themselves).

**(8)** Identify factors that help make independent silent reading more effective in supporting fluency development (e.g., ensuring that students select books at appropriate reading levels and holding them accountable for comprehension).

## Questions for Review

**8.1. What are the three key indicators of fluency?**

- Accuracy
- Rate
- Prosody

**8.2. What are some strategies a teacher might use to help students develop fluency?**

- Provide students with reading materials that are slightly below their instructional level
- Have students repeatedly read aloud the same text to develop familiarity and automaticity

**8.3. What are some factors that can disrupt fluency?**

- Weak word-analysis skills
- Lack of familiarity with vocabulary
- Lack of background knowledge
- Inappropriate level of text
- Frequent stops while reading to try to decode words

# Competency 9: Understand how to promote students' fluency development.

Including:

**(1)** Demonstrate knowledge of essential, research-based components of effective fluency instruction (e.g., guidance, practice, feedback) and how each contributes to fluency development with respect to accuracy, rate, and prosody.

**(2)** Demonstrate knowledge of research-based, systematic, explicit instruction in fluency, including when and how fluency instruction should be introduced.

(3) Demonstrate knowledge of research-based, systematic, explicit strategies for building fluency with respect to accuracy as needed (e.g., providing systematic, explicit instruction in phonemic awareness, phonics, and sight words).

(4) Demonstrate knowledge of research-based, systematic, explicit strategies for building fluency with respect to rate.

*For example:*

    **a.** for students whose decoding is not automatic—engaging in whisper reading (i.e., reading out loud to themselves) as the teacher monitors individual students

    **b.** for students whose decoding is automatic—engaging in independent silent reading with accountability for comprehension

(5) Demonstrate knowledge of research-based, systematic, explicit strategies for building fluency with respect to prosody.

*For example:*

    **a.** modeling and phrase-cued reading

    **b.** purposeful, teacher-directed instruction across subject matter to build content knowledge and academic language

(6) Demonstrate knowledge of how to address the full range of learners in the classroom with respect to their development of fluency (i.e., Universal Access).

*For example:*

    **a.** providing differentiated fluency instruction to address the needs of struggling readers and students with reading difficulties or disabilities (e.g., using texts written at students' independent reading levels; as needed, focusing on improving accuracy through additional word analysis instruction and/or focusing on improving rate through additional practice using either oral or silent reading depending on the student's automaticity)

    **b.** providing differentiated fluency instruction to support students with special needs (e.g., using texts written at students' independent reading levels, focusing on building word analysis skills and recognition of key sight words to promote automaticity, reteaching word analysis skills and sight words that are lacking, providing additional oral reading practice with appropriate-level texts)

    **c.** providing differentiated fluency instruction to address the needs of English Learners and speakers of nonstandard English (e.g., explicitly teaching English intonation patterns, phrasing, syntax, and punctuation)

    **d.** providing differentiated fluency instruction to address the needs of advanced learners (e.g., using more advanced texts to enhance and broaden fluency development)

(7) Demonstrate knowledge and ability in assessment (i.e., entry-level assessment, monitoring of progress, and summative assessment) with respect to fluency (i.e., accuracy, rate, and prosody).

*For example:*

    **a.** demonstrating ability to describe and use appropriate formal and informal assessments to determine students' fluency with respect to accuracy, rate, and prosody for different assessment purposes (i.e., entry-level assessment, monitoring of progress, and summative assessment)

    **b.** demonstrating ability to analyze and interpret results from these assessments

    **c.** demonstrating ability to use the results of assessments to plan effective instruction and interventions in fluency with respect to accuracy, rate, and prosody; adjust instruction and interventions to meet the identified needs of students; and ultimately determine whether relevant standards have been met

## Questions for Review

**9.1.** How can a teacher differentiate instruction in fluency for various populations, such as struggling readers, students with special needs, English Learners, and advanced learners?

- using texts written at students' independent reading levels
- providing additional word analysis instruction
- focusing on improving rate through additional practice using either oral or silent reading, depending on the student's automaticity
- using texts written at students' independent reading levels
- reteaching word analysis skills and sight words that are lacking, providing additional oral reading practice with appropriate-level texts
- explicitly teaching English intonation patterns, phrasing, syntax, and punctuation
- using more advanced texts to enhance and broaden fluency development

# Domain 4

# Vocabulary, Academic Language, and Background Knowledge

## Competency 10: Understand the role of vocabulary, academic language, and background knowledge in reading development and factors that affect students' development of vocabulary, academic language, and background knowledge.

Including:

**(1)** Demonstrate knowledge of the role of vocabulary, academic language, and background knowledge in reading development.

*For example:*

    **a.** the role of vocabulary knowledge in the development of word recognition and fluency

    **b.** the role of vocabulary knowledge in reading comprehension (e.g., vocabulary knowledge as both a key indicator and a predictor of comprehension ability)

    **c.** the role of academic language in reading comprehension and learning (e.g., knowledge of more complex grammatical structures supports comprehension of more advanced texts)

    **d.** the role of background knowledge in reading comprehension and learning (e.g., background knowledge of content as a key indicator of how well a student will learn new information related to that content)

    **e.** interrelationships among vocabulary, academic language, background knowledge, and comprehension (e.g., how a reader constructs understanding of a text through both knowledge of the meanings of explicit words in the text and meanings that the reader infers from relevant background knowledge)

**(2)** Demonstrate knowledge of important issues related to the development of vocabulary, academic language, and background knowledge.

*For example:*

    **a.** the critical role of early vocabulary development (prekindergarten through grade 2) in students' later achievement in vocabulary and reading

    **b.** the Matthew Effect and its impact on students' growth in vocabulary, academic language, and background knowledge and how effective instruction and intervention can reduce its negative effects

c. interrelationships between vocabulary knowledge and concept learning (e.g., how vocabulary acquisition involves concept learning and concept learning supports vocabulary development, how effective vocabulary instruction contributes to the growth of background knowledge)

d. vocabulary learning as an incremental process (e.g., more examples in context result in greater depth of understanding)

e. the open-ended nature of vocabulary and background knowledge and the implications of this for instruction (e.g., the importance of using approaches in vocabulary instruction that promote knowledge of a larger set of words than the target words)

(3) Recognize that text tends to use a larger and more sophisticated vocabulary and more complex language structures than speech and plays a critical role in the development of vocabulary, academic language, and background knowledge.

(4) Recognize the critical role of independent reading in developing students' vocabulary, academic language, and background knowledge (e.g., the correlation between the amount one reads daily and one's academic achievement) and the importance of encouraging independent reading at appropriate levels to promote development of vocabulary, academic language, and background knowledge.

(5) Demonstrate knowledge of factors to consider in developing students' vocabulary, academic language, and background knowledge.

*For example:*

a. recognizing that not all words should be given equal emphasis (e.g., the importance of evaluating the usefulness of a word and the frequency with which students will have opportunities to read it and apply it)

b. recognizing different tiers of general academic vocabulary

c. identifying academic vocabulary that has a high level of usefulness and frequency within a given content area

d. recognizing how understanding of specialized vocabulary (e.g., justify, analyze, determine) is necessary for performing comprehension tasks

e. recognizing the value of promoting students' word consciousness, including their genuine interest in and enthusiasm for words

f. recognizing the value of developing students' listening comprehension to support their vocabulary, academic language, and concept development

g. recognizing the importance of reinforcing vocabulary, academic language, and content knowledge through oral language, reading, and writing activities

h. understanding why learning vocabulary from context is a powerful strategy only when combined with wide reading by and to students

(6) Demonstrate knowledge of the components of an effective, explicit vocabulary program, including:

a. direct teaching of specific words (e.g., combining word-meaning instruction with concept development, using both definitional and contextual approaches, promoting integration ["deep processing"] of word meanings)

b. promoting development of word-learning strategies (e.g., teaching transferable, generalizable strategies; developing morphological knowledge; developing contextual strategies)

c. promoting development of word consciousness

d. promoting wide reading and providing meaningful exposure (e.g., providing multiple, meaningful exposures to new vocabulary, academic language, and background knowledge; providing opportunities to use new vocabulary, academic language, and background knowledge in a variety of topical contexts and in multiple subject areas)

## Questions for Review

**10.1. What are some of the important issues related to the development of vocabulary, academic language, and background knowledge that a teacher needs to consider?**

Possible answers might include:

1. the critical role of early vocabulary development (prekindergarten through grade 2) in students' later achievement in vocabulary and reading

2. the Matthew Effect and its impact on students' growth in vocabulary, academic language, and background knowledge and how effective instruction and intervention can reduce its negative effects

3. the interrelationships between vocabulary knowledge and concept learning (e.g., how vocabulary acquisition involves concept learning and concept learning supports vocabulary development, how effective vocabulary instruction contributes to the growth of background knowledge)

4. vocabulary learning as an incremental process (e.g., more examples in context result in greater depth of understanding)

5. the open-ended nature of vocabulary and background knowledge and the implications of this for instruction (e.g., the importance of using approaches in vocabulary instruction that promote knowledge of a larger set of words than the target words)

# Competency 11: Understand how to promote students' development of vocabulary, academic language, and background knowledge.

Including:

(1) Demonstrate knowledge of research-based, systematic, explicit instruction in vocabulary (i.e., words and their meanings).

*For example:*

    **a.** providing student-friendly definitions

    **b.** providing meaningful and contextualized examples, especially for new concepts

(2) Identify explicit oral and written strategies that promote integration of word knowledge and provide repeated, meaningful exposure to and opportunities to use new academic and content-area vocabulary.

*For example:*

    **a.** conducting guided discussions of academic content and concepts

    **b.** conducting guided discussions of new words and their meanings, including identifying synonyms and antonyms

    **c.** discussing words' origins, roots, and/or affixes

    **d.** creating semantic and morphological maps

    **e.** developing word banks and word logs

    **f.** comparing and classifying words orally and in writing

    **g.** generating metaphors and analogies with words orally and in writing

    **h.** incorporating new vocabulary in subject-matter discussions and written assignments

    **i.** using more precise words in speaking and writing

(3) Demonstrate knowledge of research-based, systematic, explicit instruction in independent strategies for building vocabulary and for determining and verifying the meanings and pronunciations of unfamiliar words or words with multiple meanings.

*For example:*

    **a.** use of contextual strategies (e.g., using semantic and syntactic context clues, including apposition, to verify the meaning of a word and/or resolve ambiguity)

    **b.** use of morphological strategies (e.g., developing knowledge of common roots and affixes, developing knowledge of the processes of word formation, applying structural analysis skills)

    **c.** use of reference materials (e.g., using a dictionary, thesaurus, or other text-based or technology-based reference tool)

**(4)** Identify explicit strategies for developing students' word consciousness and fostering a love of words (e.g., engaging students in word games, discussing the etymology and morphology of words and supporting students' investigations in etymology and morphology, drawing attention to the use of figurative language in both speech and print, encouraging students to share new and interesting words encountered in speech and print).

**(5)** Identify explicit listening-comprehension activities that promote the development of vocabulary, academic language, and background knowledge (e.g., providing word explanations, reading both literary and informational texts aloud to students and conducting guided discussions of text content and vocabulary).

**(6)** Recognize the role of wide reading in building vocabulary, academic language, background knowledge, and a love of reading and identify explicit strategies for promoting students' purposeful independent reading of a broad range of literary and informational texts at increasingly challenging levels.

**(7)** Demonstrate knowledge of explicit strategies for developing students' knowledge of language and language structures (e.g., knowledge of syntax and grammar, knowledge of elements that promote cohesion and coherence in oral and written discourse) to support their comprehension of texts at the word, sentence, paragraph, and text levels.

**(8)** Demonstrate knowledge of explicit strategies for helping students understand similarities and differences between language structures used in spoken and written language, transfer relevant skills from oral language to written language (e.g., helping students make connections between their existing oral vocabulary and new written vocabulary, engaging students in oral rehearsal in preparation for writing), and develop their knowledge of written language structures and conventions (e.g., analyzing how punctuation affects a text's meaning).

**(9)** Demonstrate knowledge of how to address the full range of learners in the classroom with respect to their development of vocabulary, academic language, and background knowledge (i.e., Universal Access).

*For example:*

    **a.** providing differentiated instruction in vocabulary, academic language, and background knowledge to address the needs of struggling readers and students with reading difficulties or disabilities (e.g., focusing on key vocabulary, academic language structures, and background knowledge; reteaching vocabulary, language structures, and concepts; using a variety of concrete examples to explain a word or concept; providing additional meaningful practice using new words and concepts)

    **b.** providing differentiated instruction in vocabulary, academic language, and background knowledge to support students with special needs (e.g., focusing on key concepts; preteaching/reteaching vocabulary and concepts; providing additional exposures to new words and concepts; using concrete examples to explain a word or concept; presenting vocabulary and concepts using visual, auditory, kinesthetic, and tactile techniques; providing additional meaningful oral and written practice using new words and concepts)

    **c.** providing differentiated instruction in vocabulary, academic language, and background knowledge to address the needs of English Learners and speakers of nonstandard English (e.g., activating students' prior knowledge by making explicit connections between their current knowledge and new vocabulary/ concepts; capitalizing on transfer of cognates; building on students' current language skills and reinforcing their knowledge of basic, functional grammar to facilitate their reading comprehension; emphasizing reading instruction that promotes development of academic language, including explicitly teaching more complex language structures and key vocabulary used in a text; contextualizing new vocabulary and concepts using visual aids, such as pictures, charts, word organizers, and graphic organizers; using "preteach-reteach-practice-review"; building students' morphological knowledge, including knowledge of the meanings of common word roots used in academic language)

**d.** providing differentiated instruction in vocabulary, academic language, and background knowledge to address the needs of advanced learners (e.g., increasing the pace and/or complexity of instruction, building on and extending current knowledge, extending the depth and breadth of assignments)

**(10)** Recognize that vocabulary, academic language, and background knowledge are indirectly assessed in reading comprehension assessments and recognize the implications of this in interpreting the results of those assessments.

**(11)** Demonstrate knowledge and ability in assessment (i.e., entry-level assessment, monitoring of progress, and summative assessment) with respect to vocabulary, academic language, and background knowledge.

*For example:*

**a.** demonstrating ability to describe and use appropriate formal and informal assessments to determine students' level of vocabulary, academic language, and background knowledge for different assessment purposes (i.e., entry-level assessment, monitoring of progress, and summative assessment)

**b.** demonstrating ability to analyze and interpret results from these assessments

**c.** demonstrating ability to use the results of assessments to plan effective instruction and interventions in vocabulary, academic language, and background knowledge; adjust instruction and interventions to meet the identified needs of students; and determine whether students have made progress in learning the content

## Questions for Review

**11.1. What steps are included in direct instruction of vocabulary words?**

- Introduce the word in child-friendly language; provide a description of the word; explain the meaning of the word
- Ask students to restate the description, explanation, or example in their own words
- Have students construct a graphic representation of the term
- Engage students in activities that help them add to their knowledge of the term
- Have students discuss the term with one another
- Engage the students in games that allow them to play with the terms

**11.2. How can a teacher use explicit instruction to build on students' prior knowledge, improve listening and speaking vocabulary, and enhance vocabulary development?**

Answers to the question should include the following:

- Use formal and informal tools to assess reading and speaking vocabulary.
- Provide a variety of activities to build vocabulary skills. These would include listening to and reading a variety of texts, playing vocabulary games, word sorts, semantic mapping, classification, word banks, and many other activities.
- Use direct, explicit instruction to teach a variety of strategies for gaining meaning from unfamiliar words, such as word analysis, decoding, prefixes, suffixes, roots, context, syntax, and root words.
- Use a variety of materials and resources to extend vocabulary and understanding of words.
- Direct instruction in vocabulary and in strategies to attain vocabulary knowledge is essential for all students. It is critical for English Learner students to acquire vocabulary. Preteaching vocabulary/concepts is a scaffolding strategy that teachers must use on a consistent basis.
- Provide many opportunities for read-alouds and independent reading in the classroom. This independent reading will help build the vocabulary knowledge of all students.

**11.3. How can a teacher differentiate vocabulary instruction for struggling readers, students with special needs, English Learners, and advanced learners?**

Possible answers might include:

a. to provide for struggling readers, focus on key vocabulary, academic language structures, and background knowledge; reteach vocabulary, language structures, and concepts; use a variety of concrete examples to explain a word or concept; provide additional meaningful practice using new words and concepts

b. to provide for students with special needs, focus on key concepts; preteaching/reteaching vocabulary and concepts; provide additional exposures to new words and concepts; use concrete examples to explain a word or concept; present vocabulary and concepts using visual, auditory, kinesthetic, and tactile techniques; provide additional meaningful oral and written practice using new words and concepts

c. to provide for the needs of English Learners and speakers of nonstandard English; activate students' prior knowledge by making explicit connections between their current knowledge and new vocabulary/ concepts; capitalize on transfer of cognates; build on students' current language skills and reinforce their knowledge of basic, functional grammar to facilitate their reading comprehension; emphasize reading instruction that promotes development of academic language, including explicitly teaching more complex language structures and key vocabulary used in a text; contextualize new vocabulary and concepts using visual aids, such as pictures, charts, word organizers, and graphic organizers; use "preteach-reteach-practice-review"; build students' morphological knowledge, including knowledge of the meanings of common word roots used in academic language

d. to provide for the needs of advanced learners, increase the pace and/or complexity of instruction, build on and extend current knowledge, extend the depth and breadth of assignments

# Domain 5

# Comprehension

## Competency 12: Understand literal, inferential, and evaluative comprehension and factors affecting reading comprehension.

Including:

(1) Recognize how a reader's knowledge and skills in word analysis, fluency, vocabulary, and academic language as well as the reader's background knowledge affect comprehension (e.g., why automaticity in word recognition facilitates comprehension, how comprehension breaks down when relevant vocabulary or background knowledge is lacking).

(2) Demonstrate knowledge of literal reading comprehension (e.g., identifying explicitly stated main ideas, details, sequences, cause-and-effect relationships, patterns, and elements of story grammar).

(3) Demonstrate knowledge of inferential reading comprehension (e.g., inferring main ideas, comparisons, and cause-and-effect relationships not explicitly stated in the text; drawing conclusions or generalizations from a text; using textual evidence to predict outcomes; inferring themes).

(4) Demonstrate knowledge of evaluative reading comprehension (e.g., recognizing instances of bias, unsupported assumptions, propaganda, and faulty reasoning in texts; distinguishing facts and opinions in texts; reacting to a text's content, characters, and use of language; analyzing themes).

(5) Recognize the role of syntax in facilitating or impeding reading comprehension and the importance of promoting students' understanding of complex grammatical structures.

(6) Recognize the role of text structures in facilitating or impeding reading comprehension and the importance of promoting students' understanding of how different types of texts are organized.

(7) Demonstrate knowledge of the relationship between students' oral language and their ability to comprehend at the word, sentence, paragraph, and text levels.

(8) Recognize the role of listening comprehension as a foundation for the development of reading comprehension and the importance of using oral language activities (e.g., strategic, purposeful read-alouds) to promote development of comprehension skills.

(9) Recognize the role that text-based discussions (e.g., instructional conversations, questioning the author, think-pair-share) play in enhancing comprehension.

(10) Recognize how writing activities (e.g., summarizing, outlining, responding) help support and reinforce students' understanding of a text and their development of reading comprehension skills.

(11) Recognize the role of independent reading in reinforcing reading comprehension skills and strategies and the importance of promoting purposeful independent reading as a pathway to healthy lifelong reading habits.

## Questions for Review

**12.1. What are the levels of comprehension? How should these levels be taught?**

Possible answers might include the following:

- Levels of Comprehension

1. Literal Comprehension Skills include clearly, explicitly identifying items such as main idea, sequence, patterns, cause and effect.

2. Inferential Comprehension Skills include making inferences concerning items not directly stated, such as comparisons, drawing conclusions, predicting, and cause/effect relationships not explicitly stated.

3. Evaluative Comprehension Skills include critical reading, such as recognizing unsupported inferences in text, distinguishing between facts and opinions, using language, and detecting propaganda and faulty reasoning.

- Instruction in levels of comprehension should include the following:

1. Direct, explicit instruction of skills

2. Modeling of each level of comprehension skills

3. Guided practice

4. Independent practice

5. Use of resources and materials and activities selected by the teacher to support effective instruction and practice in levels of comprehension

Skills and strategies represent different stages of development. A skill becomes a strategy when the student can use it independently.

**12.2. How can a teacher facilitate student attainment of comprehension?**

Possible answers might include the following:

- Provide instructional activities such as direct and indirect vocabulary building and fluency activities to build comprehension skills.
- Teach, model, practice that text comprehension is both purposeful and active.
- Teach comprehension strategies and demonstrate their application throughout the reading—for example, monitoring comprehension, using graphic and semantic organizers, answering questions, generating questions, recognizing story structure, visualizing, comparing and contrasting, previewing, predicting, retelling and summarizing, and using prior knowledge. ("Put Reading First, NIFL")
- Direct comprehension instruction, modeling, guided practice, and student independent application of comprehension skill.
- Provide a repertoire of activities that foster connections between reading and writing.

# Competency 13: Understand how to facilitate reading comprehension by providing instruction that prepares students for the reading task, scaffolds them as needed through the reading process, and prepares them to respond to what they have read.

Including:

(1) Demonstrate knowledge of explicit instructional strategies for orienting students to new texts (e.g., teacher modeling, previewing, using textual evidence to predict outcomes, using graphic features, activating and discussing prior knowledge related to the topic, developing background knowledge, setting a purpose for reading, generating questions prior to reading).

(2) Demonstrate knowledge of explicit instruction in skills that support comprehension and strategies that help students monitor their own comprehension as they read (e.g., using graphic features, visualizing, self-questioning, paraphrasing, clarifying, predicting, summarizing, rereading, adjusting reading rate based on text difficulty, note taking).

(3) Demonstrate knowledge of explicit instructional strategies for supporting students' comprehension after reading (e.g., discussing; summarizing; retelling; sharing reactions; making text-to-self, text-to-text, and text-to-world connections; creating pictures, semantic maps, Venn diagrams, and other visual/graphic representations of text meanings).

(4) Demonstrate knowledge of explicit instructional strategies for promoting students' development of listening comprehension skills and helping students transfer comprehension strategies from oral language to written language (e.g., through the use of teacher think-alouds and modeling).

(5) Demonstrate knowledge of how to address the full range of learners in the classroom with respect to facilitating their reading comprehension, including developing their use of comprehension strategies (i.e., Universal Access).

*For example:*

a. providing differentiated comprehension instruction to address the needs of struggling readers and students with reading difficulties or disabilities (e.g., as needed, focusing on building word analysis skills, fluency, vocabulary, academic language, and background knowledge to support comprehension; reteaching comprehension strategies and skills that are lacking; using a variety of concrete examples to explain a concept or task; providing additional practice applying comprehension strategies and skills; as needed, providing access to grade-level texts through oral presentation, such as reading a text aloud to students and then discussing it with them)

b. providing differentiated comprehension instruction to support students with special needs (e.g., focusing on building foundational knowledge and skills in word analysis, fluency, vocabulary, academic language, and background knowledge; providing practice with questions at different levels of comprehension; using a variety of concrete examples to explain a concept or task; reteaching comprehension skills and strategies that are lacking; providing additional practice with a variety of texts; as needed, providing access to grade-level texts through oral presentation, such as reading a text aloud to students and then discussing it with them)

c. providing differentiated comprehension instruction to address the needs of English Learners and speakers of nonstandard English (e.g., capitalizing on transfer of comprehension strategies from the primary language; explicitly teaching comprehension strategies that are lacking)

d. providing differentiated comprehension instruction to address the needs of advanced learners (e.g., increasing the pace and/or complexity of instruction, using more advanced and/or multiple texts, building on and extending current skills and strategies, extending the depth and breadth of assignments)

(6) Demonstrate knowledge and ability in assessment (i.e., entry-level assessment, monitoring of progress, and summative assessment) with respect to reading comprehension, including students' use of comprehension strategies.

*For example:*

    **a.** demonstrating ability to describe and use appropriate formal and informal assessments to determine students' comprehension and use of comprehension strategies for different assessment purposes (i.e., entry-level assessment, monitoring of progress, and summative assessment)

    **b.** demonstrating ability to analyze and interpret results from these assessments

    **c.** demonstrating ability to use the results of assessments to plan effective comprehension instruction and interventions, adjust instruction and interventions to meet the identified needs of students, and ultimately determine whether relevant standards have been met

## Questions for Review

**13.1. What are comprehension strategies? How should these strategies be taught?**

Possible answers might include the following:

- Comprehension strategies are activities that we use to gain meaning or understanding from text and to clarify text. These include strategies such as reread, retell, self-monitor, and reorganize text (outline, note-taking, summarize); predict answers and generate questions; compare and contrast; use graphic and semantic organizers; monitor comprehension; recognize story structure; use prior knowledge and visualization.

- To teach these strategies, the teacher should do the following:

1. Assess student understanding of the strategy.
2. Plan instruction to meet identified needs.
3. Include in the plan instructional strategies for direct instruction, modeling, guided practice, and independent practice. In addition, the plan should include possible resources and materials to be used in instruction and practice.
4. Instruct students using direct instruction and modeling.
5. Provide practice in both guided and independent settings.
6. Assess to monitor for mastery of skills.

## Competency 14: Understand how to promote students' comprehension and analysis of narrative/literary texts and their development of literary response skills.

Including:

    **(1)** Demonstrate knowledge of explicit instructional strategies for helping students recognize the organizational structure and key characteristics of major literary genres, including poetry (e.g., ballad, lyric, couplet, epic, sonnet), drama, and prose (e.g., short story, novel, myth, legend, biography, autobiography, historical fiction, fantasy).

    **(2)** Demonstrate knowledge of the elements of story grammar (e.g., character, plot, setting, theme) and other key elements of narrative/literary texts (e.g., mood, tone, point of view, voice) and systematic, explicit instruction in these elements.

    **(3)** Demonstrate knowledge of research-based, systematic, explicit instruction in narrative analysis and literary criticism, including explicit instructional strategies for helping students analyze and respond to narrative/literary texts.

*For example:*

    **a.** identifying the structural elements of a plot and evaluating their logic and credibility

    **b.** comparing and contrasting the motivations and reactions of characters

    **c.** evaluating the relevance of the setting

    **d.** identifying recurring themes

    **e.** identifying elements of a writer's style, including the function and effect of an author's use of figurative language (e.g., simile, metaphor, hyperbole, personification) and other literary devices (e.g., imagery, symbolism, irony, foreshadowing)

**(4)** Demonstrate knowledge of explicit oral language activities (e.g., literature circles, questioning the author, think-pair-share) that develop and reinforce students' comprehension of narrative/literary texts and their skills in narrative analysis and literary criticism.

**(5)** Demonstrate knowledge of explicit writing activities (e.g., literary response journals, summaries, character analyses) that develop and reinforce students' comprehension of narrative/literary texts and their skills in narrative analysis and literary criticism.

**(6)** Demonstrate knowledge of how to address the full range of learners in the classroom with respect to their comprehension and analysis of narrative/literary texts and their development of literary response skills (i.e., Universal Access).

*For example:*

    **a.** providing differentiated instruction in these areas of reading to address the needs of struggling readers and students with reading difficulties or disabilities (e.g., focusing on key elements of story grammar; creating and using story maps; focusing on key comprehension strategies and skills; reteaching strategies and skills that are lacking; using a variety of concrete examples to explain a concept or task; providing additional practice; as needed, providing access to grade-level texts through oral presentation, such as reading a text aloud to students and then discussing it with them)

    **b.** providing differentiated instruction in these areas of reading to support students with special needs (e.g., focusing on key elements of story grammar; creating and using story maps; using a variety of concrete examples to explain a concept or task; focusing on key skills and strategies; reteaching skills and strategies that are lacking; providing additional practice with narrative/literary texts; as needed, providing access to grade-level texts through oral presentation, such as reading a text aloud to students and then discussing it with them)

    **c.** providing differentiated instruction in these areas of reading to address the needs of English Learners and speakers of nonstandard English (e.g., clarifying the cultural context of a text, as needed; preteaching key vocabulary)

    **d.** providing differentiated instruction in these areas of reading to address the needs of advanced learners (e.g., using more advanced and/or multiple texts; building on and extending current knowledge, skills, and strategies; extending the depth and breadth of assignments)

**(7)** Demonstrate knowledge and ability in assessment (i.e., entry-level assessment, monitoring of progress, and summative assessment) with respect to comprehension and analysis of narrative/literary texts and development of literary response skills.

*For example:*

    **a.** demonstrating ability to describe and use appropriate formal and informal assessments in these areas of reading for different assessment purposes (i.e., entry-level assessment, monitoring of progress, and summative assessment)

    **b.** demonstrating ability to analyze and interpret results from these assessments

    **c.** demonstrating ability to use the results of assessments to plan effective instruction and interventions with respect to comprehension and analysis of narrative/literary texts and development of literary response skills, adjust instruction and interventions to meet the identified needs of students, and ultimately determine whether relevant standards have been met

## Questions for Review

**14.1. How can a teacher teach elements of literary analysis and criticism?**

Possible answers might include the following:

- The teacher can assess student knowledge of elements of literary analysis and criticism, such as historical fiction, biographies, autobiographies, poetry, plays, realistic fiction, multicultural literature, fact, and fantasy.
- Using the data from the assessment, the teacher can plan direct instruction, modeling, guided practice, and independent practice.
- The teacher can plan resources, materials, and student groupings to use in instruction, which will assist in meeting identified student needs and interests. Elements of literary analysis and criticism include such elements as analyzing the use of figurative language, genre, story elements, mood, theme, and time period.
- Instruction in elements of literary analysis should be direct instruction, teacher modeling, and guided practice.

**14.2. How can a teacher assist students in making connections and responding to literature?**

Possible answers might include the following:

- The teacher can engage students in reading or listening to high-quality literature.
- Students should be engaged in activities and strategies to clarify and understand text.
- Student responses to text, linked with prior knowledge, might include such activities as reading logs, literature circles, Readers' Theatre, essays, cross-curricular discussions, and writings.
- Engaging students in response activities, which include book reports; identifying main problem in the story, semantic webs, trait charts; and analyzing different types of literature.

## Competency 15: Understand how to promote students' comprehension of expository/informational texts and their development of study skills and research skills.

Including:

(1) Demonstrate knowledge of explicit instructional strategies for helping students recognize key characteristics of various expository/informational materials (e.g., textbook, news article, consumer manual, research report, website).

(2) Demonstrate knowledge of explicit instructional strategies for promoting students' comprehension of expository/informational texts at the word, sentence, paragraph, and text levels by helping them understand common text structures used in these texts (e.g., chronological, cause/effect, comparison/contrast, problem/solution) and helping them recognize and attend to common transition words and other features (e.g., topic sentence, concluding sentence) associated with different text structures.

(3) Demonstrate knowledge of explicit instructional strategies for helping students recognize and use a variety of text features that help support comprehension of expository/informational texts.

*For example:*

  **a.** organizational/explanatory features (e.g., table of contents, index, glossary)

  **b.** typographic features (e.g., italics, boldfacing, underlining, color coding)

  **c.** graphic features (e.g., charts, maps, diagrams, illustrations)

(4) Demonstrate knowledge of explicit instructional strategies for promoting students' comprehension of expository/informational texts.

# Glossary of Reading Terms, Concepts, and Assessments

This section summarizes important key terms, concepts, and reading assessment tools that are beneficial in developing a reading instructional knowledge base. Your success on both the multiple-choice and written constructed-responses of the RICA requires your familiarity of suitable reading instruction terminology and reading assessment strategies. Use this glossary as a starting point for your instructional reference resource and to help you optimize your RICA preparation.

## Terms and Concepts

**Affix**   A bound (nonword) morpheme that changes the meaning or function of a root or stem to which it is attached, as the prefix *ad–* and suffix *–ing* in *adjoining*.

**Alphabetic Principle**   The assumption underlying alphabetic writing systems that each speech sound or phoneme of a language should have its own distinctive graphic representation, which is a letter or group of letters of the alphabet.

**Analytic Phonics**   A whole-to-part approach to word study in which the student is first taught a number of sight words and then relevant phonic generalizations, which are subsequently applied to other words; deductive phonics.

**Auditory Blending**   The ability to fuse discrete phonemes into recognizable spoken words.

**Auditory Discrimination**   The ability to hear phonetic likenesses and differences in phonemes and words and to distinguish among the sounds.

**Auditory Processing**   The full range of mental activity involved in reacting to auditory stimuli, especially sounds, and in considering their meanings in relation to past experience and to their future use.

**Automaticity**   The ability to recognize a word (or series of words) in text effortlessly and rapidly.

**Basal Reading Program**   A collection of student texts and workbooks, teacher's manuals, and supplemental materials used for development of reading/language arts and sometimes writing instruction, used chiefly in the elementary and middle school grades.

**Blend**   To combine the sounds represented by letters to pronounce a word; to sound out; the instance of two or more consonants appearing together in a word but each of the consonant sounds remaining an independent phoneme.

**Comprehension**   The essence and ultimate purpose of reading, comprehension is the ability to gain meaning from what is read. The hierarchy of comprehension skills ranges from concrete to abstract, and it includes levels such as literal, inferential, analytical, and evaluative. The various levels of comprehension skills are also referred to as lower-order and higher-order skills.

**Concepts of Print**   Familiarity with print conventions, such as reading left to right, top to bottom; the direction of print on a page; the use of spaces to denote words; the idea that print represents words and punctuation. An important predictor of learning to read.

**Consonant**   **1.** A speech sound made by partial or complete closure of part of the vocal tract, which obstructs air flow and causes audible friction in varying amounts. **2.** Letters of the alphabet that are not vowels. (See "Vowel" also.)

**Context Clue**   Information from the immediate textual setting that helps identify a word or word group, as by recognizing words, phrases, sentence illustrations, syntax, typography, etc.

**Cueing System**   A cueing system can include any of the various sources of information that might aid identification of a word unrecognized at first glance. These are cues that every good reader uses to decode words in the context of the text to help predict or guess. The three main cueing systems are: **1. semantics** (meaning), **2. syntax** (syntactical or structural), and **3. grapho-phonemic** (visual or letter-sound information).

**Curriculum-Based Assessment**   The appraisal of student progress by using materials and procedures directly from the curriculum taught.

**Decodable Text**   A type of text used in beginning reading instruction, often from Little Books, for the purpose of fluency practice. Decodable text can be independently decoded or sounded out based on what the student knows. The text contains many repetitions of sounds and phonic elements that students have already been taught, along with a limited number of high-frequency words.

**Decode**   To analyze spoken or graphic symbols of a familiar language in order to ascertain their intended meaning. **Note:** To learn to read, one must learn the conventional code in which something is written in order to decode the written message. In reading practice, the term is used primarily to refer to word identification rather than to identify higher units of meaning.

**Decoding**   A series of strategies used selectively by readers to recognize and read written words. The reader locates cues (e.g., letter-sound correspondences) in a word that reveals enough about it to help in pronouncing it and attaching meaning to it.

**Diagnosis**   The act, process, or result of identifying the specific nature of a disorder or disability through observation and examination. **Note:** Technically, diagnosis means only the identification and labeling of a disorder. As the term is used in education, however, it often includes the planning of instruction and an assessment of the strengths and weaknesses of the student.

**Diagnostic Teaching**   The use of the results of student performance on current tasks to plan future learning activities; instruction in which diagnosis and instruction are fused into a single ongoing process.

**Diagnostic Test**   A test used to analyze strengths and weaknesses in content-oriented skills. **Note:** Diagnostic tests may permit comparison among several subabilities of the same individuals and sometimes comparisons of strong and weak points of a group or class. Available instruments for the diagnosis of reading difficulties vary widely in the thoroughness of analysis they permit and in the specific procedures followed.

**Digraph**   A combination of two letters, either consonants or vowels, representing a single speech sound. The consonant digraphs in English are *th, sh, ch,* and *wh, ph, ck, tch.*

**Diphthong**   A vowel sound produced when the tongue moves or glides from one vowel sound toward another vowel or semivowel sound in the same syllable, as /i/ in *buy* and vowel sounds in *boy* and *bough.* A vowel diphthong is represented by two or more vowels together.

**Dyslexia**   A medical term for a developmental reading disability, which is presumably congenital and often hereditary, and which may vary in degree from mild to severe. **Note:** Dyslexia, originally called word blindness, occurs in persons who have adequate vision, hearing, intelligence, and general language functioning. People with dyslexia frequently have difficulty in spelling and in acquiring a second language, suggesting that dyslexia is part of a broad type of language disability. Difficulties with phonology are typical in most cases.

**Emergent Literacy**   The beginning stage of the development of the association of print with meaning that starts early in a child's life and continues until the child reaches the stage of conventional reading and writing; "the reading and writing concepts and behaviors of young children that precede and develop into conventional literacy."

**Encode**   To change a message into, as encode oral language into writing, encode an idea into words, or encode physical law into mathematical symbols.

**Etymology**   The study of the history of words.

**Explicit Instruction**   The intentional design and delivery of information by the teacher to the students. It begins with (1) the teacher's modeling or demonstration of the skill or strategy; (2) a structured and substantial opportunity for students to practice and apply newly taught skills and knowledge under the teacher's direction and guidance; and (3) an opportunity for feedback.

**Fluency**   The clear, easy, and quick written or spoken expression of ideas. In reading, this means freedom from word-identification problems that might hinder comprehension in silent reading or hinder the expression of ideas in oral reading; automaticity.

**Fluent Reader**   A reader whose performance meets or exceeds normal expectations with respect to age and ability; an independent reader. A reader who reads at an adequate pace with sufficient accuracy and correct intonation to enable comprehension to occur.

**Frustration Reading Level**   A readability or grade level of material that is too difficult to be read successfully by a student, even with normal classroom instruction and support. The frustration level is reached when a student cannot read a selection with more than 89 percent word-recognition or decoding accuracy.

**Genre**   A term used to classify literary works into categories such as novel, mystery, historical fiction, biography, short story, and poem.

**Graded Word List**   A list of words ranked by grade level, reader level, or other level of difficulty of complexity, often used to assess competence in word identification, knowledge of word-meanings, and spelling.

**Grapheme**   A written or printed representation of a phoneme as *b* for /b/ or *oy* for /oi/ in boy.

**Grapheme-Phoneme Correspondence**   The relationship between a grapheme and the phoneme(s) it represents; letter-sound correspondence, as *c* representing /k/ in *cat* and /s/ in *cent*.

**Graphic Organizer**   A visual representation of facts and concepts from a text and their relationships within an organized frame. Graphic organizers are effective tools for thinking and learning. They help teachers and students represent abstract or implicit information in more concrete form, they depict relationships among facts and concepts, they aid in organizing and elaborating ideas, they relate new information with prior knowledge, and they effectively store and retrieve information.

**Guided Reading**   Reading instruction conducted in small, flexible groups in which everyone reads simultaneously and for which the teacher provides the structure and purpose for reading and for responding to the material read. Little Books are often used for guided reading.

**High-Frequency Word**   A word that appears much more often than most other words in spoken or written language; it is also known as a sight word.

**Informal Reading Inventory (IRI)**   The use of a graded series of passages of increasing difficulty to determine students' strengths, weaknesses, and strategies in word identification and comprehension and to determine a student's independent, instruction, and frustration reading levels. Comprehension questions are often asked after each passage is read.

**Interactive Writing**   A shared writing experience used to assist emergent readers in learning to read and write. With help from the teacher, students dictate sentences about a shared experience, such as a story, movie, or event. The teacher stretches each word orally so students can distinguish its sounds and letters as they use chart paper to write the letter while repeating the sound. After each word has been completed, the teacher and students reread it. The students take turns writing letters to complete the words and sentences. The completed charts are posted on the wall so the students can reread them or rely on them for standard spelling.

**Invented Spelling**   Spelling of sounds processed phonologically. (A child's attempt to map speech to print.) It is also known as phonetic spelling and temporary spelling.

**Learning Center or Station**   A location within a classroom in which students are presented with instructional materials, specific directions, clearly defined objectives, and opportunities for self-evaluation.

**Metacognition**   Awareness and knowledge of one's mental processes. Metacognition is simply "thinking about thinking." One example of a metacognitive task is when readers self-monitor their comprehension of text. While "thinking about" their understanding of text, readers may adjust their reading speed to fit the difficulty level.

**Minimally Contrasting Pairs**   Words that differ only in the initial or medial or final sound (e.g., pest/best, scrapple/scrabble, cat/cap).

**Mnemonic Device**   A method for improving memory, especially the use of pattern strategies to improve memorizing strings of facts.

**Morpheme**   The smallest unit of meaning. It can be a letter, syllable, affix, root, or base word. The addition of a morpheme to a word adds a meaningful element or changes the meaning, as the addition of an *s* to the word *book* changes the meaning from one book to more than one book.

**Morphology**   The study of the structure and forms of words, including derivation, inflection, roots, base words, and combining forms.

**Nonphonetic Word**   In teaching practice, a word whose pronunciation may not be accurately predicated from its spelling.

**Nonsense Syllable**   A pronounceable combination of graphic characters, usually trigrams, that do not make a word, as in *kak, vor, mek,* but are pronounced as English spellings.

**Orthographic**   Pertains to orthography, the art or study of correct spelling according to established usage.

**Orthography**   The way a language is written (encoded); spelling.

**Peer Editing**   A form of collaborative learning in which students work with their peers in editing a piece of writing.

**Phoneme**   The smallest unit of speech that, when contrasted with another phoneme, affects the meaning of words in a language, as /b/ in *book* contrasts with /t/ in *took*, /k/ in *cook*, /h/ in *hook*.

**Phoneme Grapheme Correspondence**   The relationship between a phoneme and its graphemic representation(s), as /s/, spelled *s* in *sit, c* in *city, ss* in *grass*.

**Phonemic Awareness or Phoneme Awareness**   Phonemic awareness is awareness of the sounds (phonemes) that make up spoken words. Such awareness does not appear when young children learn to talk; this ability is not necessary for speaking and understanding spoken language. However, phonemic awareness is important to understand the code of alphabetic languages and letters (and letter sounds). Having phonemic awareness provides some understanding of the notion that words are made up of phonemes. This insight is not always easily achieved. Phonemes are abstract units, and when one pronounces a word one does not produce a series of discrete phonemes; rather phonemes are folded into one another and are pronounced as a blend. Although most young children have no difficulty segmenting words into syllables, many find it very difficult to segment at the phoneme level. Phonemic awareness is an important predictor of success for beginning readers.

**Phonics**   A way of teaching, reading, and spelling that stresses symbol-sound relationships, used most often in beginning instruction. Phonics also refers the correspondence of sounds to the letters that represent them.

**Phonic Analysis**   In teaching practice, the identification of words by their sounds.

**Phonogram**   A graphic character or symbol that can represent a phonetic sound, phoneme, or word.

**Phonology**   The permissible part of accepted arrangements of speech sounds in forming morphemes and words; the rules for producing the phonemes in words.

**Phonological Awareness**   A broader term than phonemic awareness, phonological awareness refers to language sensitivity and ability to manipulate language at the levels of words, syllables, rhymes, and individual speech sounds.

**Prefix**   A meaningful affix attached before a base word or root, as *re–* in *reprint*.

**Preprimer**   In a basal reading program, a booklet used before the first reader to introduce students to features in texts and books and sometimes to introduce specific characters found later in a series.

**Prereading**   Referring to activities designed to develop needed attitudes and skills before formal instruction in reading.

**Prewriting**   The initial creative and planning stage of writing, prior to drafting, in which the writer formulates ideas, gathers information, and considers ways in which to organize a piece of writing. The first step in the writing process.

**Primer**   A beginning book for the teaching of reading; specifically, the first formal textbook in a basal reading program, usually preceded by a readiness book and one or more preprimers.

**Primary Language**   The first language a child learns to speak.

**Print Awareness**   In emergent literacy, a learner's growing recognition of the conventions and characteristics of a written language.

**Print-Rich Environment**   An environment in which students are provided many opportunities to interact with printed language, and an abundance and variety of printed materials are available and accessible. Students have many opportunities to read and to be read to. In such an environment, reading and writing are modeled by the teacher and used for a wide variety of authentic everyday purposes.

**Prosody**   A component of fluency that refers to reading with expression, which includes the use of appropriate emphasis, stress, intonation, pitch, pauses, and phrasing that demonstrates understanding of syntax and mechanics.

**R-Controlled Vowel Sound**   The modified sound of a vowel immediately preceding /r/ in the same syllable, as in *care, never, sir, curse,* etc.

**Recognition Vocabulary**   The number of different words that are recognized without word analysis, words understood quickly and easily; sight vocabulary.

**Rhyme**   Correspondence of ending sounds of words or lines of verse.

**Rime**   A vowel and any of the following consonants of a syllable, as /ook/ in *book* or *brook*, /ik/ in *strike*, and /a/ in *play*.

**Scaffolding**   Temporary support, guidance, or assistance provided to a student on a new or complex task. For example, students work in partnership with a more advanced peer or adult who scaffolds the task by engaging in appropriate instructional interactions designed to model, assist, or provide necessary information. These interactions should eventually lead to independence.

**Schwa**   A diacritical mark that indicates the vowel sound in an unstressed syllable of a word. It can be spelled with any of the vowel letters and is represented by the symbol ə.

**Semantics**   The study of meaning in language, as the analysis of the meanings of words, phrases, sentences, discourse, and entire texts.

**Sight Word**   A word that is immediately recognized as a whole and does not require word analysis for identification. A word taught as a whole. It is also known as a high-frequency word.

**Sound O**   The application of phonics skills in reproducing the sound(s) represented by a letter or letter group in a word.

**Story Frame/Map**   A graphic organizer of major events and ideas from a story to help guide students' thinking and heighten their awareness of the structure of stories. The teacher can model this process by filling out a chart on a projected image while reading. Or students can complete a chart individually or in groups after a story is read, illustrating or noting the characters, setting, compare/contrast, problem/solution, climax, conflict, and so forth.

**Structural Analysis**   The identification of word-meaning elements, as *re* and *read* in *reread,* to help understand the meaning of a word as a whole, morphemic analysis.

**Suffix**   A meaningful affix attached to the end of a base, root, or stem that changes meaning or grammatical function of the word, as *–en* added to *ox* to form *oxen.*

**Syllable**   In phonology, a minimal unit of sequential speech sounds composed of a vowel sound or a vowel-consonant combination, as in /a/, /ba/, /ab/, /bab/, etc.

**Syllabication**   The division of words into syllables.

**Syntax**   **1.** The study of the way sentences are formed and of the grammatical rules that govern their formation. **2.** The pattern or structure of word order in sentences, clauses, and phrases. Syntax examines the various ways that words can be combined to create meaning. The direct teaching of syntactic patterns is critical for comprehension of higher-level texts as well as for the development of good writing skills.

**Synthetic Method of Phonics**   A way of teaching beginning reading by starting with word parts or elements, as sounds, or syllables, and later combining them into words.

**Visual Discrimination**   **1.** The process of perceiving similarities and differences in stimuli by sight. **2.** The ability to engage in such a process.

**Vowel**   **1.** A voiced speech sound made without stoppage or friction of the air flow as it passes through the vocal tract. **2.** A letter or letters that represent a vowel sound.

**Web**   A graphic organizer that is used to involve students in thinking about and planning what they will study, learn, read about, or write about within a larger topic. A teacher may begin with a brainstorming discussion of topics related to a particular theme and then represent subtopics through the use of a web drawn on the board. Webbing can be used to encourage students to consider what they know about each subtopic or what they want to learn.

**Word Bank**   A list of related words posted in the classroom, often written on cards, to increase students' exposure to infrequently occurring vocabulary words that they would usually encounter only in specialized contexts. The words can all be related to one topic of study, or in other cases can be related by common spelling patterns.

**Word Family**   A group of letters consisting of a vowel or vowel team followed by a consonant or consonant blend (rime), to which many different onsets (consonants or consonant blends) can be added. Word families are also known as spelling patterns or phonograms.

**Word Play**   A child's manipulation of sounds and words for language exploration and practice or for pleasure (using alliteration, creating rhymes, singing songs, clapping syllables, etc.).

**Word Wall**   A word wall is a systematically organized collection of words displayed in large letters or on cards on a wall or other large display space in the classroom. The words are usually listed under their beginning letter. The purpose of word walls is to work on spelling by displaying sight words and words that belong to word families.

**Writing Process**   The series of sequential steps involved in a writing project including prewriting, drafting, revising, editing, and publishing. Repeated drafting, revising, and editing may occur several times during the process.

| Assessment Tools | What's Assessed? |
|---|---|
| Word Recognition (San Diego Quick Reading Assessment) | – Approximate reading level<br>– General decoding skills<br>– Word level automaticity |
| Oral Reading Inventory (Fry Oral Reading Test) | – Approximation of instructional, independent, and frustration level<br>– Fluency<br>– Reading strategies<br>– Comprehension (if retelling is added) |
| Phonics Inventory (BPST–Beginning Phonics Skills Test by Shefelbine) | – Decoding skills<br>– Level of phonics skills<br>– Specific phonetic skills<br>– High frequency word knowledge |
| Phonics Inventory (Fry Phonics Patterns Diagnostics Test) | – Level of phonic knowledge<br>– Application of phonics skills<br>– Short and long vowel patterns<br>– Analysis of additional phonics skills is possible |
| Phoneme Awareness (Yopp-Singer, Test of Phoneme Segmentation) | – Phoneme segmentation (Yopp-Singer)<br>– Phoneme deletion (Rosner) |

# Review of Reading Terms, Concepts, and Assessments

"Reading is at the heart of education. The knowledge of almost every subject in school flows from reading."

—Jim Trelease (2001)

Teaching children to read effectively may be the single most significant contribution toward the educational achievement of the developing child. The acquisition of solid reading skills opens the doorway to all other academic disciplines as it provides children with an unlimited access to new information while strengthening cognitive brain structures. The path toward literacy begins during early childhood and continues through adolescence and into adulthood. Children do not have to be highly intelligent to become successful readers, but it is important for children to develop early reading skills in order to gain opportunities for future learning possibilities. The RICA identifies the need for potential teachers to demonstrate their competency at providing children with skilled reading and language instruction.

| Stages of Reading Development | | |
|---|---|---|
| Age | Developmental Expectation | Reading Instruction |
| *THE EMERGENT READER* | | |
| Early Childhood to Pre-K<br><br>Pre-alphabetic | Beginning of awareness that text progresses from left to right. Children scribble and recognize distinctive visual clues in environmental print, such as of letters in their names. | Begin phonemic awareness<br>■ Help to recognize print in environment<br>■ Help to make predictions in stories<br>■ Observe pretending to read<br>■ Help to recognize letter shapes |

continued

| Stages of Reading Development *(continued)* | | |
|---|---|---|
| **Age** | **Developmental Expectation** | **Reading Instruction** |
| ***THE BEGINNING READER*** | | |
| K to Second (Third) Grade<br><br>Alphabetic | Letters are associated with sounds. Children begin to read simple CVC words (such as mat, sun, pin). They usually represent such words with a single sound, and later spell with the first and last consonant: for example, CT for cat. When writing later, vowels are included in each syllable. Children now rhyme and blend words. When reading later, they begin to recognize "chunks," or phonograms. | Systematic and explicit instruction, including:<br>▪ Phonics, phonemic awareness, blending, decoding<br>▪ Vocabulary word-attack skills, spelling<br>▪ Text comprehension<br>▪ Listening and writing |
| ***THE FLUENT READER*** | | |
| Fourth to Eighth Grade<br><br>Orthographic | Students read larger units of print and use analogy to decode larger words. Decoding becomes fluent. Accuracy and speed when reading are stressed. | Systematic and explicit instruction, including:<br>▪ Word-attack skills (multisyllabic words)<br>▪ Decoding<br>▪ Spelling<br>▪ Vocabulary<br>▪ Fluency<br>▪ Text comprehension (context skills)<br>▪ Strategic reading skills |
| ***THE REMEDIAL READER*** | | |
| Third to Eighth Grade<br><br>Students who do not demonstrate competency | The key approach to successful reading programs is preventive rather than remedial while understanding that there is a full range of learners in the classroom. Therefore, students who are struggling to read are taught from the same systematic framework taught in early grades of successful readers. | Reading instruction includes reteaching all of the modalities taught as a "beginning reader" listed above and emphasizing:<br>▪ Assessment of identified reading weakness<br>▪ Teaching explicit strategies based on diagnosis<br>▪ Linking instruction to prior knowledge<br>▪ Increasing instruction time<br>▪ Teaching systematically and breaking skills into smaller steps |

## Phonemic Awareness

**Phonemic awareness** is the ability to notice, think about, and work with the individual sounds in spoken words. This awareness is strongly related to reading achievement. To become proficient readers, children must be able to perceive and produce specific sounds of the English language and understand how the sound system works. Before children learn to read print, they need to become aware of how the sounds in words work. They must understand that words are made up of speech sounds, or phonemes. Phonemes are the smallest parts of sound in a spoken word that make a difference in the word's meaning.

Although phonemic awareness is a widely-used term in reading, **phonemic** awareness is *not* phonics. Phonemic awareness is the understanding that the sounds of *spoken* language work together to make words. Phonics is the understanding that there is a predictable relationship between phonemes and graphemes, the letters that represent those sounds in *written* language. If children are to benefit from phonics instruction, they need phonemic awareness. The reason is that children who cannot hear and work with the phonemes of spoken words will have a difficult time learning how to relate these phonemes to the graphemes when they see them in written words.

## Implications of Teaching Phonemic Awareness in the Classroom

1. Teachers help children recognize which words in a set of words begin with the same sound. ("*Bell, bike,* and *boy* all have /b/ at the beginning.")
2. Teachers help children isolate and say the first or last sound in a word. ("The beginning sound of *dog* is /d/." "The ending sound of *sit* is /t/.")
3. Teachers help children combine or blend separate sounds in a word to say the word ("/m/, /a/, /p/—map").
4. Teachers help children break or segment a word into its separate sounds ("up—/u/, /p/").

## Classroom Expectations: How to Teach Phonemic Awareness

Effective phonemic awareness instruction teaches children to notice, think about, and work with (manipulate) sounds in spoken language. This helps children become aware of English sound systems, consonants, and vowels. Teachers can use a variety of instructional methods, however, teaching one or two types of phoneme manipulation—specifically, blending and segmenting phonemes in words—is likely to produce greater benefits. Instruction should also be explicit about the connection between phonemic awareness and reading.

| An Example of Teaching Phoneme Manipulation—Blending and Segmenting | | |
|---|---|---|
| Step One | | Teacher: Listen: I'm going to say the sounds in the word jam—/j/ /a/ /m/. What is the word? |
| Step Two | Say the word out loud | Teacher: You say the sounds in the word jam. |
| Step Three | Write the word down | Teacher: Now let's write the sounds in **jam**: /j/, write j; /a/, write a; /m/, write m. |
| Step Four | Read the word together | Teacher: (Writes jam on the board). Now we're going to read the word jam. |

# Phonological Awareness

A common misunderstanding about phonemic awareness is that it means the same as phonological awareness. The two names are *not* interchangeable. Phonemic awareness is a subcategory of phonological awareness. The focus of phonemic awareness is narrow—identifying and manipulating the individual sounds in words. The focus of **phonological awareness** is much broader. It includes identifying and manipulating larger parts of spoken language, such as words, syllables, and onsets and rimes—as well as phonemes. It also encompasses awareness of other aspects of sound, such as rhyming, alliteration, and intonation.

## Implications of Teaching Phonological Awareness in the Classroom

1. Teachers help children identify and make oral rhymes. "*The pig has a (wig)."*

    "*Pat the (cat)."*

    "*The sun is (fun)."*

2. Teachers help children identify and work with syllables in spoken words: "*I can clap the parts in my name: An-drew."*
3. Teachers help children identify and work with onsets and rimes in spoken syllables or one-syllable words.

    "*The first part of sip is s-.*" "*The last part of win is in."*

## Phonics

Phonics instruction teaches children the relationships between the letters (graphemes) of written language and the individual sounds (phonemes) of spoken language. It teaches children to use these relationships to read and write words. Teachers of reading programs sometimes use different labels to describe these relationships, including the following:

- graphophonemic relationships
- letter-sound associations
- letter-sound correspondences
- sound-symbol correspondences
- sound-spellings

Regardless of the label, the goal of phonics instruction is to help children learn and use the alphabetic principle—the understanding that there are systematic and predictable relationships between written letters and spoken sounds. Knowing these relationships will help children recognize familiar words accurately and automatically, and "decode" new words. In short, knowledge of the alphabetic principle contributes greatly to children's ability to read words both in isolation and in connected text.

## Criticisms of Phonics Instruction

Critics of phonics instruction argue that English spellings are too irregular for phonics instruction to really help children learn to read words. The point is, however, that phonics instruction teaches children a system for remembering how to read words. Once children learn, for example, that *phone* is spelled this way rather than *foan,* their memory helps them to read, spell, and recognize the word instantly and more accurately than they could read *foan.* The same process is true for all irregularly spelled words. Most of these words contain some regular letter-sound relationships that can help children remember how to read them. In summary, the alphabetic system is a mnemonic device that supports our memory for specific words.

---

### Implications of Teaching Phonics in the Classroom

1.  **Assess** phonics and other word identification strategies. Select and use formal and informal tools such as decoding tests, fluency tests, and sight word checks to collect data, and analyze to plan instruction.
2.  **Plan** instruction that is systematic, explicit, and sequenced according to the increased complexity of linguistic units including sounds, phonemes, onsets and rimes, letters, letter combination syllables, and morphemes.
3.  **Explicitly** teach and model phonics, decoding, and other word identification strategies in reading for meaning. Positive explicit feedback for word identification errors is an essential strategy in this process.
4.  **Select** and design resource material and strategies for assessment and instruction. Resources include materials for teaching decoding, word identification strategies, and sign word mastery in multiple and varied reading and writing experiences.
5.  **Provide fluency practice** in a variety of ways:
    - Practice **decoding** and word-attack skills so that they become **automatic** in reading text.
    - Provide **application** and practice decoding skills to fluency in decodable (controlled vocabulary) text and word recognition skills taught out of context.
    - Continue to **develop fluency** through the use of decodable texts and other texts written at the student's instructional level.
6.  **Ongoing assessment** to demonstrate student progress toward mastery of State Standards.

---

**Systematic and Explicit Instruction**

Programs of systematic phonics instruction clearly identify a carefully selected and useful set of letter-sound relationships and then organize the introduction of these relationships into a logical instructional sequence. Children learn to use these relationships to decode words that contain them. Systematic instruction is *particularly beneficial for children who are having difficulty learning to read* and who are at risk for developing future reading problems.

Effective programs offer phonics instruction that:

- help teachers explicitly and systematically instruct students in how to relate letters and sounds, how to break spoken words into sounds, and how to blend sounds to form words.
- help students understand why they are learning the relationships between letters and sounds.
- help students apply their knowledge of phonics as they read words, sentences, and text.
- help students apply what they learn about sounds and letters to their own writing.
- can be adapted to the needs of individual students, based on assessment.
- include alphabetic knowledge, phonemic awareness, vocabulary development, and the reading of text, as well as systematic phonics instruction.

**Non-Systematic Instruction**

Programs of phonics instruction that are not systematic do not teach consonant and vowel letter-sound relationships in a prescribed sequence. Rather, they encourage informal phonics instruction based on the teacher's perceptions of what students need to learn and when they need to learn it. Nonsystematic instruction often neglects vowels, even though knowing vowel letter-sound relationships is a crucial part of knowing the alphabetic system. Nonsystematic programs do not provide practice materials that offer children the opportunity to apply what they are learning about letter-sound relationships.

Nonsystematic programs often include:

- literature-based programs that emphasize reading and writing activities. Phonics instruction is embedded in these activities, but letter-sound relationships are taught incidentally, usually based on key letters that appear in student reading materials.
- basal reading programs that focus on whole-word or meaning-based activities. These programs pay only limited attention to letter-sound relationships and provide little or no instruction in how to blend letters to pronounce words.
- sight-word programs that begin by teaching children a sight-word reading vocabulary of 50–100 words. Only after they learn to read these words do children receive instruction in the alphabetic principle.

# Fluency

**Fluent readers read aloud effortlessly and with expression. Their reading sounds natural, as if they are speaking.**

**Fluency** is the ability to read a text accurately and quickly. When fluent readers read silently, they recognize words automatically. They group words quickly to help them gain meaning from what they read. Fluent readers read aloud effortlessly and with expression. Their reading sounds natural, as if they are speaking. Readers who have not yet developed fluency read slowly, word by word. Their oral reading is choppy and plodding.

Fluency is important because it provides a bridge between word recognition and comprehension. Because fluent readers do not have to concentrate on decoding the words, they can focus their attention on what the text means. They can make connections among the ideas in the text and between the text and their background knowledge. Fluent readers recognize words and comprehend at the same time and focus their attention on making connections among the ideas in a text and between these ideas and their background knowledge. Less fluent readers focus their attention on figuring out the words and tend to have little attention left for comprehending the text.

Fluency develops gradually over considerable time and through substantial practice. At the earliest stage of reading development, students' oral reading is slow and labored because students are just learning to "break the code"—to attach sounds to letters and to blend letter sounds into recognizable words. Even very skilled readers may read in a slow, labored manner when reading texts with many unfamiliar words or topics.

Even when students recognize many words automatically, their oral reading still may be expressionless, not fluent. To read with expression, readers *must be able to divide the text into meaningful chunks.* These chunks include phrases and clauses. Readers must know to pause appropriately within and at the ends of sentences and when to change emphasis and tone.

---

## Implications of Teaching Fluency Instruction in the Classroom

1. Teachers are good models of fluent reading. By listening, students learn how a reader's voice can help written text make sense.
2. Teachers should read aloud to students daily.
3. Teachers should help students practice orally rereading text that is reasonably easy for them—that is, text containing mostly words that they know or can decode easily. In other words, the texts should be at the students' independent reading level and relatively short (probably 50–200 words) depending upon the age.
4. Teachers should assess to see if the text is at students' independent reading level. The student should be able to read with about 95 percent accuracy, or misread only about 1 of every 20 words. If the text is more difficult, students will focus so much on word recognition that they will not have an opportunity to develop fluency.
5. Teachers use a variety of reading materials, including stories, nonfiction, and poetry. Poetry is especially well suited to fluency practice because poems for children are often short and they contain rhythm, rhyme, and meaning, making practice easy, fun, and rewarding.

---

## Reading Fluency Assessment

**Easy Text:** Readers show that no more than 1 in 20 words are difficult (95 percent success).

**Challenging Text:** Readers show that no more than 1 in 10 words are difficult (90 percent success).

**Difficult Text:** Readers show that more than 1 in 10 words are difficult (less than 90 percent success).

---

**Instructional Strategy: How to Calculate Fluency**

*Total words read–errors = words correct per minute*

1. Select two or three brief passages from appropriate grade-level material (regardless of students' instructional levels).
2. Have individual students read each passage aloud for exactly 1 minute.
3. Count the total number of words the student read for each passage. Compute the average number of words read per minute.
4. Count the number of errors the student made on each passage. Compute the average number of errors per minute.
5. Subtract the average number of errors read per minute from the average total number of words read per minute. The result is the average number of words correct per minute (WCPM).
6. Repeat the procedure several times during the year. Graphing students' WCPM throughout the year easily captures their reading growth.
7. Compare the results with published norms or standards to determine whether students are making suitable progress in their fluency. For example, according to one published norm, students should be reading approximately 60 words per minute correctly by the end of first grade, 90–100 words per minute correctly by the end of second grade, and approximately 114 words per minute correctly by the end of third grade.

| Reading Aloud Exercises | | | | |
|---|---|---|---|---|
| **Student-Adult Reading** | **Choral Reading** | **Tape-Assisted Reading** | **Partner Reading** | **Readers' Theatre** |
| In student-adult reading, the student reads one-on-one with an adult. The adult can be you, a parent, a classroom aide, or a tutor. The adult reads the text first, providing the students with a model of fluent reading. Then the student reads the same passage to the adult with the adult providing assistance and encouragement. The student rereads the passage until the reading is quite fluent. This should take approximately three to four rereadings. | In choral, or unison, reading, students read along as a group with you (or another fluent adult reader). They might follow along as you read from a big book, or they might read from their own copy of the book you are reading. Predictable books are particularly useful for choral reading, because their repetitious style invites students to join in. Begin by reading the book aloud as you model fluent reading. Students should read the book with you three to five times total (though not necessarily on the same day). At this time, students should be able to read the text independently. | In tape-assisted reading, students read along in their books as they hear a fluent reader read the book on an audiotape. For tape-assisted reading, you need a book at a student's independent reading level and a tape recording of the book read by a fluent reader at about 80–100 words per minute. The tape should not have sound effects or music. For the first reading, the student should follow along with the tape, pointing to each word in her or his book as the reader reads it. Next, the student should try to read aloud along with the tape. Reading along with the tape should continue until the student is able to read the book independently, without the support of the tape. | In partner reading, paired students take turns reading aloud to each other. More fluent readers can be paired with less fluent readers. The stronger reader reads a paragraph or page first, providing a model of fluent reading. Then the less fluent reader reads the same text aloud. The stronger student gives help with word recognition and provides feedback and encouragement to the less fluent partner. The less fluent partner rereads the passage until he or she can read it independently. Partner reading need not be done with a more and less fluent reader. Two readers of equal ability can practice rereading after hearing the teacher read the passage. | In Readers' Theatre, students rehearse and perform a play for peers or others. They read from scripts that have been derived from books that are rich in dialogue. Students play characters who speak lines or a narrator who shares necessary background information. Readers' Theatre provides readers with a legitimate reason to reread text and to practice fluency. Readers' Theatre also promotes cooperative interaction with peers and makes the reading task appealing. |

# Vocabulary

Vocabulary refers to the words we must know to communicate effectively. In general, vocabulary can be described as oral vocabulary or reading vocabulary. Oral vocabulary refers to words that we use in speaking or recognize in listening. Reading vocabulary refers to words we recognize or use in print.

## Implications of Teaching Vocabulary Instruction in the Classroom

### Implement Strategies for Teaching Specific Words

A teacher plans to have his third-grade class read the novel *Stone Fox* by John Reynolds Gardiner. In this novel, a young boy enters a dogsled race in hopes of winning prize money to pay the taxes on his grandfather's farm. The teacher knows that understanding the concept of taxes is important to understanding the novel's plot. Therefore, before his students begin reading the novel, the teacher may do several things to make sure they understand what the concept means and why it is important to the story. For example, the teacher may:

- engage students in a discussion of the concept of taxes.
- read a sentence from the book that contains the word *taxes* and ask students to use context and their prior knowledge to try to figure out what it means.
- ask students to use taxes in their own sentence.

### Repeated Exposure to Words

A second-grade class is reading a biography of Benjamin Franklin. The biography discusses Franklin's important role as a scientist. The teacher wants to make sure that her students understand the meaning of the words *science* and *scientist*, both because the words are important to understanding the biography and because they are obviously very useful words to know in school and in everyday life.

### Using Word Parts

Knowing some common prefixes and suffixes (affixes), base words, and root words can help students learn the meanings of many new words. For example, if students learn just the four most common prefixes in English (*un-, re-, in-, dis-*), they will have important clues about the meaning of about two thirds of all English words that have prefixes. Prefixes are relatively easy to learn because they have clear meanings (for example, *un-* means *not* and *re-* means *again*); they are usually spelled the same way from word to word; and, of course, they always occur at the beginnings of words.

### Using Context Clues

Context clues are hints about the meaning of an unknown word that are provided in the words, phrases, and sentences that surround the word. Context clues include definitions, restatements, examples, or descriptions. Because students learn most word meanings indirectly, or from context, it is important that they learn to use context clues effectively.

### Using Dictionaries and Other Reference Aids

When students use reference aids, they can easily eliminate inappropriate definitions based upon context of the defined word. For example, in searching for the definition of the word *board* in a dictionary, students can eliminate the wrong definitions of *board* by looking at the word in the context of the sentence. In this example, one definition of *board* is, "to get on a train, an airplane, a bus, or a ship." The teacher next has students substitute the most likely definition for *board* in the original sentence to verify that the sentence makes sense. "The children were waiting to *get on* the buses."

## Text Comprehension

Even teachers in the primary grades can begin to build the foundation for reading comprehension. Reading is a complex process that develops over time. Although the basics of reading—word recognition and fluency—can be learned in a few years, reading to learn subject matter does not occur automatically. Teachers should emphasize text comprehension from the beginning, rather than waiting until students have mastered "the basics" of reading. Instruction at all grade levels can benefit from showing students how reading is a process of making sense out of text, or constructing meaning. Beginning readers, as well as more advanced readers, must understand that the ultimate goal of reading is comprehension.

---

**Metacognition**

*Metacognition* can be defined as "thinking about thinking." Good readers use metacognitive strategies to think about and have control over their reading. Before reading, they might clarify their purpose for reading and preview the text. During reading, they might monitor their understanding, adjusting their reading speed to fit the difficulty of the text and "fixing up" any comprehension problems they have. After reading, they check their understanding of what they read.

---

## Implications of Teaching Comprehension Instruction in the Classroom

Multiple strategies are available to help students gain reading comprehension competency. Multiple-strategy instruction teaches students how to use strategies flexibly as they are needed to assist their comprehension. In a well-known example of multiple-strategy instruction called "reciprocal teaching," the teacher and students work together so the students learn comprehension strategies. Teachers can do the following:

- ask questions about the text they are reading.
- ask students to summarize parts of the text.
- help students clarify words and sentences they don't understand.
- ask students to predict what might occur next in the text.
- talk about the content.
- model, or "think aloud," about their own thinking and understanding.
- lead students in a discussion about text meaning.
- help students relate the content of their reading to their life experiences and to other texts they have read.

**The first four of the above are the primary strategies.**

### TEXT COMPREHENSION CLASSROOM ACTIVITIES

| | |
|---|---|
| **Monitoring Comprehension** | Students who are good at monitoring their comprehension know when they understand what they read and when they do not. They have strategies to "fix" problems in their understanding as the problems arise.<br>- Identify **where** the difficulty occurs. ("I don't understand the second paragraph on page 76.")<br>- Identify **what** the difficulty is. ("I don't get what the author means when she says, 'Arriving in America was a milestone in my grandmother's life.'")<br>- **Restate** the difficult sentence or passage in their own words. ("Oh, so the author means that coming to America was a very important event in her grandmother's life.")<br>- **Look back** through the text. ("The author talked about Mr. McBride in chapter 2, but I don't remember much about him. Maybe if I reread that chapter, I can figure out why he's acting this way now.")<br>- **Look forward** in the text for information that might help them to resolve the difficulty. ("The text says, 'The groundwater may form a stream or pond or create a wetland. People can also bring groundwater to the surface.' Hmm, I don't understand how people can do that . . . Oh, the next section is called 'Wells.' I'll read this section to see if it tells how they do it.") |
| **Using Graphic and Semantic Organizers** | **Graphic organizers** illustrate concepts and interrelationships among concepts in a text, using diagrams or other pictorial devices. Graphic organizers are known by different names, such as maps, webs, graphs, charts, frames, or clusters. **Semantic organizers** (also called semantic maps or semantic webs) are graphic organizers that look somewhat like a spider web. In a semantic organizer, lines connect a central concept to a variety of related ideas and events. |
| **Answering Questions** | Question-answering instruction encourages students to learn to answer questions better and, therefore, to learn more as they read. One type of question-answering instruction simply teaches students to look back in the text to find answers to questions that they cannot answer after the initial reading. Another type helps students understand question-answer relationships—the relationships between questions and where the answers to those questions are found. In this instruction, readers learn to answer questions that require an understanding of information. |
| **Generating Questions** | Teaching students to ask their own questions improves their active processing of text and their comprehension. By generating questions, students become aware of whether they can answer the questions and whether they understand what they are reading. Students learn to ask themselves questions that require them to integrate information from different segments of text. |

*continued*

| TEXT COMPREHENSION CLASSROOM ACTIVITIES *(continued)* | |
|---|---|
| **Recognizing Story Structure** | **Story structure** refers to the way the content and events of a story are organized into a plot. Students who can recognize story structure have greater appreciation, understanding, and memory for stories. In story structure instruction, students learn to identify the categories of content (setting, initiating events, internal reactions, goals, attempts, and outcomes) and how this content is organized into a plot. Often, students learn to recognize story structure through the use of story maps. Story maps, a type of graphic organizer, show the sequence of events in simple stories. Instruction in the content and organization of stories improves students' comprehension and memory of stories. |
| **Summarizing** | A **summary** is a synthesis of the important ideas in a text. Summarizing requires students to determine what is important in what they are reading, to condense this information, and to put it into their own words. Instruction in summarizing helps students identify or generate main ideas, connect the main or central ideas, eliminate redundant and unnecessary information, and remember what they read. |
| **Making Use of Prior Knowledge** | Good readers draw on prior knowledge and experience to help them understand what they are reading. You can help your students make use of their prior knowledge to improve their comprehension. Before your students read, preview the text with them. As part of previewing, ask the students what they already know about the content of the selection (e.g., the topic, the concept, the time period). Ask them what they know about the author and what text structure he or she is likely to use. Discuss the important vocabulary used in the text. Show students some pictures or diagrams to prepare them for what they are about to read. |
| **Using Mental Imagery** | Good readers often form mental pictures, or images, as they read. Readers (especially younger readers) who visualize during reading understand and remember what they read better than readers who do not visualize. Help your students learn to form visual images of what they are reading. For example, urge them to picture a setting, character, or event described in the text. |

# PART III

# TWO FULL-LENGTH PRACTICE TESTS

This section contains two full-length practice RICA Written Examinations. The practice tests are followed by complete answers, explanations, sample essays, and analysis techniques. The format, levels of difficulty, question structures, and number of questions are similar to those on the actual RICA Written Exam. **The actual RICA is copyrighted and may not be duplicated, so these questions are not taken from the actual tests.**

When taking these exams, try to simulate the test conditions. Remember, the total testing time for each practice test is 4 hours. Although you may divide your time between the two sections any way you want, be sure you budget your time effectively to finish all of the sections. Try to spend about 1 to 1½ minutes on each multiple-choice question, about 15 minutes each for written Assignments A and B, approximately 25 minutes each for written Assignments C and D, and about 1 hour for written Assignment E, the case study.

**On the actual RICA test you will be given:**

1. A **Test Booklet** with all the questions (multiple-choice and essay assignments);
2. An **Answer Document** to record your multiple-choice answers and Assignments A–D responses; and
3. A **Case Study Responses Booklet** to record your responses to the case study (Assignment E).

**Note:** On the actual RICA you will NOT be tearing out any pages as your answers and essays will be written in separate documents or booklets.

# Practice Test 1

## Practice Test 1 Answer Document

### Multiple-Choice Answer Sheets

| | | |
|---|---|---|
| 1 Ⓐ Ⓑ Ⓒ Ⓓ | | 36 Ⓐ Ⓑ Ⓒ Ⓓ |
| 2 Ⓐ Ⓑ Ⓒ Ⓓ | | 37 Ⓐ Ⓑ Ⓒ Ⓓ |
| 3 Ⓐ Ⓑ Ⓒ Ⓓ | | 38 Ⓐ Ⓑ Ⓒ Ⓓ |
| 4 Ⓐ Ⓑ Ⓒ Ⓓ | | 39 Ⓐ Ⓑ Ⓒ Ⓓ |
| 5 Ⓐ Ⓑ Ⓒ Ⓓ | | 40 Ⓐ Ⓑ Ⓒ Ⓓ |
| 6 Ⓐ Ⓑ Ⓒ Ⓓ | | 41 Ⓐ Ⓑ Ⓒ Ⓓ |
| 7 Ⓐ Ⓑ Ⓒ Ⓓ | | 42 Ⓐ Ⓑ Ⓒ Ⓓ |
| 8 Ⓐ Ⓑ Ⓒ Ⓓ | | 43 Ⓐ Ⓑ Ⓒ Ⓓ |
| 9 Ⓐ Ⓑ Ⓒ Ⓓ | | 44 Ⓐ Ⓑ Ⓒ Ⓓ |
| 10 Ⓐ Ⓑ Ⓒ Ⓓ | | 45 Ⓐ Ⓑ Ⓒ Ⓓ |
| 11 Ⓐ Ⓑ Ⓒ Ⓓ | | 46 Ⓐ Ⓑ Ⓒ Ⓓ |
| 12 Ⓐ Ⓑ Ⓒ Ⓓ | | 47 Ⓐ Ⓑ Ⓒ Ⓓ |
| 13 Ⓐ Ⓑ Ⓒ Ⓓ | | 48 Ⓐ Ⓑ Ⓒ Ⓓ |
| 14 Ⓐ Ⓑ Ⓒ Ⓓ | | 49 Ⓐ Ⓑ Ⓒ Ⓓ |
| 15 Ⓐ Ⓑ Ⓒ Ⓓ | | 50 Ⓐ Ⓑ Ⓒ Ⓓ |
| 16 Ⓐ Ⓑ Ⓒ Ⓓ | | 51 Ⓐ Ⓑ Ⓒ Ⓓ |
| 17 Ⓐ Ⓑ Ⓒ Ⓓ | | 52 Ⓐ Ⓑ Ⓒ Ⓓ |
| 18 Ⓐ Ⓑ Ⓒ Ⓓ | | 53 Ⓐ Ⓑ Ⓒ Ⓓ |
| 19 Ⓐ Ⓑ Ⓒ Ⓓ | | 54 Ⓐ Ⓑ Ⓒ Ⓓ |
| 20 Ⓐ Ⓑ Ⓒ Ⓓ | | 55 Ⓐ Ⓑ Ⓒ Ⓓ |
| 21 Ⓐ Ⓑ Ⓒ Ⓓ | | 56 Ⓐ Ⓑ Ⓒ Ⓓ |
| 22 Ⓐ Ⓑ Ⓒ Ⓓ | | 57 Ⓐ Ⓑ Ⓒ Ⓓ |
| 23 Ⓐ Ⓑ Ⓒ Ⓓ | | 58 Ⓐ Ⓑ Ⓒ Ⓓ |
| 24 Ⓐ Ⓑ Ⓒ Ⓓ | | 59 Ⓐ Ⓑ Ⓒ Ⓓ |
| 25 Ⓐ Ⓑ Ⓒ Ⓓ | | 60 Ⓐ Ⓑ Ⓒ Ⓓ |
| 26 Ⓐ Ⓑ Ⓒ Ⓓ | | 61 Ⓐ Ⓑ Ⓒ Ⓓ |
| 27 Ⓐ Ⓑ Ⓒ Ⓓ | | 62 Ⓐ Ⓑ Ⓒ Ⓓ |
| 28 Ⓐ Ⓑ Ⓒ Ⓓ | | 63 Ⓐ Ⓑ Ⓒ Ⓓ |
| 29 Ⓐ Ⓑ Ⓒ Ⓓ | | 64 Ⓐ Ⓑ Ⓒ Ⓓ |
| 30 Ⓐ Ⓑ Ⓒ Ⓓ | | 65 Ⓐ Ⓑ Ⓒ Ⓓ |
| 31 Ⓐ Ⓑ Ⓒ Ⓓ | | 66 Ⓐ Ⓑ Ⓒ Ⓓ |
| 32 Ⓐ Ⓑ Ⓒ Ⓓ | | 67 Ⓐ Ⓑ Ⓒ Ⓓ |
| 33 Ⓐ Ⓑ Ⓒ Ⓓ | | 68 Ⓐ Ⓑ Ⓒ Ⓓ |
| 34 Ⓐ Ⓑ Ⓒ Ⓓ | | 69 Ⓐ Ⓑ Ⓒ Ⓓ |
| 35 Ⓐ Ⓑ Ⓒ Ⓓ | | 70 Ⓐ Ⓑ Ⓒ Ⓓ |

CUT HERE

**Note:** On the actual RICA you will NOT be tearing out any pages as your answers and essay will be written in separate documents or booklets.

## Assignment A

CUT HERE

## Assignment B

## Assignment C

CUT HERE

## Assignment D

CUT HERE

CUT HERE

# Practice Test 1 Case Study Response Booklet

## Assignment E

CUT HERE

CUT HERE

# General Directions

The RICA test is composed of two sections: a multiple-choice question section, which contains 70 multiple-choice questions, and an open-ended assignment section. This assignment section contains five assignments, A to E, requiring written responses. The weight of each section toward the total examination score is approximately 50 percent. Therefore, your performance on both sections is equally important.

The directions for each section appear immediately before that section. The multiple-choice questions and the open-ended assignments may be worked on or completed in any order that you choose. On the actual RICA test you will be given a checklist to help you keep track of the sections you have completed. Plan your time carefully to make sure that you can complete the entire test within the time allotted.

**For security reasons, you may not take notes or remove any of the test materials from the room.** Since no scratch paper is allowed, you may use the margins of this test booklet for your notes. Keep in mind that only the responses recorded in your Answer Document and your Case Study Response booklet will be scored.

Following the last open-ended assignment (E) you will see the words "End of Test." You may go back and review your answers at any time during the testing session if time permits. When you are sure you have answered all the multiple-choice questions, completed all the assignments, and properly recorded all of your responses in your Answer Document and Case Study Response Booklet, alert the proctor by raising your hand. At that time, your test materials will be collected, and you will be allowed to leave.

If you have any questions when you are taking the actual RICA test, be sure to ask them before beginning the test.

GO ON TO THE NEXT PAGE

# Directions for Section I: Multiple-Choice Questions

**Questions 1 to 70**

This section is composed of 70 multiple-choice questions. Each question is followed by four answer choices. Carefully read each question and choose the **one** best answer. Make sure that you record each answer on page 1 or 2 of the Answer Document in the space that corresponds to the question number. Completely fill in the circle having the same letter as the answer you have chosen. *Use only a No. 2 lead pencil.*

---

<u>Sample Question:</u>

1. Which of the following cities is farthest south?

   **A.** Los Angeles
   **B.** Sacramento
   **C.** San Diego
   **D.** San Francisco

---

The correct answer to this question is **C.** You would indicate that on the Answer Document as follows:

**1**

You should try to answer all the questions. If you have some knowledge about the subject of a question, you should try to use that knowledge to help answer it. You will not be penalized for guessing, because no points are deducted for incorrect answers.

DO NOT GO ON UNTIL YOU ARE TOLD TO DO SO.

1. At the beginning of the school year, Mrs. Harvey uses the results of an entry-level IRI (Informal Reading Inventory) to determine each child's independent, instructional, and frustration reading level. She will then group students for Universal Access according to similar reading needs. She should remember that:

A. frustration level refers to books above the child's current grade. Students reading books above their level are frustrated and cannot comprehend the material because it is too difficult.

B. knowledge of independent, instructional, and frustration reading levels is important. However, she needs to select grade-level texts for all learners.

C. instructional level refers to students being able to read 90–95% of the words correctly and answer most comprehension questions accurately.

D. independent level refers to what children can independently read. They should be able to choose books they are interested in and discuss them with their peers. Students should be able to read 90% of the words accurately.

2. A first-grade teacher notices one of her students is struggling with reading. He is in the lowest-achieving reading group. The teacher has tried some strategies to improve his reading, but he seems to make no progress. The next step the teacher should take in working with this student is to:

A. assess his reading and target instruction to meet identified skill needs.

B. request the help of specialists at her school—such as the reading specialist, resource specialist, or counselor— to make a joint decision on how to best help the student.

C. send home more homework for the child to practice reading skills with his parents.

D. read more often with the child to help develop confidence, and provide buddy reading time with more capable students.

3. A fourth-grade student is able to read fluently but is unable to identify the main idea of what he has read. The teacher notices the difficulties this student is having, individually assesses his comprehension, and tries to help him connect his experiences to what he is reading through discussions before, during, and after his reading. Additional activities might help this student bring meaning to the text during and after reading. Some suggested activities to help this student could include:

A. making word banks, using computer reading programs, and performing contextual analysis.

B. reading response logs, adjusting reading rate, and increasing library visits.

C. playing word games, sharing books, and observing teacher modeling of how to connect text to experiences.

D. paraphrasing text, self-questioning, summarizing and retelling, and using graphic organizers.

4. A first-grade teacher is using the reading program adopted by her school district. The program includes decodable texts. The instructional advantage of using decodable texts with beginning readers is that:

A. decodable texts provide abundant practice with previously taught phonic elements and sight words.

B. decodable texts can provide beginning readers with a controlled vocabulary that will enable them to read more books.

C. books with controlled vocabulary are predictable and can be used as literature in a reading program.

D. decodable texts allow the school to accumulate more books in primary classrooms.

GO ON TO THE NEXT PAGE

5. Mr. Vasquez is planning phonemic awareness instruction for his kindergarten class. He gives each student the Yopp-Singer assessment. He then uses the test data to determine student needs and form groups. When planning instruction groups for Universal Access, Mr. Vasquez should be primarily concerned with:

   A. creating flexible skill groups and providing differentiated instruction.

   B. balancing his phonemic awareness groups in a stimulating learning environment.

   C. considering the classroom behavior and special needs of each student.

   D. seeking outside intervention for students below grade-level standards.

6. It is the beginning of the school year in Mr. Jones' third-grade class. He is examining the results of a standardized reading test that uses norm-referenced, grade-equivalent scores. One student's score was 5.2. This student's score indicates that her reading performance on this test:

   A. corresponds to what an average fifth grader in the second month of school would achieve.

   B. represents a top third-grade stanine score for students in the same school.

   C. places her in the 51st percentile of all students who have taken this norm-referenced test.

   D. was as good as or better than 51% of students in the same grade nationwide.

7. Mr. Tonning gives each of his sixth-grade students an entry-level reading assessment at the beginning of each school year. At the end of the school year, he administers a summative assessment. Each time he ranks his students' performance and determines who is reading at the grade-level benchmark, and who is reading above and below that mark. Mr. Tonning uses this data in a variety of ways. Mr. Tonning is *least* likely to use the results to:

   A. plan interventions for students below grade level.

   B. communicate to students, parents, and school personnel performance information regarding progress on the standards-based assessment.

   C. plan reading groups based on student needs.

   D. interpret use of the three cueing systems and concepts about print and use them to report student achievement on the standards-based report card.

8. In preparation for administering the fourth-grade California Standards Test, Mrs. Slotnikow reviews the guidelines for administering the test to students with special needs. She recognizes that students with Individualized Education Programs (IEPs) may require accommodations during assessment. Which is the most logical action to ensure appropriate testing protocols have been implemented?

   A. Make arrangements with the resource teacher to individually assess all IEP students.

   B. Preteach material systematically to provide Universal Access for students with IEPs.

   C. Consult the manual for a list of possible accommodations available to students with special needs.

   D. Provide individual students with the accommodations that have been specified in their IEPs.

9. A first-grade teacher has 20 students with varying abilities in reading. How should the teacher group the students for reading instruction during Universal Access time?

   A. The teacher should create small groups that remain constant throughout the school year to enable students to form bonds that further their reading progress.

   B. Primary classes should have children grouped for reading throughout the day. The teacher can often use the same groups for all instruction.

   C. Grouping is an effective practice, but the groups should remain flexible. The teacher should regroup students as a result of frequent assessment of their skill needs.

   D. Research has proven that children do best in whole-group instruction. This type of grouping provides for higher and lower-ability children and meets the needs of all learners.

10. Mr. Nordquist regularly conducts curriculum-based assessments with his second-grade class. As a result, it is clear to him that Juan, a nonnative speaker, can decode and comprehend at a higher reading level than the majority of the class. What is the most important factor for Mr. Nordquist to consider when planning classroom interventions?

    A. He should always group Juan with other advanced students during the language-arts block so he can fully access the English Language curriculum.

    B. He should vary the complexity of Juan's assignments so Juan can continually access the challenging English vocabulary.

    C. He should vary the pacing and complexity of the teaching so Juan is appropriately challenged during small-group and whole-group instruction.

    D. He should assess Juan for the Gifted and Talented Education program.

11. Ms. Ramirez notices many of her eighth-grade students making spelling errors. She wants to gain more specific understanding of her students' spelling needs. In order to understand their spelling strengths and weaknesses and plan remediation in this problem area, Ms. Ramirez is most likely to begin by:

    A. giving direct instruction in spelling, complete with weekly pre-tests and post-tests.

    B. administering a comprehensive spelling assessment and analyzing student writing samples.

    C. assigning extra spelling homework to go along with her comprehensive spelling program.

    D. examining spelling in student journals, essays, and reports on a regular basis and taking anecdotal records.

12. Mr. Karabines, a primary teacher, is developing his daily schedule as well as his long-range classroom goals. According to the California Language Arts Framework, what is the minimum amount of time per day to be allocated for language arts instruction?

    A. 2½ hours
    B. 2 hours
    C. 1½ hours
    D. 1 hour

13. In Ms. Winters' fifth-grade classroom, students create academic vocabulary journals and regularly record newly introduced academic vocabulary. Which of the following should *not* be included in an academic vocabulary journal?

    A. synonyms and antonyms
    B. spelling word lists that focus on a particular pattern
    C. meaningful example sentences
    D. student-friendly definitions

GO ON TO THE NEXT PAGE

14. A primary teacher is aware of the Matthew Effect and its potential impact on student growth. The teacher plans numerous interventions to reduce its negative effects. Which of the following is *least* likely to make a difference in addressing the gap in the Matthew Effect?

    A. direct instruction in the use of figurative language and morphemic analysis combined with meaningful independent practice

    B. systematic, explicit instruction in word analysis

    C. helping students select books at their independent reading levels

    D. providing students with reading material that holds their interest

15. A second-grade teacher listens to students read orally in a small guided reading group. She notices one student who is continually struggling with fluency. What intervention strategies would best provide for the needs of this student?

    A. The teacher should model reading with expression. In addition, the teacher should provide decodable text for this student and encourage the child to whisper read and reread passages to develop automaticity and appropriate phrasing.

    B. The teacher needs to concentrate on using related workbook pages in prosody and word-recognition skills for this student to become an automatic reader.

    C. The teacher should increase time for read-alouds, which would provide this reader with more exposure to good literature. Doing this would also result in the added benefits of increasing the student's vocabulary and helping develop automaticity.

    D. The teacher should give time for sustained, silent reading, which increases fluency and reading rate when the student is reading books at the student's reading level.

16. After completing his entry-level reading assessments, a fifth-grade teacher notes that one of his students, Maya, reads 80 WCPM (words correct per minute). Which of the following strategies would the teacher be *least* likely to use when planning his next steps?

    A. Analyze Maya's reading to see whether she has been focusing her attention on decoding the words and perhaps needs to read lower-level material.

    B. Work to develop automaticity so Maya can translate letters into sounds effortlessly and accurately.

    C. Record WCPM and then begin systematic instruction in phonological awareness and word attack skills.

    D. Directly teach and model appropriate prosodic features.

17. In a May assessment of a kindergarten student's performance, the teacher notes that the student is able to name the letters of the alphabet and has mastered print concepts. However, the student is unable to identify rhyming words. What should the teacher conclude about this student?

    A. The student has completed most of the requirements of kindergarten and will be successful in first-grade reading.

    B. The student has not mastered a phonemic awareness skill (that is, rhyming words) that should be mastered by the end of kindergarten.

    C. The student will not be able to perform at grade level in first grade.

    D. The student needs direct instruction and practice in phonemic letter recognition skills.

18. When evaluating a student's reading, a primary teacher notes that when reading text orally, the student continually omits the silent *e* and reads:

   hat for hate      tap for tape      cop for cope

   What are the instructional implications of this behavior?

   A.  The student is performing poorly in spelling, and the teacher needs to focus on teaching silent *e* endings to the student.
   B.  The teacher needs to focus the student's attention on making sense of what she is reading.
   C.  The teacher needs to have the student reread the passage to clarify meaning.
   D.  The student would benefit from more explicit skills instruction with attention to vowel sounds.

19. According to the California Language Arts Framework, many learning difficulties can be corrected during Universal Access time. Which strategy is *not* included?

   A.  good diagnostic teaching
   B.  repetition of instruction with lots of opportunities for student practice
   C.  a focus on key skills and understanding
   D.  a referral to the Student Success Team

20. According to the California Language Arts Framework, to plan appropriate intervention strategies to help students who are experiencing learning difficulties, teachers should consider the degree of severity according to the three major groups:

   A.  benchmark, strategic, and intensive
   B.  advanced, intensive, and strategic
   C.  English Learner and English Only
   D.  low, middle, and high

21. A third-grade student is confusing consonant pairs when writing in her daily journal. She writes *JUNCL* for jungle, *EFRYONE* for everyone, and *CARROD* for carrot. Which is an appropriate instructional strategy to use with this student?

   A.  The teacher should assign related workbook pages from their reading series to help this student overcome these errors.
   B.  The student would benefit from worthwhile practice in sound blending to make meaning of words.
   C.  The teacher needs to instruct the student in articulating phonemes.
   D.  The student needs to add similar words to her spelling lists and study them.

22. During daily writing, a third-grade student continually confuses long vowel sounds and writes *hiev* for *hive*, *bote* for *boat*, and *trea* for *tree*. The instructional strategies the teacher should use to meet this student's identified need include which of the following?

   A.  increasing independent reading, assigning additional homework with long vowel sounds, and making frequent assessments
   B.  providing crossword puzzles and word hunts and encourage independent reading, so the student can encounter similar vocabulary
   C.  developing weekly spelling words using the look-see-say method; sorting pictures; and adding vocabulary hunts
   D.  direct instruction in long vowel patterns, word sorts, and the use of word study notebooks and other activities to practice vowel patterns

GO ON TO THE NEXT PAGE

23. A fourth-grade teacher is working on syllabication with her class. When she says "misunderstanding," her students clap on the syllables and segment the word into *mis-un-der-stand-ing*. Next, she says "hospitality" and asks students to clap on the syllables and segment the word into *hos-pi-tal-i-ty*. Later, during a writing assignment, she encourages students to softly clap on syllables before writing difficult words. Which is the best reason for students to practice segmenting words?

   A. Syllabication will increase their ability to encode the first 100 high-frequency words.

   B. The ability to break words into syllables will have an impact on their spelling accuracy with multisyllabic words.

   C. Syllabication helps students connect new words to existing words in their oral vocabularies.

   D. Awareness of syllabication and word origin is necessary for students to become proficient readers.

24. What are the instructional implications regarding a primary student who reads the word *yell* as *will*?

   A. The student needs added practice with letters and blending sounds into words.

   B. Some examples of activities that would benefit the student are picture sorts and spelling puzzles.

   C. Maintenance of critical word skills is imperative to this student's progress.

   D. The ability to distinguish between letters and sounds is apparent, and the child should be moved to the next level.

25. Fifth-grade students are studying traditional literature. As part of the fables genre, students will perform a Readers' Theatre version of *Androcles and the Lion* for a second-grade class. This type of activity helps teachers informally gather data about the fifth-grade students' ability to:

   A. change the way they speak to fit main character traits while reading and develop automaticity at an independent level.

   B. develop listening skills in younger students.

   C. learn roles and read lines with fluency and expression.

   D. work with younger students while performing literary analysis.

26. Some effective ways to teach letter recognition to kindergarten students include the use of:

   A. a pocket chart, reciting nursery rhymes, and singing songs.

   B. magnetic letter sorts, creating alphabet books, and calling students' attention to individual letters that the teacher writes in a morning message.

   C. clapping syllables, word segmentation, and blending.

   D. alphabet-sound charts, sound boxes, and the modeling of stretching words when writing.

27. A teacher prepares a lesson using a series of boxes that correspond to the number of sounds that are heard in a word. For example, a kindergarten teacher provides her students with the following boxes along with round plastic markers. Next, the teacher pronounces the word *c-a-t* slowly, stretching the word into its sounds. Finally, she asks the students in her reading group to move their plastic markers into the boxes as she says the sounds in the word. Why is this lesson effective for these students?

   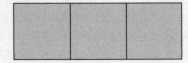

   A. These students are learning to segment the sounds in a word that is spoken.

   B. These students are "playing with language," which research has shown is an essential precursor to reading.

   C. The teacher is guiding these students in an activity that develops their oral language and has proven to be an indicator of early reading success.

   D. The teacher understands that similar activities help students to develop an interest in language and how it works and will help them develop into proficient readers.

28. Which of the following strategies is the most effective in teaching spelling to children?

    A. memorizing lists of words that are related to reading material introduced at the beginning of each theme
    B. studying spelling patterns such as those found in CVCC, CCVC, and CVVC words
    C. taking a spelling test every week
    D. developing alphabetic principles and using phonemic analysis by spelling words aloud

29. A fourth-grade teacher is working with Tony, a student who is trying to decode the word *upsetting*. Read the following dialog and use it to answer the question about their conversation.

    | | |
    |---|---|
    | **Teacher:** | Can you read this word? |
    | **Student:** | Yes. It's *upsing*. |
    | **Teacher:** | Does *upsing* make sense? |
    | **Student:** | No. I guess not. |
    | **Teacher:** | You've read part of the word. Try again. |
    | **Student:** | Oh! It's *upping*. |
    | **Teacher:** | You've read the first syllable and the last syllable. Now I want you to focus on the middle part of the word. Can you try the word again? |
    | **Student:** | up-set-ting. |
    | **Teacher:** | You just read all of the syllables in the word. Try to put them together quickly to read the word. |
    | **Student:** | *upsetting, upsetting.* I got it. The word is *upsetting!* |
    | **Teacher:** | Great job! You figured out the word *upsetting.* |

    Based on the preceding conversation, this student would most clearly benefit from:

    A. participating in a systematic, organized phonics program.
    B. paying attention to structure and syntactic cues.
    C. explicit instruction and guided practice decoding multisyllabic words.
    D. systematic instruction in decoding prefixes and suffixes.

30. Anwar is a fourth grader who reads at grade level. When asked to choose a book from the classroom library, he generally selects texts that are at his frustration level. It is clear that he is unable to read his chosen material. The teacher's best response to this behavior would be to:

    A. choose easier material for Anwar so he is able to accurately decode and comprehend the text.
    B. continue allowing Anwar to select books at his frustration level for as long as he appears to be enjoying his choices.
    C. teach Anwar the five-finger rule of reading so he will be able to monitor his own reading selections. When Anwar makes more than five errors per page, he will know the book is too difficult for him and choose another.
    D. review Anwar's book selections during Guided Reading and give mini-lessons on difficult reading concepts so Anwar will be able to read at his instructional level.

31. Which of the following are *not* examples of phonological awareness tasks?

    A. deleting and identifying word boundaries
    B. distinguishing initial, medial, and final sounds
    C. blending sounds together
    D. adding letters to form words

32. Advanced students and those with learning difficulties in the language arts often require systematically planned differentiation to ensure that curriculum and instruction are appropriately challenging. The strategies for modification of curriculum and instruction are similar for both groups and can be considered variations along four dimensions: pacing, depth, complexity, and novelty. Which strategy (or strategies) is most commonly used?

    A. novelty
    B. complexity and novelty
    C. pacing and complexity
    D. depth

GO ON TO THE NEXT PAGE

33. Grouping students for instruction is a tool and an aid to instruction, not an end to itself. When grouping for instruction, the teacher should focus on all of the following, *except*:

    A. it should be used flexibly to ensure all students achieve the standards.

    B. it should be used so all students have a chance to meet with the teacher in a small instructional group.

    C. it should be used to group those students who do not understand a concept or skill and to reteach the concept or skill in a different way by providing additional practice.

    D. instructional objectives should always be based on the standards and should dictate grouping strategies.

34. A teacher uses a Big Book to do a shared reading with her students. What are some advantages of using this strategy?

    A. The children can hear good quality literature, which fosters good reading, good listening skills, and better study skills.

    B. Kids can self-select their books and read independently. The teacher can explicitly teach phonemic awareness skills that students will later read independently.

    C. Word attack skills can be taught in context, building from simple to complex.

    D. The teacher can directly instruct concepts of print, such as title, author, left/right direct print, and table of contents.

35. The most important advantage of using invented spelling activities in the primary classroom is that:

    A. children are able to move through the stages of the writing process even though they still cannot spell in the conventional manner.

    B. the teacher is developing phonemic awareness and furthering the child's understanding of the alphabetic principle.

    C. the teacher is encouraging the students to become independent spellers and encouraging an active interest in correct spelling.

    D. it is a good way to explain the developmental processes of spelling to parents.

36. A fifth-grade teacher asks his students to break into groups, and each student then reads a different passage from the same story in his or her respective group. The students are to discuss their passage in their group and then report the important story elements back to the whole class. What would be the primary reason a teacher would use this type of technique?

    A. The teacher can cover more material in a shorter period of time.

    B. The students can gain a deeper understanding of their passage and have the opportunity for more clarity by discussing with peers.

    C. The teacher can evaluate each student's reading ability during text-based discussion.

    D. Cooperative learning can be a powerful instructional strategy.

37. Which of the following is *not* an effective strategy for encouraging independent reading and fluency at home?

    A. Students complete at-home reading logs and receive rewards as incentives.

    B. Students take home book bags with classroom books at their independent reading level.

    C. The teacher regularly gives comprehension quizzes on reading that was completed at home.

    D. The teacher provides lists of books that can be checked out from the local public library.

**38.** Jemma is a sixth grader experiencing difficulty with comprehension. Her teacher has noted that her reading fluency is weak despite her proven ability to decode words accurately. The teacher might help improve Jemma's fluency by:

**A.** providing direct, explicit instruction in fluency. Jemma can then practice reading aloud books at her independent level to a partner or small group.

**B.** modeling phrasing and reading with expression. Jemma can practice orally retelling stories to build her text fluency and comprehension.

**C.** providing direct instruction in phonics to build decoding skills and automaticity before reading aloud. Jemma can practice reading aloud to a younger student to help build her confidence.

**D.** providing meaningful opportunities for Jemma to listen to classmates reading aloud fluently. When Jemma is ready, she will read with expression.

**39.** During the reading period in a fourth-grade classroom, the teacher reads aloud a short, difficult piece of nonfiction. After completing the passage, the teacher retells what she has read to the class and then evaluates her own comprehension. Immediately after, she reads the piece a second time, retells it again, and subsequently re-evaluates her own comprehension. The students witness that the teacher's understanding is increased after the second reading. What reading strategy is the teacher demonstrating to her students?

**A.** Rereading is a very effective reading strategy.

**B.** The demonstration of this strategy provides a model for what students may do when they have difficulty understanding vocabulary in a passage.

**C.** The teacher is helping her students prepare for state testing by reviewing material twice.

**D.** Modeling a reading technique for students is an optimum way to teach.

**40.** The teacher leads a fifth-grade class in composing the following chart:

### OUR "SURVEY" STRATEGIES

| What to examine: | Pages when strategies are used: |
|---|---|
| ■ heading<br>■ captions<br>■ graphs<br>■ photos<br>■ maps | |

Together as a class, they decide what should be listed under the first column. The teacher explains that the class will fill out the second column after they finish reading some articles. Next, the teacher passes out articles from the newspaper and magazines to previously formed cooperative groups. The students are to read the selections within their groups and note on the chart when they use the strategies that are listed. What reading skill or strategy are these students practicing?

**A.** The students are receiving practice with comprehension strategies.

**B.** This lesson has been carefully planned so each student is able to participate in the lesson.

**C.** The students are applying surveying strategies.

**D.** Students are being taught how to increase their comprehension.

**GO ON TO THE NEXT PAGE**

41. A third-grade teacher writes on the board the following chart headings (in the shaded part) before reading a new story to her class:

| Character | Is a. . . . . | Description of Appearance | Behavior: nice/mean/angry |
|-----------|---------------|---------------------------|---------------------------|
| Mandy | young lion | small, scraggly | very sweet, helpful |
| Samba | mother lion | strong, protective | angry when her cub is threatened |

After reading, the students respond to the story by naming the characters and the teacher writes them on the chart. Next, they complete the rest of the chart. At this point, the best activity the teacher could assign to his students would be to:

A. write their own story.
B. write character descriptions.
C. read the story again.
D. copy the chart.

42. A first-grade teacher decides to reread a story to her class instead of selecting a new story. Which of the following describes the greatest benefit of this technique?

A. Rereading a book promotes good listening skills that are required for all texts.
B. Rereading is a valuable technique that leads to more enjoyment of literature for the students.
C. Reading a selection/book over again engages the students in a familiar text, enhances their understanding of author's style, and builds overall comprehension.
D. The rereading of a story builds excitement and is a delightful technique to use with young children.

43. A fifth-grade teacher notices that some of her English Language Learners and speakers of nonstandard English are unable to read fluently. The best strategy for her to use with those students would be to:

A. systematically use reading books in which the students can correctly read all the words.
B. encourage shared reading and prosody as part of an organized word study program.
C. explicitly teach English intonation patterns, phrasing, and syntax, and give students the opportunity to practice rereading.
D. differentiate instruction by choosing books that are on the students' reading levels.

**Use the information below to answer the three questions that follow.**

Ms. Montell and her kindergarten students have been studying many books in the Curious George series, including *Curious George Rides a Bike*. Each day, she sends a "Curious George suitcase" home with a different student. In this suitcase, the student will find a copy of *Curious George Rides a Bike,* a Curious George stuffed animal, a set of instructions, and a journal. Students are asked to read the book together with their parents. Students are then asked to dictate a story to their families while an adult records it in the class journal labeled "Adventures with Curious George." Each kindergartener will then illustrate a picture to go with the writing.

44. In the classroom, Ms. Montell asks students to brainstorm events from *Curious George Rides a Bike.* She records the events on sentence strips and asks students to organize them in a pocket chart. This strategy is likely to be particularly useful in helping Ms. Montell evaluate students' ability to:

A. apply inferential knowledge about the story in context.
B. identify cause-effect relationships and patterns and sequence them in proper order.
C. identify story grammar and story developments in the order they appear in the text.
D. determine main ideas from the story and organize them in sequential order.

45. When the students return the suitcase to the classroom the following day, Ms. Montell is most likely to ask her students to:

    A.  read the journal aloud. Fellow students are asked to comment on their favorite parts from the writing and illustrations.
    B.  ask the student to correct spelling and grammatical errors. The students are asked to publish the writing in a class book.
    C.  read other Curious George stories. Ask students to retell the story in paragraph form.
    D.  place the journal in the class library. Well-behaved students will be able to read the "Adventures of Curious George" as a reward for finishing their work.

46. Ms. Montell most likely chose to send this Curious George suitcase home because she wanted to:

    A.  motivate students while encouraging and providing support for families to read at home with their children.
    B.  enjoy reading and writing while practicing a written topic that will be on the next district-wide literacy assessment.
    C.  acknowledge that parents are busy and give them study tools to work with their students at home.
    D.  motivate students while building literal, inferential, and evaluative comprehension skills in a nonthreatening home environment.

47. In the word *snack,* which of the following letters or letter clusters is a rime?

    A.  *sn*
    B.  *snack*
    C.  *ack*
    D.  *ck*

48. A first-grade teacher frequently assesses students' reading to determine instructional levels and select guided reading books. When listening to one of her students read an unknown text, the teacher notices the student is able to read all the words in the text without making any errors but when asked to recall the story, the student is unable to do so in detail. What does this information tell the teacher about the student's reading ability?

    A.  This information tells the teacher she is selecting books for the student at an independent reading level.
    B.  The student is able to read text at a very high level, and the teacher needs to select more difficult text for the student to read.
    C.  The student is able to decode the text but does not comprehend what she is reading.
    D.  The student should be reading with other students who are reading at her level and needs to be further challenged.

49. During small group reading, the teacher notices that one of her third-grade students is struggling with understanding the story and is unable to make logical inferences about it. After determining that the text is correctly matched to the child's reading ability, what strategies should the teacher use with this student?

    A.  The teacher needs to emphasize decoding strategies with this student to further his understanding of inferential comprehension during the story.
    B.  The teacher should continually assess the student to determine the instructional reading level of the student and be sure that the text isn't too difficult.
    C.  The student should be encouraged to do more silent reading with suitable text that matches his ability in order to develop inferential thinking skills.
    D.  The teacher should reread the story with the student and model the use of comprehension strategies such as drawing conclusions and using textual evidence to predict outcomes.

GO ON TO THE NEXT PAGE

50. A first-grade student is capable of fluently reading a grade-level story. However, when asked by the teacher to recall details about the story just read, she is unable to recall specific information and often answers, "I liked the story." What are some instructional implications for this student?

    A. The student needs direct instruction in comprehension skills, which should be followed with guided and independent practice of the comprehension skills.

    B. The student needs to be given more structured situations for writing about stories so she can better express herself.

    C. Instructional suggestions would include cooperative groups and paired learning that focus on retelling.

    D. The teacher needs to structure her day to include opportunities for student interaction and oral language development.

51. A new first-grade teacher correctly understands that she needs to spend time during her instructional day teaching her students to focus on reading words automatically. However, she thinks she does not need to teach students how to understand what they are reading in the text. Is this assumption correct?

    A. Yes, during most of the day in a first-grade classroom the teacher needs to focus on phonics, decoding skills, and correctly reading words to enable students to read texts accurately.

    B. No, all students beginning in the early grades need to be taught that reading is about making sense of text in addition to decoding the words.

    C. Yes, this teacher understands what she needs to spend the most time on during her instructional day. Automaticity and fluency are keys to reading.

    D. No, this teacher has not included writing as part of her instructional day, a necessary part of reading and language instruction.

52. After reviewing a summative assessment, Ms. Jones realizes she must spend more time providing vocabulary instruction for her eighth graders. She decides she will take several steps toward developing word consciousness. Which of the following strategies would Ms. Jones be *least* likely to consider when planning vocabulary instruction?

    A. Assist students in learning word roots and researching a word's origin or history when reading from a content-area textbook.

    B. Encourage students to participate in word play, such as puns, palindromes, word games, and using figurative language.

    C. Clarify and enrich the meaning of known words, such as the distinctions between words like *say, state, advocate, mention, speak, reveal,* and *exclaim.*

    D. Directly teach the meaning of all unknown words found in their reading and organize in word study notebooks.

53. During Universal Access time, a first-grade teacher is working with a small reading group that is having difficulty with literal comprehension. She draws the following diagram on the board after reading a selection from the grade-level text. What is the purpose of using this graphic organizer?

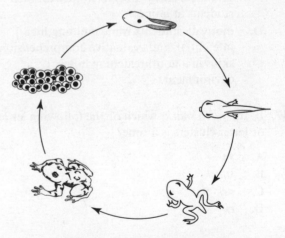

    A. This type of diagram can clarify for students what the text is trying to represent.

    B. Charts enable a teacher to promote an artistic understanding for students.

    C. This type of chart can compare and contrast the information that is presented in the text.

    D. Students are able to apply their understanding to decoding the grade-level text.

**54.** Mr. Farley reads aloud the book *The Three Little Pigs,* a story in which a wolf tries to destroy the home of three pigs. The next day, Mr. Farley reads aloud *The True Story of the Three Little Pigs,* in which the wolf explains how he was framed by the pigs. The teacher leads a discussion comparing the two stories. This discussion is most likely to promote student reading proficiency by:

A. guiding students to compare stories and determine a character's perspective or bias.

B. helping students self-monitor and identify common themes in related stories.

C. guiding students to distinguish fact versus opinion in similar stories.

D. helping students to use evaluative comprehension skills to determine the mood and theme in literary analysis.

**55.** Which of the following statements about phonics instruction is *false?*

A. The most effective phonics programs are systematic, with skills taught in a predetermined, logical sequence.

B. Effective phonics programs provide ample opportunities for students to apply what they are learning about letters and sounds to the reading of words, sentences, and stories.

C. Systematic phonics is the most important component of literacy and should be the focus of all reading instruction.

D. Explicit phonics is most effective when it begins in kindergarten.

**56.** Students from Mr. Ghali's class have been reading *Alexander and the Wind-Up Mouse.* Upon completion, they are asked to work with a partner to fill-in this graphic organizer.

| Title and Author: |
| --- |
| Main Characters: |
| Problem: |
| Main Events: |
| Outcome: |

Completing this story map is most likely to promote student reading proficiency by:

A. fostering students' ability to use reciprocal teaching strategies when working with a partner.

B. enhancing students' ability to identify cause and effect in story grammar.

C. helping students use Bloom's Taxonomy to organize literary details in the text frame.

D. guiding students to think about the structure of the text and how story elements relate to each other.

GO ON TO THE NEXT PAGE

57. A first-grade teacher is teaching a class with students from diverse cultural and ethnic backgrounds. As she prepares her reading lessons, her greatest concern should be:

   A.  to make sure that her lessons include pictures or realia (real objects) for the English Language Learner.

   B.  to be aware of making connections from new information to existing knowledge.

   C.  to be sensitive to the different languages that each child speaks.

   D.  to consider and plan strategies to meet the instructional needs of each child.

58. A fourth-grade teacher has been assigned to teach a newly organized class at her school. The class is made up of 30 students, many of whom are English Language Learners from different cultural backgrounds. When the teacher is selecting reading material for her classroom, she should:

   A.  be sure to select standards-based reading material that is sensitive to each culture in her class.

   B.  provide grade-level curriculum materials as well as reading material at many different text levels to reach all her students' abilities.

   C.  use the same material that she used with her previous fourth-grade class to make sure her students are at benchmark.

   D.  use the same reading material that the other fourth-grade classes are using and include culturally sensitive material.

59. Mr. Ovadia is evaluating several supplemental reading programs for his second graders. He is particularly interested in providing systematic effective phonics instruction. Mr. Ovadia is most likely to select:

   A.  a literature-based program that emphasizes reading and writing activities in an unstructured, yet interesting way.

   B.  an explicit program that helps teachers instruct students to relate letters and sounds, break spoken words into sounds, and blend sounds to form words.

   C.  a basal reading program that focuses on whole-word or meaning-based activities.

   D.  a sight-word program that begins by teaching a sight-word vocabulary of 50–100 words followed by instruction in the alphabetic principle.

60. A fifth-grade teacher is incorporating vocabulary building into her lessons. Which of the following is the *least effective* method for building vocabulary?

   A.  encouraging wide reading and providing effective, language-rich instructional activities.

   B.  memorizing vocabulary word lists and recording them in a notebook.

   C.  demonstrating how to use word parts, such as affixes and base words, to "unlock" unknown words.

   D.  modeling appropriate usage of academic language and allowing students to practice it in their writing.

61. Irena is an English Language Learner who joins Ms. Hightower's seventh-grade class mid-year. Following a round of assessments, Ms. Hightower determines that Irena decodes extremely well and reads fluently. However, her comprehension performance is inconsistent. Sometimes she seems to understand everything in a grade-level text, while other times she has difficulty retelling a story with accuracy. Ms. Hightower then assesses Irena's vocabulary knowledge and notes some weak areas. What are some logical next steps for instruction?

   A.  Provide Irena easier reading material that is at her instructional reading level.

   B.  Place Irena in a group with other English Language Learners. They should focus on vocabulary and phonics instruction.

   C.  Provide systematic vocabulary and phonemic awareness instruction. Irena needs more exposure to the sounds of the English language.

   D.  Use this information to plan appropriate vocabulary and academic language interventions in relation to Irena's specific reading needs.

62. A third-grade teacher asks her students to create "idiom posters." Each student is to choose the idiom he or she would like to illustrate on his or her poster from a posted chart of idioms. What is the teacher's primary purpose in assigning this project to her students?

A. Differentiating instruction by teaching her students to learn new vocabulary.

B. Understanding that many children, including English Language Learner students, have difficulty learning figurative sayings. She is exposing her students to these expressions.

C. Learning this concept will help the students use more vivid language in their writing.

D. This type of instruction will aid the students in unlocking their background knowledge.

63. Mrs. Ng has numerous English Language Learner students in her fifth-grade class. She pairs the students and gives each pair a piece of paper folded in half and one sentence from the following sheet:

| It rained cats and dogs. |
| He walks with his head in the clouds. |
| She was walking on air. |
| She had a frog in her throat. |
| He spilled the beans. |
| He has a heart of gold. |

The students are asked to write the sentence on both sides of the folded paper. On one side they draw the literal definition, and on the other they draw an idiomatic illustration. Afterward, students will share their illustrations with the class, and then the student idioms will be displayed.

The primary objective of Ms. Ng is to:

A. shelter instruction so that her second language learners will read as well as her native English speakers.

B. illustrate idioms to bolster concepts about print for second language learners.

C. scaffold using graphic organizers to help meet the needs of all students.

D. support her vocabulary instruction with pictures to convey the true meaning of the sentence.

64. A first-grade teacher asks her students to illustrate an activity they did with their families during the summer break. She then circulates throughout the room asking students to tell her about their drawings. She writes what students have told her on the individual drawings. The work is posted throughout the classroom. Over the course of the next few weeks, the students read together what their classmates did over the summer. Why might the teacher do this?

A. This is a purposeful writing opportunity to help students understand that oral language and written language are interrelated and that we can write what we say.

B. This teacher is providing a meaningful opportunity for students to share their experiences.

C. This experience is giving students a first experience with writing.

D. This teacher is fostering the students' self-confidence by allowing them to share their experiences and artistic abilities.

65. A second-grade teacher provides time for students to write in journals daily. After the students make a written entry, often accompanied by an illustration, the teacher responds by writing a comment or a question. What is the principal benefit of this activity for English Language Learner (ELL) students?

A. This kind of activity provides the teacher with an opportunity to provide new vocabulary for an ELL student.

B. This type of journal gives the teacher an opportunity to model correct writing, questioning, and academic language for the ELL student.

C. This activity allows the ELL student to have access to the teacher and provides the teacher with insight into the student's strengths and weaknesses.

D. This is an excellent way for the teacher to provide additional instruction to her ELL students.

GO ON TO THE NEXT PAGE

66. A second-grade teacher distributes pieces of a puzzle to her students and instructs them to place the pieces in their proper order. The "puzzle" is composed of words, punctuation, and phrases that form a single, complex sentence, taken directly from their reading. The cut-up pieces have been taken from sentence strips that were printed with the sentences. Partners are told to sequence the cut-up words and phrases into a proper sentence. After correctly ordering one sentence puzzle, students mix up the parts again and trade with their classmates. They then begin sequencing a new sentence. This instructional activity is likely to be most effective in helping students:

A. strengthen their ability to assemble sentences, sequence words, and use language conventions when reading and writing complex sentences.

B. improve general inferential comprehension skills through sequencing and analysis of semantic and orthographic patterns.

C. organize instructional materials in a systematic, direct manner to clarify text meaning.

D. use deliberate multisensory techniques that contribute to vocabulary development and reinforce reading development in context.

67. A first-grade teacher plans to read several books about animals. Before reading the first text, students are given animal pictures to sort into categories during literacy center time. Why is this technique likely to be effective?

A. This technique is effective because animal words can be challenging for many students.

B. This is an effective technique because words with multiple meanings, such as "dear/deer" and "aunt/ant" can be confusing.

C. This technique can be effective because building vocabulary is a precursor to reading acquisition.

D. This technique expands on children's natural tendency to sort and classify and assists in building vocabulary and the understanding of words.

68. A teacher uses an Informal Reading Inventory (IRI) to assess a bilingual eighth-grade student who is having difficulty with reading. The teacher has noticed this student does not participate in whole-group discussions but seems to possess adequate oral language skills in English. After administering the IRI, she determines that he makes frequent errors on words with the –ed ending but does understand "past tense," and these errors do not affect his reading comprehension. She also notes that he has recurrent errors with multisyllabic words, which do seem to impede his comprehension. From the IRI, the teacher can see that he does not recognize frequently occurring word patterns or common prefixes and suffixes in multisyllabic words. What would be the most effective intervention for this student?

A. This teacher can provide explicit instruction in prefixes, suffixes, and roots to promote this student's ability to analyze and understand new words.

B. The teacher can model strategies for figuring out new words, such as using the dictionary and word searches.

C. The teacher can provide opportunities for this student that will promote self-selected reading and in this way increase the student's vocabulary.

D. The teacher can provide more instruction in developing vocabulary and model strategies for unlocking new words.

69. What is a simple definition of *scaffolding* in the context of language and literacy development?

A. Scaffolding is a temporary means of support to assist students with more complex tasks in reading, writing, thinking, and understanding until they are ready to proceed at a higher level on their own.

B. Scaffolding is a technique used with students that provides needed instruction to complete literacy tasks.

C. Scaffolding in the context of language and literacy development provide students with the needed skills in order to function within a classroom.

D. Scaffolding is a means to assess English Language Learner students so they can function within the regular classroom and achieve proficiency in quickly developing reading and reading comprehension skills.

**70.** What are the potential benefits for a struggling fifth-grade reader if he is assigned to write a text for younger students?

    **A.** This is a good technique to balance reading and writing skills.

    **B.** Producing student-written text is a highly motivating technique because it provides a real-life purpose for writing.

    **C.** This is a good opportunity to use cross-age tutors.

    **D.** Word-work can be created from that text and provide meaningful learning opportunities for the older student.

**END OF SECTION I**

Proceed to Section II of the test.

# Directions for Section II: Open-Ended Assignments

## Assignments A to E

This section of the test consists of four focused educational problems and instructional tasks and one case study. You are required to prepare a written response for each of these assignments and record each in the appropriate area provided in the Written Response Sheet in the Answer Document or, for the case study, in the Case Study Response Booklet.

Before you begin to write your response to an assignment, read the assignment carefully. Take some time to plan and organize your response. Blank space is provided in this test booklet following each assignment so that you can make notes, write an outline, or do any prewriting necessary. *Your final responses, however, must be written on the appropriate page(s) of the Answer Document. The case study must be written in the Case Study Response Booklet.*

The evaluation of your written responses will be based on how well the responses demonstrate knowledge and skills important for effective delivery of a balanced, comprehensive reading program. Make sure that you address all aspects of each given assignment and demonstrate your understanding of relevant content and pedagogical knowledge. Your responses will be evaluated on the following criteria: (1) fulfilling the purpose of the assignment; (2) effectively applying relevant content and academic knowledge; and (3) supporting your responses with appropriate evidence, examples, and rationales.

Considering that the multiple-choice section is weighted 50% of the total RICA score, each of the individual assignments will be weighted approximately as follows:

| | |
|---|---|
| Assignment A | 10% |
| Assignment B | 5% |
| Assignment C | 5% |
| Assignment D | 10% |
| Assignment E | 20% |
| | |
| Total | 50% |

The assignments are intended to assess knowledge and skills of reading instruction and, although writing ability is not directly assessed, your responses must be written clearly enough to allow for a valid judgment of your knowledge and skills. As you plan your responses, keep in mind that the audience is composed of educators knowledgeable about reading instruction. Each written response should conform to the conventions of edited American English.

Your responses to the assignments should be your original work. They should be written in your own words and not copied or paraphrased from some other work. Citations, however, may be used when appropriate.

To maintain your anonymity during the scoring process of the written assignments, the multiple-choice section of the Answer Document containing your name will be removed from your written responses. Do not write your name on any other portion of the Answer Document and do not separate any of the sheets from the document.

You may work on the assignments in any order you choose, but be sure to record your final responses in the appropriate locations, as listed in the directions for each individual assignment.

# Assignment A

**Record your written response to Assignment A on the Assignment A Response Sheet** on page 3 of the Answer Document. The length of your response is limited to the lined space available on the Assignment A Response Sheet.

---

**Use the information here to complete the exercise that follows.**

A first-grade teacher administers a phonics survey to his class at the beginning of the school year.

**<u>Examinee Task</u>**

Write a response in which you describe how a first-grade teacher would use the data from a phonics survey administered at the beginning of the school year.

---

Remember to record your final response on the **ASSIGNMENT A RESPONSE SHEET**
on page 3 of the Answer Document.

**(On the actual RICA test you will be warned NOT TO REMOVE THIS OR ANY OTHER PAGE,
or any portion of any page, from the test booklet.)**

**You may use the space below to make notes. These notes will not be scored.**

GO ON TO THE NEXT PAGE

# Assignment B

**Record your written response to Assignment B on the Assignment B Response Sheet** on page 5 of the Answer Document. The length of your response is limited to the lined space available on the Assignment B Response Sheet.

---

**Use the information here to complete the exercise that follows.**

A second-grade teacher notices that a student is struggling with reading grade-level text. The student is decoding slowly, sound by sound, and is unable to accurately retell what she has read. What should the teacher do to address the problem?

**Examinee Task**

Using your knowledge of reading, write a response in which you: (1) describe how the teacher would identify the specific need of the student; (2) state an instructional strategy and student activity to address the identified need; and (3) explain why the strategy and activity would be effective in addressing the problem.

---

Remember to record your final response on the **ASSIGNMENT B RESPONSE SHEET**
on page 5 of the Answer Document.

**(On the actual RICA test you will be warned NOT TO REMOVE THIS OR ANY OTHER PAGE,
or any portion of any page, from the test booklet.)**

**You may use the space below to make notes. These notes will not be scored.**

# Assignment C

**Record your written response to Assignment C on the Assignment C Response Sheet** on pages 7 and 8 of the Answer Document. The length of your response is limited to the lined space available on the Assignment C Response Sheet.

---

**Use the information here to complete the exercise that follows.**

A kindergarten teacher knows her students are from diverse language backgrounds and have varying abilities, foundations, and experience in the English language.

**<u>Examinee Task</u>**

Describe three instructional strategies the teacher can use to develop and enhance the English language skills and ability of all her students. Briefly explain why these strategies would be effective for assisting students in developing English language skills.

---

Remember to record your final response on the **ASSIGNMENT C RESPONSE SHEET**
on pages 7 and 8 of the Answer Document.

**(On the actual RICA test you will be warned NOT TO REMOVE THIS OR ANY OTHER PAGE,
or any portion of any page, from the test booklet.)**

**You may use the space below to make notes. These notes will not be scored.**

GO ON TO THE NEXT PAGE

# Assignment D

**Record your written response to Assignment D on the Assignment D Response Sheet** on pages 9 and 10 of the Answer Document. The length of your response is limited to the lined space available on the Assignment D Response Sheet.

---

**Use the information here to complete the exercise that follows.**

A first-grade teacher notices that a student is struggling with reading grade-level text. The student is able to retell what she has read but is decoding slowly, sound by sound, and seems confused when encountering long vowel patterns in text. What should the teacher do to address the problem?

**Examinee Task**

Using your knowledge of reading, write a response in which you: (1) describe how the teacher would identify the specific decoding need of the student; (2) state an instructional strategy and student activity to address the identified need; and (3) explain why the above process would be effective in addressing the problem.

---

Remember to record your final response on the **ASSIGNMENT D RESPONSE SHEET**
on pages 9 and 10 of the Answer Document.

**(On the actual RICA test you will be warned NOT TO REMOVE THIS OR ANY OTHER PAGE,
or any portion of any page, from the test booklet.)**

**You may use the space below to make notes. These notes will not be scored.**

# Assignment E

## Case Study

**Record your written response to the case study in the Case Study Response Booklet.** Your response is limited to the lined space available in the Case Study Response Booklet.

> The following case study gives information about a second-grade student named Brianna. Brianna is 7 years old, and her primary language is English. After carefully reading and reviewing the information on the following pages, write an analysis in which you apply your knowledge of reading assessment and instruction. Your response should include three parts:
>
> **1.** identify the strengths and weaknesses in Brianna's reading;
>
> **2.** describe at least two methods or strategies that would assist her reading development; and
>
> **3.** explain how these methods or strategies would work.

Remember to record your final response in the **CASE STUDY RESPONSE BOOKLET.**

**(On the actual RICA test you will be warned NOT TO REMOVE THIS OR ANY OTHER PAGE, or any portion of any page, from the test booklet.)**

**You may use the space below to make notes. These notes will not be scored.**

GO ON TO THE NEXT PAGE

## Reading Attitude Survey

Brianna's teacher, Ms. Smith, first recorded Brianna's answers on a Reading Attitude Survey. Ms. Smith read the survey questions and let Brianna respond orally. The survey follows.

## Reading Attitude Survey

Name **Brianna**                                        Date **3/20/2010**

Directions: Make one check for each of your choices.

☑ I like reading a lot.          ☐ Reading is O.K.          ☐ I'd rather do other things.

What kinds of books do you like to read?

☐ realistic fiction          ☑ picture books          ☐ poetry          ☐ true facts

☐ fantasy          ☐ folktales and fables          ☐ myths          ☐ mysteries

☐ historical fiction          ☐ biographies (about real people)          ☐ plays

☐ science fiction          ☐ _____ (write any other kind you like here)

How do you choose something to read?

☐ I listen to a friend                    ☑ I look to see if it's easy enough

☑ I look at the front cover              ☐ I look to see if it's hard enough

☐ if it's part of a series I like         ☐ I read the back cover or jacket flap

☐ I read the first few pages             ☑ follow my teacher's suggestion

☐ if I liked other books by that author

When do you prefer to read?

☐ in my spare time          ☑ at home          ☑ as part of my class work

How do you like to read?

☐ with friend                    ☐ with kids who read about the same as I do

☑ by myself                     ☑ with my teacher in the group

**GO ON TO THE NEXT PAGE**

## Family Survey

The following family survey was completed by her mother. The survey was mailed to her mother and was completed at home.

## Family Survey

Date __3/20/2010__

Dear Family

    Please take several minutes to help me learn more about your child as a reader and writer by responding to the questions below.

Sincerely,

__Ms. Smith__

**Child's Name** __Brianna__      **Family Member's Name** __Kathy (mother)__

1. What are some of your child's favorite activities at home? __Brianna likes reading, arts and crafts, and doing activities with her family. She is an accomplished gymnast.__

2. What kinds of books does your child look at or read at home? Which books are your child's favorites? __She is beginning to read chapter books. She likes the "Henry and Mudge" series.__

3. What kind of drawing or writing does your child do outside of school? __She writes stories and illustrates them.__

4. In what everyday situations does your child read something other than books (for example, food packages, catalogs, posters)? __She will read recipe directions to me. She also will read signs when we go somewhere.__

5. In what ways do you and other family members share reading and writing with your child? __We read stories to Brianna every night.__

6. What are your hopes for your child's reading and writing studies this year? __I hope that Brianna will read more "smoothly" this year.__

GO ON TO THE NEXT PAGE

## Running Record

For the running record, Brianna read a story from an anthology, her school's adopted reading textbook for second grade. She had been exposed to the story previously in her guided reading group but had not seen it lately. Her teacher, Ms. Smith, listened to her read the text and marked her responses on the running record that follows. Ms. Smith analyzed her running record and noted the cueing systems she used for decoding words.

## RUNNING RECORD OF READING BEHAVIOUR

Name: **Brianna**                                             Age: **7.6**   Date: **3/27/2010**

Title/Text: **Moon Mouse**          Emergent ☐  Early ☐  Fluency ☐  Seen ☐  Unseen ☐

Error Rate (ER) = $\frac{\text{Running Words}\ (138)}{\text{Errors}\ \ \ 7}$ = 1:19   % Accuracy (ACC) = **94%**

Self-Correction Rate = $\frac{(E) + (SC)}{(SC)}$ = $\frac{(7) + (3)}{(3)}$ = 1:**2.5**

(Percent Accuracy Chart on back of this sheet)

Easy ☐
Instructional ☐
Too Challenging ☐

| M | Meaning (Semantic) |
|---|---|
| S | Structure (Syntactic) |
| V | Visual (Graphophonic) |

**Analysis of Errors:** Using primarily meaning and structure cues and mostly ignoring visual cues.
Is reading text again to check for meaning.

**Summary:**
Brianna read slowly, about 53 words per minute. She is beginning to monitor & cross-check her reading.
She is starting to use some phrasing and expression.

| Page # | | # of E | # of SC | Analysis E | SC |
|---|---|---|---|---|---|
| | ✓ ✓ ✓ ✓ ✓ ✓ ✓<br>One night Mother Mouse call to her baby. | | | | |
| | ✓ ✓ ✓<br>"Come, Arthur," she said | | | | |
| | ✓ ✓ ✓ ✓ ✓ st✓<br>"Now that you are old enough, you may stay | | | | |
| | ✓ ✓ ✓ ✓ ✓ ✓ ✓<br>up after dark. Let us look up at the night sky." | | | | |
| | ✓ ✓ ✓ ✓ ✓ ✓ ✓<br>Arthur ran happily to the door of the next | | | | |
| | ✓ ✓ ✓ ✓ ✓ ✓ ✓<br>and looked out. The black sky was all around | | | | |
| | dark-ness ✓ ✓ ✓ ✓<br>⌐him⌐ Darkness was everywhere. The night was | | | | |
| | ✓ ✓ cold ✓<br>⌐still and ⌐cool. | 1 | | Ⓜ Ⓢ V | |
| | ✓ called ✓ coldness ✓ ✓ ✓<br>Arthur ⌐could ⌐feel the coolness on his little | 2 | | Ⓜ Ⓢ V<br>Ⓜ Ⓢ V | |
| | ✓ called sc ✓ ✓ ✓ ✓ ✓<br>nose. He ⌐could ⌐feel it on his whiskers and his | 1 | | Ⓜ Ⓢ V | Ⓜ Ⓢ V |
| | ✓ ✓ ✓<br>round little ears | | | | |

GO ON TO THE NEXT PAGE

| Page # | Moon Mouse | # of E | # of SC | Analysis | |
|---|---|---|---|---|---|
| | | | | **E** | **SC** |
| | ✓ ✓ ✓ ✓ night's ✓ sc ✓ ✓<br>"So this is what the night is like!" he said | 1 | | Ⓜ S Ⓥ | M Ⓢ V |
| | happy-happy sc<br>happily. | 1 | | Ⓜ S V | M Ⓢ Ⓥ |
| | ✓ ✓ ✓ ✓ ✓<br>"It is wonderful!" Arthur looked up. There | | | | |
| | ✓ ✓ darkness ✓ ✓ ✓ ✓<br>in the blackness was something big and round | 1 | | Ⓜ Ⓢ V | |
| | ✓ ✓<br>and shining. | | | | |
| | ✓ ✓ ✓ ex-expression<br>"Look!" he cried in excitement. | 1 | | Ⓜ S V | |
| | ✓ ✓ ✓<br>"Oh, look! Look!" | | | | |
| | ✓ ✓<br>Mother Mouse smiled. | | | | |
| | It's - ✓ ✓ ✓ ✓ ✓<br>"It is only the moon," she said. | 2 | | Ⓜ S V<br>Ⓜ Ⓢ V | |
| | ✓ ✓ ✓ ✓ ✓<br>"It is the big, round, yellow moon." | | | | |
| | **TOTALS** | 7 | 3 | M-10<br>S-6<br>V-1 | M-1<br>S-3<br>V-2 |

| ERROR RATE | % ACCURACY | |
|---|---|---|
| 0: | | 100 |
| 1:200 | | 99.5 |
| 1:100 | | 99 |
| 1:50 | **Easy** | 98 |
| 1:35 | | 97 |
| 1:25 | | 96 |
| 1:20 | | 95 |
| 1:17 | | 94 |
| 1:14 | **Instructional** | 93 |
| 1:12.4 | | 92 |
| 1:11.75 | | 91 |
| 1:10 | | 90 |
| 1:8 | | 87.5 |
| 1:6 | | 83 |
| 1:5 | **Too** | 80 |
| 1:4 | **Challenging** | 75 |
| 1:3 | | 66 |
| 1:2 | | 50 |

## Story Discussion

Following the completion of the running record, Brianna discussed the story with her teacher. Brianna was able to retell the story she had just read with some accuracy. She remembered many details. The teacher then asked Brianna questions about the story. Brianna could answer almost all of the questions that her teacher asked her related to the story.

GO ON TO THE NEXT PAGE

## Additional Reading and Summary

Brianna was asked to read another short story silently. Afterward, she was asked to write about the story. Brianna's writing about the short story actually told the story quite well and gave some good details. She did seem to have trouble spelling a few of the words. Although she appeared to read the story slowly, she seemed to enjoy the reading and the chance to write about it.

## Teacher's Comments

Ms. Smith also made the following comments about Brianna's classroom work and behavior.

Brianna is an outstanding student. She is a hard worker and completes her assignments on time.

She enjoys reading in class and usually volunteers to read aloud.

Brianna has many friends in class and her group appears to be the top students and the most motivated.

Brianna takes advantage of her spare time in class using our reading corner.

Brianna also seems to enjoy writing, and although she still needs work on her spelling, her writing is very good. She also has outstanding penmanship.

**End of Test**

# Answers and Explanations for Practice Test 1

## Section I: Multiple-Choice Questions

### Answer Key

1. C (Domain 1, Content Specification 002)
2. A (Domain 1, Content Specification 002)
3. D (Domain 5, Content Specification 013)
4. A (Domain 2, Content Specification 006)
5. A (Domain 1, Content Specification 001)
6. A (Domain 1, Content Specification 002)
7. D (Domain 1, Content Specification 002)
8. D (Domain 1, Content Specification 002)
9. C (Domain 1, Content Specification 001)
10. C (Domain 1, Content Specification 001)
11. B (Domain 1, Content Specification 002)
12. A (Domain 1, Content Specification 001)
13. B (Domain 4, Content Specification 011)
14. A (Domain 4, Content Specification 010)
15. A (Domain 3, Content Specification 009)
16. C (Domain 3, Content Specification 008)
17. B (Domain 2, Content Specification 003)
18. D (Domain 2, Content Specification 006)
19. D (Domain 1, Content Specification 001)
20. A (Domain 1, Content Specification 001)
21. C (Domain 2, Content Specification 003)
22. D (Domain 2, Content Specification 007)
23. B (Domain 2, Content Specification 007)
24. A (Domain 2, Content Specification 003)
25. C (Domain 3, Content Specification 009)
26. B (Domain 2, Content Specification 004)
27. A (Domain 2, Content Specification 003)
28. B (Domain 2, Content Specification 007)
29. C (Domain 2, Content Specification 004)
30. C (Domain 3, Content Specification 008)
31. D (Domain 2, Content Specification 003)
32. C (Domain 1, Content Specification 001)
33. B (Domain 1, Content Specification 002)
34. D (Domain 2, Content Specification 003)
35. B (Domain 2, Content Specification 004)
36. B (Domain 5, Content Specification 012)
37. C (Domain 3, Content Specification 009)
38. A (Domain 3, Content Specification 009)
39. A (Domain 5, Content Specification 013)
40. C (Domain 5, Content Specification 015)
41. B (Domain 5, Content Specification 013)
42. C (Domain 5, Content Specification 013)
43. C (Domain 3, Content Specification 009)
44. D (Domain 5, Content Specification 014)
45. A (Domain 4, Content Specification 011)
46. A (Domain 4, Content Specification 011)
47. C (Domain 2, Content Specification 005)
48. C (Domain 1, Content Specification 002)
49. D (Domain 5, Content Specification 012)
50. A (Domain 5, Content Specification 013)
51. B (Domain 5, Content Specification 012)
52. D (Domain 4, Content Specification 011)
53. A (Domain 5, Content Specification 015)
54. A (Domain 5, Content Specification 014)
55. C (Domain 2, Content Specification 005)
56. D (Domain 5, Content Specification 014)
57. D (Domain 4, Content Specification 010)
58. B (Domain 1, Content Specification 001)
59. B (Domain 2, Content Specification 005)
60. B (Domain 4, Content Specification 011)
61. D (Domain 4, Content Specification 011)
62. B (Domain 4, Content Specification 010)
63. D (Domain 4, Content Specification 010)
64. A (Domain 4, Content Specification 011)
65. B (Domain 4, Content Specification 011)
66. A (Domain 4, Content Specification 011)
67. D (Domain 4, Content Specification 011)
68. A (Domain 4, Content Specification 011)
69. A (Domain 4, Content Specification 010)
70. B (Domain 2, Content Specification 007)

# Explanations

1. **C.** Awareness of independent, instructional, and frustration reading levels is crucial for creating flexible reading groups during Universal Access time. Knowing a student's instructional level is important because it provides the teacher with information useful for planning interventions when differentiating instruction. If too many errors are made, it becomes frustrating for the student to read, and text meaning is lost. Frustration means reading 89 percent or less correctly; instructional refers to 90 percent to 95 percent accurately; and independent means reading 96 percent to 100 percent correctly. If the student is making four errors or less in a 100-word passage, this signifies that the text can be read independently by the student. This is a good passage to provide reading practice for the student. Generally, at least 70 percent of the comprehension questions must also be answered accurately. (Some experts cite a different percentage for comprehension questions, but teachers can assume that the vast majority must be correctly answered.) Choice A is incorrect because it inaccurately states that frustration level refers to any book above grade level. Choice B is incorrect because it assumes that all students can independently read at grade level. Choice D incorrectly lists 90 percent accuracy as independent. (Domain 1, Content Specification 002)

2. **A.** While the actions suggested by answers B, C, and D may be helpful, A is the best answer choice overall. The first level of intervention should occur in the classroom. Teachers need to realize the importance of entry-level assessment and continued monitoring of reading as tools for targeting instruction and planning interventions. (Domain 1, Content Specification 002)

3. **D.** Some graphic organizers that would be helpful to this student could include Venn diagrams, which compare and contrast different text elements; story maps; or K-W-L charts. Other visual/graphic representations of text meanings would also work. These graphic organizers could help this student bring meaning to the text. In choice A, word banks would not help this student with his reading difficulties, although computer reading programs and contextual analysis might assist him. Similarly, choices B and C do not adequately address the understanding of main ideas or assessing comprehension. (Domain 5, Content Specification 013)

4. **A.** Decodable text with controlled vocabulary provides meaningful practice for beginning readers. The books should be aligned with the phonic element that is being taught. They should also present the phonic element of focus at least 12 times. Decodable readers should be reread many times to develop automaticity and fluency with the identified phonic element. Decodable readers are not meant to replace other literature in the classroom. (Domain 2, Content Specification 006)

5. **A.** When organizing and planning phonemic awareness instruction, it is important that the teacher use data to plan flexible groups to meet identified student skill needs and provide differentiated or individualized instruction. Mr. Vasquez may consider balancing his groups, behavior, and special needs (choices B and C), but these are not the key factors. Choice D is incorrect because it suggests going outside the classroom rather than placing the child in his or her appropriate group and individualizing instruction. (Domain 1, Content Specification 001)

6. **A.** For this type of scoring, the first number refers to the grade, and the second number refers to the month of school. (Domain 1, Content Specification 002)

7. **D.** Choices A, B, and C are all effective methods of using test results to evaluate student performance in relation to the standards. Some uses for assessments are to plan interventions, communicate about performance, and to plan groupings based on student needs. Choice D is inaccurate because concepts about print are generally mastered in the early grades and would not be assessed or reported for sixth-grade students on the standards-based report card by Mr. Tonning. (Domain 1, Content Specification 002)

8. **D.** While the resource teacher may end up assessing individuals, this may be done only in compliance with testing protocols. Choice B is incorrect because it is not acceptable to "teach to the test." Although a teacher certainly may consult the manual of accommodations (choice C), testing accommodations must comply with their IEP specifications to preserve the integrity of the exam. (Domain 1, Content Specification 002)

9. **C.** To accommodate the individual differences of all students, every classroom should provide a balance in types of grouping. Some examples of grouping types are whole groups, small groups, pairs of students, or individual students. Grouping should always be flexible when teaching reading (choice C), therefore, choices A and B can be eliminated. Consistently teaching reading instruction to the whole group (choice D) is not effective. (Domain 1, Content Specification 001)

10. **C.** Choice C is correct because it is the only answer that specifically addresses appropriate modifications for Juan. Choices A and B assume that Juan is lacking in vocabulary. However, the question stated that Juan has good comprehension. Although he is a nonnative speaker, we should not assume he has difficulties with vocabulary. Choice A is also incorrect because it suggests that Juan should always be with other advanced students. Choice D can be eliminated because while Juan may qualify for Gifted and Talented Education (GATE), Mr. Nordquist still must differentiate instruction to appropriately challenge Juan. (Domain 1, Content Specification 001)

11. **B.** The question specifically asks about determining student spelling needs. It is best to use multiple assessments when analyzing student performance to determine instructional needs. Choices A and D do not adequately address both understanding spelling strengths and planning intervention strategies. Choice C, assigning extra homework, is neither a good practice, nor is it an appropriate assessment tool. (Domain 1, Content Specification 002)

12. **A.** According to the California Language Arts Framework, in an effective primary language arts program, a minimum of $2\frac{1}{2}$ hours of instructional time should be allotted to language arts instruction daily. "This time is given priority and is protected from interruption. It is the responsibility of both teachers and administrators to protect language arts instructional time. In grades four through eight, 2 hours (or two periods) of instructional time are allocated to language arts instruction daily through core instructional periods or within a self-contained classroom." (Domain 1, Content Specification 001)

13. **B.** Choice B is the exception because it focuses on spelling and phonics rather than meaning. The goal of academic language instruction is teaching students to accurately use academic words in their writing and speaking across content areas. When introducing a new term, the teacher should share a synonym to help make the connection between the new vocabulary and students' background knowledge. The teacher can provide examples of using the sentence in context. She then can help facilitate student use of the academic language in context. Rather than rely on rote memorization, students will have a much greater chance of internalizing the word if they have the opportunity to use it accurately. (Domain 4, Content Specification 011)

14. **A.** The Matthew Effect refers to the idea that good readers tend to read more and therefore become even better readers. Another way of expressing the concept is "The rich get richer and the poor get poorer." Since poor readers often read slowly or avoid reading, the gap between good readers and poor readers grows over time. The Matthew Effect has an impact on student growth in vocabulary, academic language, and background knowledge as well as fluency. Students who struggle with attaining automaticity with decoding get much less practice reading and are likely to lag behind their peers. Without strategic intervention, poor readers can fall behind in language arts classes as well as the content areas. (Domain 4, Content Specification 010)

15. **A.** The teacher needs to provide systematic, direct instruction in prosody, including reading with expression, paying attention to punctuation, and variations in pitch and intonation. There is also ample documentation that repeated readings of text develop young reader's fluency. Repeated reading must be at the independent level, beginning with decodable text. A child's ability to make visual discriminations between words has a positive effect on his or her reading. (Domain 3, Content Specification 009)

16. **C.** Choices A, B, and D *are* appropriate strategies for increasing reading fluency. Choice C is the least appropriate strategy for several reasons. Although it states the teacher should record Maya's reading information, it does not mention analyzing the data, the real reason for assessment. Also, choice C focuses on phonological awareness, which is a skill usually mastered in the early grades. Maya's 80 WCPM indicates a very slow reader. Ideally, a fifth grader would be reading a minimum of 100 WCPM, and 180 WCPM is considered fluent. Automaticity, reading rate, and prosodic features such as expression, attention to punctuation, appropriate phrasing, and pitch are necessary for fluent reading. Lack of fluency can also have an impact on comprehension because nonfluent readers must place so much effort on decoding rather than focusing on the author's purpose and message. (Domain 3, Content Specification 008)

17. **B.** The greatest predictors of a child's success in beginning to read are a mastery of the alphabetic principle, phonemic awareness, and concepts of print. *The English-Language Content Standards for California Public Schools* states that phonemic awareness skills such as rhyming, counting syllables, substituting sounds, and blending phonemes are kindergarten skills. Answer D is incorrect because "phonemic letter recognition" is not a reading term. Phonemes are single speech sounds, not letters. (Domain 2, Content Specification 003)

18. **D.** The student needs explicit skills instruction with attention to vowel sounds. Activities could include word sorting. *Words Their Way* by Donald Bear provides many ideas for phonics and word instruction, such as word sorting and games with words. Additional strategies for practicing vowel sounds can be found in Patricia Cunningham's books, *Phonics We Use*, *Making Words*, and *Classrooms That Work*. (Domain 2, Content Specification 006)

19. **D.** Students are referred to the Student Success Team only after the teacher has provided good diagnostic teaching (choice A), repetition of instruction with many opportunities for student practice (choice B), and a focus on key skills and understanding (choice C). If the student is still scoring at the intensive level after multiple assessments have been completed, then a referral to the Student Success Team is appropriate. (Domain 1, Content Specification 001)

20. **A.** When student assessment data is sorted into the benchmark, strategic, and intensive groups, the teacher is aware of the kinds of additional intervention strategies that can be employed based on the student's level of proficiency. See the California Language Arts Framework (pages 264–65) for intervention strategies. (Domain 1, Content Specification 001)

21. **C.** The errors this student is making show a lack of discrimination between two very similar consonant sounds. Nine pairs of consonants (in English) differ only in that one of the pair is quiet (unvoiced) and the other is heard (voiced). These nine pairs of consonants are

/p/, /b/ pet, bet
/t/, /d/ tip, dip
/k/, /g/ cake, gate
/f/, /v/ fast, vast
/th/, /th/ thin, this
/s/, /z/ cease, seize
/sh/, /zh/ attention, measure
/ch/, /j/ hatch, Madge
/wh/, /w/ when, was

Some activities that would help this child with this skill are articulating phonemes, looking in a mirror and feeling the throat while articulating the sounds, and reading/spelling contrasting pairs of words and establishing the distinctions. (Domain 2, Content Specification 003)

22. **D.** At this stage of spelling development, the student is using but confusing long vowel patterns. The student is aware of how long vowels are represented but is using them incorrectly. Some activities for children at this stage are word sorts and working in a word study notebook. A sequence the teacher might follow when working with this skill is to focus on the spelling patterns of one long vowel, compare and contrast short and long vowels, and collect words that have the long vowel sound. (Domain 2, Content Specification 007)

23. **B.** Syllabication is useful in supporting decoding and spelling of multisyllabic words. Choice A is incorrect because most of the top 100 words are one syllable words, which cannot be segmented into syllables. Choices C and D are also incorrect statements. Although knowledge of syllable division helps with decoding, word origin is not necessary for reading proficiency. (Domain 2, Content Specification 007)

24. **A.** Making mistakes with letters and their sounds is common for beginning readers and demonstrates the need and importance for explicit teaching in distinguishing between letter names and letter sounds. The student is in an early alphabetic stage of reading. (Domain 2, Content Specification 003)

25. **C.** This strategy encourages rereading of familiar text and enhances students' phrasing and oral expression. Choices A and D are only partly correct. Although the teacher could assess how a student changes his speech to reflect the main character, choice A is wrong because it mentions independent reading levels. Choice D is incorrect because students are not completing literary analysis. Choice B is also incorrect because second-grade listening skills are not the focus of the question. (Domain 3, Content Specification 009)

26. **B.** Answer choice B includes some effective ways to provide letter recognition instruction. The ability to recognize and name the letters of the alphabet and understand that each letter makes a certain sound has been correlated to success in beginning reading. It is important that the teacher engage his or her students by teaching letter recognition instruction in meaningful contexts. Choices A and D are incorrect because these activities relate to developing phonological and/or auditory skills. All of the activities mentioned in choice C relate to phonemic awareness, which does not contribute to letter recognition. (Domain 2, Content Specification 004)

27. **A.** Choices B, C, and D contain misleading statements. Remember to be sure you understand exactly what the question is asking. Choice A is the correct answer because it states the objective of this lesson with a specific instructional strategy. These boxes, known as Elkonin Boxes, help students understand that a word can be segmented into sounds and that those sounds can be isolated and reconnected. Choices B and D are not specific instructional strategies, and therefore, incorrect. The activity described in choice C would not be the best for developing oral language and so it is an incorrect choice. Choice D is incorrect because although students enjoy working with the boxes, that does not lead to helping students to develop an interest in language. (Domain 2, Content Specification 003)

28. **B.** Choices A and C are not the *most* effective ways of teaching spelling. Looking at patterns in words should be part of every organized word study program. Looking at spelling patterns and vocabulary is most effective in teaching spelling. Teachers should provide systematic, explicit instruction in phonics and sight words during spelling instruction. D is an incorrect choice because it suggests using phonemic analysis by spelling words aloud. That statement uses words that "sound right" but are not actual classroom spelling tasks. (Domain 2, Content Specification 007)

29. **C.** At first glance, choice D may seem correct. However, Tony is having difficulty reading the whole word. He actually read the prefix and suffix correctly. Although choices A and B are important for word identification, they may not remediate Tony's specific decoding problem. (Domain 2, Content Specification 004)

30. **C.** Choice C is the best answer because the five-finger rule is an effective tool that Anwar can use to self-monitor his reading selections. The teacher needs to ensure that students self-select books at their appropriate reading levels and hold them accountable for comprehension. Choice A is incorrect because Anwar, rather than his teacher, should be allowed to select motivating material in the library. Providing a mini-lesson and reviewing material does not necessarily make a book an appropriate selection for guided reading; therefore, choice D is also wrong. The teacher might also install a system of book leveling in the classroom for students to use when making independent reading choices. (Domain 3, Content Specification 008)

31. **D.** Answers A, B, and C all *are* phonological awareness activities. Examples of appropriate tasks are deletion (for example, "saying *pill* without the *p*"), manipulation (reordering phonemes in a syllable), and addition (adding extra phonemes to a word or syllable). Phonological awareness strongly correlates with reading achievement. It is important that students recognize oral language is composed of smaller units, such as spoken words and syllables. Choice D is incorrect because adding letters to form words is not a phonological awareness task. (Domain 2, Content Specification 003)

32. **C.** Pacing, indicating that the teacher slows down or speeds up the rate of instruction, is perhaps the most commonly used strategy for differentiation. Complexity for advanced students means enriched instruction that encourages students to address topics, time periods, or connections across disciplines not normally expected at that grade level. But complexity for struggling students means the teacher should focus on the key concepts within the standards and eliminate confusing activities. (Domain 1, Content Specification 001)

33. **B.** According to the California Language Arts Framework, research shows that <u>what</u> students are taught has a far greater effect on their achievement than <u>how</u> they are grouped. The purpose of grouping students is to provide additional time for students who need help understanding the fundamental concepts and skills needed to master later standards. (Domain 1, Content Specification 002)

**34. D.** The teacher is providing direct instruction through modeling. Students can hear the text while following along with their eyes. The teacher can explicitly teach the more specific points, such as concepts about print, during subsequent readings. (Domain 2, Content Specification 003)

**35. B.** The most important advantage of using invented spelling activities in the primary classroom is the development of phonemic awareness and furthering the child's understanding of the alphabetic principle. In addition, early writing activities promote and enhance a child's interest in learning about words and improve linguistic readiness for reading. Encouraging children to write complements instruction in reading. (Domain 2, Content Specification 004)

**36. B.** Text-based discussions play a role in enhancing comprehension. This technique helps with Universal Access by allowing students to read material among peers. It can help students of lower reading ability absorb the grade level's curriculum with their peers. It also allows for small discussion groups in which each student can have the opportunity to interact, affording a deeper understanding of the material. Choice A is incorrect because although the strategy may seem to make it easier to cover more material in a shorter period of time, students read and discuss in depth, and more time may be needed for lesson. Choice C is incorrect because what it describes is not an effective assessment tool. Choice D is incorrect because, although cooperative learning can be effective, it is not the primary reason for using the strategy. (Domain 5, Content Specification 012)

**37. C.** Regular quizzes are <u>not</u> likely to promote enjoyment of independent reading. On the other hand, choices A, B, and D each describe effective ways to support at-home reading. The more practice students have in reading, the more fluent they become. (Domain 3, Content Specification 009)

**38. A.** Direct instruction and practice in reading aloud will help Jemma to increase fluency. Choice B is partially correct, because it does mention modeling phrasing and reading with expression; however, retelling a story orally will not be as helpful as direct instruction in developing reading fluency. In addition, both choices B and D are incorrect because Jemma is never given the opportunity to read aloud, which is an appropriate strategy for building fluency. The question states that Jemma decodes accurately. Although reading aloud to a younger student might be an appropriate strategy, choice C is wrong because the focus should not be on phonics. (Domain 3, Content Specification 009)

**39. A.** Research consistently shows that rereading is one of the best strategies to help struggling readers, although it is rarely taught. Choice A is correct, therefore, because this teacher is demonstrating firsthand how to increase comprehension by rereading. Choice B is incorrect because the teacher is not modeling how students deal with understanding vocabulary. Choice D may be a correct statement, but it is not the best answer because it addresses reading, not <u>re</u>reading. Choice C is not a relevant answer for this question. (Domain 5, Content Specification 013)

**40. C.** When students are able to concentrate on the really essential information, they can be more discriminating when reading. The correct answer is choice C; these students are practicing "surveying" techniques. Even though choices A and D also mention "comprehension," neither one is the best answer for this particular question. Choice B is neither a reading skill nor a strategy. (Domain 5, Content Specification 015)

**41. B.** This chart provides the students with character descriptions. A good follow-up activity would be to take the information from the chart and use it as a basis for writing descriptions about the characters. Choices A, C, and D would not be effective follow-up activities because they do not ask the students to use the information they gained from charting. (Domain 5, Content Specification 013)

**42. C.** One of the most important strategies the teacher can use is to read aloud to her students, often by rereading a favorite story. The teacher is helping her students build vocabulary and increase their and appreciation of literature, while exposing them to literary-level language and a variety of authors' styles. Rereading aloud is one of the most important strategies for a teacher who wants to improve attitudes, to enhance her students' motivation, and to instill the love of reading in students. (Domain 5, Content Specification 013)

**43. C.** By modeling phrasing, syntax, and intonation, the teacher is differentiating fluency instruction for her students. A result of rereading a passage is that the reader becomes more fluent. Some good ways to incorporate repeated reading within the classroom are to conduct Readers' Theatre, to have students record and then listen to their taped passages, to do partner reading, and to whisper read. (Domain 3, Content Specification 009)

44. **D.** The purpose of this activity is to have students determine main ideas from the story and organize them in sequential order. Choice D is correct because identifying the main ideas and organizing sequentially are the comprehension strategies Ms. Montell is going to be evaluating with this task. Choice A is incorrect because the question is about literal rather than inferential comprehension. Notice that choices B, C, and D all mention sequencing, one of Ms. Montell's goals, but the activity does not help students identify cause-effect relationships or story grammar as suggested by choices B and C. Therefore, choices B and C are also incorrect. (Domain 5, Content Specification 014)

45. **A.** Choice A is the correct answer because it celebrates student writing and helps make the connection between reading, writing, and oral language. Choice B is wrong because it focuses on the conventions rather than the ideas in a piece of writing completed at home with parents. Choice C is incorrect because it is asking kindergartners to read and write in paragraphs without teacher support. Although it would be appropriate to place the journal in the class library (choice D), such a motivating piece of writing should not be reserved only for fast workers and well-behaved students. (Domain 4, Content Specification 011)

46. **A.** Improved student motivation and providing increased support for reading at home are the primary reasons for sending home the *Curious George Suitcase*. Choice B is incorrect because it suggests that a teacher would send home something that would be tested in a formal assessment. Choice C does not address the importance of self-motivation in reading. Choice D is incorrect because it states that students will be working on all types of comprehension, which is a questionable assumption. (Domain 4, Content Specification 011)

47. **C.** One-syllable words and syllables within multisyllabic words can be broken into two parts, the onset and the rime. *Onset* refers to the consonant that comes before the vowel. The *rime* is the vowel and any sounds that come after it. In the word *trout, tr* is the onset and *out* is the rime. In the word *bake, b* is the onset and *ake* is the rime. The words *if* and *on* do not have onsets. The rimes are *f* and *n*. When teaching rimes, an effective teacher can use the term "word families" and teach similar words with the rime *ock,* such as *sock, rock, shock, block, clock,* and *stock.* (Domain 2, Content Specification 005)

48. **C.** The student has the ability to decode the text but not the skills necessary to comprehend it. Reading involves not just reading words accurately but fluency and comprehension as well. If a student is able to decode but does not comprehend, then he or she is unable to enjoy and appreciate the real reason for reading. The goal of beginning reading programs should be for all students to comprehend the grade-level material they have read. The teacher must demonstrate knowledge of literal, inferential, and evaluative reading comprehension. The teacher should support the struggling reader by helping the student monitor her own comprehension, and teach her to visualize, question, and make connections. In addition, the teacher can model inferring main ideas, comparisons, and other relationships not explicitly stated in the text. (Domain 1, Content Specification 002)

49. **D.** Choice D suggests that the student is correctly matched to the text but is not applying comprehension strategies to understand the text. Choice A, decoding strategies, would not help this student with comprehension. Choice B, assessment, is something that should always be ongoing in the classroom. Choice C should also be happening in the classroom; however, since no one is monitoring the silent reader, this option does not address the problem of comprehension strategies. (Domain 5, Content Specification 012)

50. **A.** The student needs direct instruction in comprehension skills followed by practice. A significant number of poor readers enter school with poor verbal abilities. To be successful readers, children need to develop oral language skills. Although choices C and D focus on retelling, oral language, and comprehension skills, they do not emphasize direct explicit instruction in retelling for the individual students. Choice B is incorrect because students who have difficulty with comprehensive skills will lack the advanced skills necessary for structured writing. Students should be given meaningful opportunities to practice verbal skills. (Domain 5, Content Specification 013)

51. **B.** Teachers should emphasize word decoding, but not at the expense of teaching comprehension, therefore, choices A and C are incorrect. Comprehension skills, along with decoding and fluency skills, should be protected to attain automaticity and should start in early primary grades. Although writing should also be included as part of a balanced literacy program, choice D is incorrect because comprehension is not mentioned. (Domain 5, Content Specification 012)

52. **D.** Choices A, B, and C are all effective methods for teaching vocabulary. There are many reasons why a teacher should not directly teach all unknown words. First, students need opportunities to develop their own word-learning skills. In addition, students can understand much text without knowing the meaning of every word. Students can deduce some definitions from context. A passage might have so many unknown words that direct vocabulary instruction would take up valuable class time that could be better spent having students read. Teachers should choose vocabulary words carefully because only about 7 to 10 per week can be taught thoroughly. (Domain 4, Content Specification 011)

53. **A.** This chart will help students understand the order of the concept presented by the text. Charting information is helpful to all readers, especially English Language Learner students. Graphic organizers such as story maps and Venn diagrams are frequently used to improve comprehension. They help clarify information that is presented. (Domain 5, Content Specification 015)

54. **A.** Choice B is incomplete because it does not mention perspective or bias. Since the stories are clearly fiction, determining fact versus opinion is not relevant, thus eliminating choice C. Choice D is also incorrect. Although the activity does help develop evaluative comprehension, the focus is not on mood and theme. Thus, Choice A is the best answer; additionally, it is the only choice that addresses <u>comparing</u> the two stories. (Domain 5, Content Specification 014)

55. **C.** Choices A, B, and D all present true statements. Choice C is incorrect because although systematic phonics is extremely important, this answer suggests that phonics should be taught in isolation. Learning to encode (spell) and decode phonetically must be combined with other areas of reading instruction. To fully understand reading material, students must be taught strategies for comprehension, fluency, and vocabulary acquisition along with phonics instruction in a balanced, comprehensive program. (Domain 2, Content Specification 05)

56. **D.** Completing a story map, as in choice A, will not help develop reciprocal teaching strategies. Cause and effect are addressed in choice B, so it might seem like a possible answer, but it does not address other aspects of story structure. Choice D provides a more complete answer. The incorrect use of Bloom's Taxonomy eliminates choice C. (Domain 5, Content Specification 014)

57. **D.** Because the students in this class are from diverse cultural and ethnic backgrounds, the needs of each student could vary widely. The teacher must be careful in planning her strategies to make sure they meet the unique needs of each child. (Domain 4, Content Specification 010)

58. **B.** In a balanced comprehensive reading program, the teacher must provide reading materials to meet the reading level of every student in the class. She can provide for Universal Access by differentiating instruction to meet the needs of all learners. (Domain 1, Content Specification 001)

59. **B.** Choice B offers the most effective, systematic phonics program. The programs described in the other choices lack this essential, systematic element. (Domain 2, Content Specification 005)

60. **B.** Although choice B mentions vocabulary, memorizing lists of words is less effective than using words in a meaningful context. Therefore, choice B is the least effective method for building vocabulary. Choices A, C, and D all describe effective methods for building vocabulary. Vocabulary can be developed both directly and indirectly. One important way to build a vocabulary is by reading. There is a strong correlation between the amount of time that children spend reading independently and increases in vocabulary. (Domain 4, Content Specification 011)

61. **D.** This question mentions that Irena is a second-language learner. However, it is important to remember that finding what is best for each student is a central theme in teaching. A teacher should never assume that all English Language Learners have the same needs and must be assigned to the same groups (choices A and B). Because Irena already decodes well, reads fluently, and frequently retells accurately, we can conclude that she would benefit from effective vocabulary instruction before reading complex passages. Phonemic awareness instruction (choice C) would not effectively remediate her problem. (Domain 4, Content Specification 011)

62. **B.** The best answer to this question is choice B because idioms use figurative language and are often confusing to students, especially those who are learning English as a second language. Even though choice A does mention vocabulary, this teacher is not differentiating instruction. Choice C might perhaps be true, but getting students to use vivid language is not the primary reason why lower primary teachers introduce idiom posters. Choice D is not an accurate statement. (Domain 4, Content Specification 010)

63. **D.** The majority of instructional strategies that are helpful for English Language Learner (ELL) students are also beneficial for all students. Choice A is incorrect because the answer assumes that all ELLs perform at a lower level than native English speakers. Choice B at first appears plausible because it mentions idioms; however, idioms are not a part of concepts about print. Choice C also appears to be plausible, but a graphic organizer is not used in this question. The graphic nature of the grid may have been misleading. (Domain 4, Content Specification 010)

64. **A.** This weeks-long project is a relevant opportunity to relate oral language, reading, and writing. Choices B, C, and D may be correct statements but none provides the best <u>reason </u>for the teacher's activities. (Domain 4, Content Specification 011)

65. **B.** This activity provides students with a reading and writing activity at their level, an activity in which the teacher can provide targeted assistance in literacy development. The new activity might also provide new vocabulary, and/or access to the teacher, and/or additional instruction, as suggested in choices A, C, and D, but these potential outcomes are not the "principal benefit" of the activity. (Domain 4, Content Specification 011)

66. **A.** To successfully complete this activity, students must pay attention to phrasing, sequencing, and other English language conventions, including punctuation and grammar. A basic understanding of these elements helps improve their reading and writing competence. This activity does not directly relate to orthography or inferential comprehension, as in choice B. Choices C and D are both attractive, but they are distracters. Choice C sounds appropriate but is not as thorough as choice A. Choice D is incorrect because the focus is on vocabulary development. (Domain 4, Content Specification 011)

67. **D.** Expanding on a child's natural tendency to sort and classify is an effective technique to assist in vocabulary building. Additionally, the use of picture and word sorts can help to expand a student's grasp of simple concepts. Choice A is incorrect because early readers can build their vocabulary with challenging words when sorting and classifying. Choice B is incorrect because this activity will not address multiple meanings. Although the statement in choice C is true, it does not address the activity the teacher assigned to the students. (Domain 4, Content Specification 011)

68. **A.** The teacher has determined that this student's inability to read multisyllabic words is due to his lack of knowledge about English root words, suffixes, and prefixes. Strengthening this student's skills in these areas will not only address word formation but will also aid in building his vocabulary. Choices B, C, and D are not the best interventions the teacher can use, although each one contains some true information. (Domain 4, Content Specification 011)

69. **A.** Scaffolding can help students function at a higher level than they can when unassisted. Activities that provide scaffolding are designed to have teacher or peer assistance built-in. (Domain 4, Content Specification 010)

70. **B.** Student-written text has proven to be an excellent technique to help to motivate struggling readers. A, C, and D are incorrect statements. (Domain 2, Content Specification 007)

# Section II: Open-Ended Questions

## Sample Essays and Evaluations

### Domain 2/Assignment A

### Sample Essay

Data from this entry-level survey can be used in a variety of ways.

First, the teacher could use the data to inform his systematic phonics instruction. He would provide targeted and direct instruction and practice in the phonics elements identified in the survey. Data could be shared with other teachers on his team. They may decide to form flexible skill groups among several classes.

The teacher may share this data with the student and parent during a beginning of the year conference. This would provide an understanding of where the student is in phonics skill attainment. Data could also be shared with administrators and/or coaches. This data demonstrates a beginning point for targeting phonics/decoding instruction.

### Evaluating the Essay

The essay fulfills the task by identifying several ways to use the data. The data (information) must be communicated to several individuals or groups. The writer describes the recipients of the data (information) and describes how each would use it. The answer is clearer when the writer includes the description of how each recipient would use the data. This is entry-level data and, therefore, is essential for beginning planning.

# Domain 3/Assignment B

## Sample Essay

If the student cannot accurately retell what she is reading, she is weak in comprehension. Comprehension is difficult without effective fluency, and because the student is decoding sound by sound, the teacher should begin by assessing the student's fluency. To assess, the teacher should give the student a timed oral reading test and calculate how many correct words per minute the student reads.

The next step would be to plan fluency lessons and activities that would help the student improve. The student can be assigned to read easy materials, such as decodable books, several times over because repeated readings help improve fluency. This strategy is effective for increasing fluency because, when practicing reading for fluency, the text needs to be at the student's independent level, so she has few unknown words to decode and can work just on speed and phrasing.

## Evaluating the Essay

The essay addresses all three parts of the Examinee Task. It starts by identifying the domain that is involved, which is fluency.

Next, the writer tells how he or she would identify the specific need of the student by explaining how to assess the student's fluency.

Then the writer describes an instructional strategy for working on fluency, which is repeated readings of easy, familiar text. She provides detail by giving an example of a specific type of material that contains this type of text—decodable books.

The writer concludes by explaining why repeated readings of text that is easy and familiar helps to improve fluency.

# Domain 4/Assignment C

## Sample Essay

Children start kindergarten with a vocabulary of about 5,000 words and need to learn 3,000 to 4,000 new words each year to keep up with the academic demands of school. English Learners start with a language deficit because they do not know many English words. The teacher needs to develop the vocabulary of her students.

She can: (1) Use semantic webs and maps, such as the Frayer Model, to teach new words. This is an effective way to give children visual representations for helping them organize concepts and learning relationships among words. (2) Read extensively to students. They figure out the meanings of new words by hearing them repeatedly in different contexts. (3) Point out cognates between the student's first language and English. Doing this helps them make connections from what is known to new unknown material.

## Evaluating the Essay

This essay is effective because it begins by identifying the appropriate domain, which is vocabulary. The writer explains the importance of having an extensive vocabulary and gives specific details about how many vocabulary words need to be learned for school success.

Three instructional strategies for addressing vocabulary are then offered: using graphic organizers; reading aloud to students, so they can hear words in a variety of contexts; and pointing out cognates. This question is about kindergarten students, and the suggested strategies are age appropriate. For learning words in context, the writer suggests that the teacher read to the students, rather than having them read to themselves, because the writer is aware that most kindergarten students aren't yet proficient readers. In addition, the writer provides a detail by giving a specific example of a graphic organizer—the Frayer Model.

After describing each of the three strategies, the writer explains why they will be effective for vocabulary development with English learners. She especially targets English Learners when choosing the strategy of comparing cognates because a teacher would only use cognates for vocabulary development with English Learners.

# Domain 5/Assignment D

## Sample Essay

To identify the student's decoding need, the teacher would use a phonics survey such as John Shefelbine's Basic Phonics Skills Test (BPST). The BPST may reveal that the student has difficulties recognizing long vowel patterns such as –*ake, –eed, –ike, –oat,* or –*une.*

The instructional strategy to address this need would be direct instruction of the vowel pattern such as –*ike.* After blending the sound, the teacher would guide the student in practicing reading the word family for –*ike.*

- bike
- hike
- mike
- pike
- like

The next step would be guided practice with the word family in a meaningful manner in connected text, i.e., decodable text. The student activity would be independent practice with the word family. The first activity would be to use a word wheel to substitute initial consonants in reading the word family. The next step in the student activity would be to practice automaticity reading the word family in connected text that is a decodable text.

The above process would assist the student to attain automaticity in decoding. With practice in automaticity, the student would become able to read grade level text with fluency.

## Evaluating the Essay

The essay clearly states the three steps the teacher must take in addressing the problem. These three steps or tasks guide the writing of the case study and often structure the questions in one or more essay questions. These "Big Three" guiding steps are:

1. Tell what's happening: data, findings, strengths, and needs.
2. Tell what you (teacher) will do: instructional strategies and student tasks (intervention).
3. Tell why you chose to do the steps 1 and 2. Give a rationale.

To clearly describe the three tasks the author uses a bullet format. This format demonstrates the sequence of steps from assessment to instruction, practice, and finally the explanation or rationale.

# Case Study Information

**Your case-study essay should have included some of the following information.**

This student's 94 percent accuracy rate makes it an ideal text for guided reading instruction. An analysis of her running record shows that when confronted with an unknown word, Brianna relies primarily on meaning and structure cues. She rereads the text to check for understanding, using her knowledge of language. She uses structure and visual cues when self-correcting. She is able to self-correct one out of every three errors.

In some of the student's errors, the miscue had a similar meaning to the correct word, *(cold/cool, coldness/coolness, darkness/blackness)*. She was able to retell the story accurately to her teacher and so was able to preserve meaning. She also demonstrated an awareness of English structure or grammar several times *(night's/night sc, happy/happily sc, it's/it is)*.

In recommending areas for additional instruction or practice, Brianna could benefit from rereading familiar text to improve her fluency rate and increase her speed. Her teacher can also encourage her to read more like she talks. Even though she was able to use expression and phrasing, her teacher noted that Brianna read very slowly. In addition, the running record shows her confusion with some vowel digraph patterns: *oo* in *cool, ou* in *could.* These skills could be included in a word study program in her class. Brianna also needs to be encouraged to look at the whole word, not just at the beginning of words, *(expression/excitement, cold/cool, coldness/coolness, darkness/blackness)*. She could also benefit from practice with suffixes like *ily* (happily). Suffixes are usually a second-grade skill so she should have many opportunities to work in these areas.

Brianna's running record suggests that she is on her way to being a fluent reader. She needs to continue to be encouraged to use meaning and structure to decode words, and her skills in word knowledge and vocabulary need to be further developed and strengthened. A teacher should also continue to expand Brianna's comprehension strategies and vocabulary skills as she reads more complex text. In order to improve fluency, Brianna needs to read a lot of familiar material and to write about what she is reading. Her teacher might model such reading behavior in order to make the instruction more explicit.

Some suggested activities for Brianna might include preparing for oral speaking parts, participating in Readers' Theatre, practice for reading aloud to another child or an adult, or practice reading prior to reading into a tape recorder to make a tape of "Brianna's Very Best Reading." A program of word study coupled with at least an hour of reading on her independent level will develop her fluency rate, improve her reading rate, extend her vocabulary, and advance her comprehension.

# Analyzing Your Test Results

Use the following charts to carefully analyze your results and spot your strengths and weaknesses. Complete the process of analyzing each subject area and each individual question for Practice Test 1. Examine your results for trends in types of error (repeated errors) or poor results in specific subject areas. This re-examination and analysis is of tremendous importance for effective test preparation.

## Practice Test 1 Analysis Sheets

| Multiple-Choice Questions | | | | |
|---|---|---|---|---|
| | Possible | Completed | Right | Wrong |
| Domain 1 | 16 | | | |
| Domain 2 | 18 | | | |
| Domain 3 | 7 | | | |
| Domain 4 | 16 | | | |
| Domain 5 | 13 | | | |
| Total: | 70 | | | |

## Analysis/Tally Sheet for Multiple-Choice Questions

One of the most important parts of test preparation is analyzing why you missed a question so that you can reduce the number of mistakes. Now that you've taken Practice Test 1 and corrected your answers, carefully tally your multiple-choice mistakes by marking in the proper column.

| Reasons for Mistakes | | | | |
|---|---|---|---|---|
| | Total Mistakes | Simple Mistake | Misread Question | Lack of Knowledge |
| Domain 1 | | | | |
| Domain 2 | | | | |
| Domain 3 | | | | |
| Domain 4 | | | | |
| Domain 5 | | | | |
| Total: | | | | |

# Open-Ended Questions (The Essays)

See the discussion of essay scoring that begins on page 2 to evaluate your essays. Have someone knowledgeable in reading instruction read and evaluate your responses using the checklists that follow.

## Domain 2/Assignment A

# RICA Practice Essay Evaluation Form

**Use this checklist to evaluate your essay:**

1.  To what extent does this response reflect an **understanding of the relevant content** and academic knowledge from the applicable RICA domain?

    | **thorough** | **adequate** | **limited or no** |
    |---|---|---|
    | understanding | understanding | understanding |

2.  To what extent does this response **fulfill the purpose of the assignment?**

    | **completely** | **adequately** | **partially** |
    |---|---|---|
    | fulfills | fulfills | fulfills or fails to |

3.  To what extent does this essay **respond to the given task(s)?**

    | **fully** | **adequately** | **limited or inadequately** |
    |---|---|---|
    | responds | responds | responds |

4.  How **accurate** is the response?

    | **very** | **generally** | **inaccurate** |
    |---|---|---|
    | accurate | accurate | |

5.  Does the response **demonstrate an effective application** of the relevant content and academic knowledge from the applicable RICA domain?

    | **yes** | **reasonably** | **no** |
    |---|---|---|
    | effective | effective | ineffective and inaccurate |

6.  To what extent does the **response provide supporting examples, evidence, and rationale** based on the relevant content and academic knowledge from the applicable RICA domain?

    | **strong** | **adequate** | **limited or no** |
    |---|---|---|
    | support | support | support |

# Domain 3/Assignment B

# RICA Practice Essay Evaluation Form

**Use this checklist to evaluate your essay:**

1. To what extent does this response reflect an **understanding of the relevant content** and academic knowledge from the applicable RICA domain?

   | **thorough** | **adequate** | **limited or no** |
   |---|---|---|
   | understanding | understanding | understanding |

2. To what extent does this response **fulfill the purpose of the assignment?**

   | **completely** | **adequately** | **partially** |
   |---|---|---|
   | fulfills | fulfills | fulfills or fails to |

3. To what extent does this essay **respond to the given task(s)?**

   | **fully** | **adequately** | **limited or inadequately** |
   |---|---|---|
   | responds | responds | responds |

4. How **accurate** is the response?

   | **very** | **generally** | **inaccurate** |
   |---|---|---|
   | accurate | accurate | |

5. Does the response **demonstrate an effective application** of the relevant content and academic knowledge from the applicable RICA domain?

   | **yes** | **reasonably** | **no** |
   |---|---|---|
   | effective | effective | ineffective and inaccurate |

6. To what extent does the response **provide supporting examples, evidence, and rationale** based on the relevant content and academic knowledge from the applicable RICA domain?

   | **strong** | **adequate** | **limited or no** |
   |---|---|---|
   | support | support | support |

# Domain 4/Assignment C

# RICA Practice Essay Evaluation Form

**Use this checklist to evaluate your essay:**

1.  To what extent does this response reflect an **understanding of the relevant content** and academic knowledge from the applicable RICA domain?

    | **thorough** | **adequate** | **limited or no** |
    |---|---|---|
    | understanding | understanding | understanding |

2.  To what extent does this response **fulfill the purpose of the assignment?**

    | **completely** | **adequately** | **partially** |
    |---|---|---|
    | fulfills | fulfills | fulfills or fails to |

3.  To what extent does this essay **respond to the given task(s)?**

    | **fully** | **adequately** | **limited or inadequately** |
    |---|---|---|
    | responds | responds | responds |

4.  How **accurate** is the response?

    | **very** | **generally** | **inaccurate** |
    |---|---|---|
    | accurate | accurate | |

5.  Does the response **demonstrate an effective application** of the relevant content and academic knowledge from the applicable RICA domain?

    | **yes** | **reasonably** | **no** |
    |---|---|---|
    | effective | effective | ineffective and inaccurate |

6.  To what extent does the response **provide supporting examples, evidence, and rationale** based on the relevant content and academic knowledge from the applicable RICA domain?

    | **strong** | **adequate** | **limited or no** |
    |---|---|---|
    | support | support | support |

# Domain 5/Assignment D

# RICA Practice Essay Evaluation Form

**Use this checklist to evaluate your essay:**

1.  To what extent does this response reflects an **understanding of the relevant content** and academic knowledge from the applicable RICA domain?

    | **thorough** | **adequate** | **limited or no** |
    |---|---|---|
    | understanding | understanding | understanding |

2.  To what extent does this response **fulfill the purpose of the assignment?**

    | **completely** | **adequately** | **partially** |
    |---|---|---|
    | fulfills | fulfills | fulfills or fails to |

3.  To what extent does this essay **respond to the given task(s)?**

    | **fully** | **adequately** | **limited or inadequately** |
    |---|---|---|
    | responds | responds | responds |

4.  How **accurate** is the response?

    | **very** | **generally** | **inaccurate** |
    |---|---|---|
    | accurate | accurate | |

5.  Does the response **demonstrate an effective application** of the relevant content and academic knowledge from the applicable RICA domain?

    | **yes** | **reasonably** | **no** |
    |---|---|---|
    | effective | effective | ineffective and inaccurate |

6.  To what extent does the response **provide supporting examples, evidence, and rationale** based on the relevant content and academic knowledge from the applicable RICA domain?

    | **strong** | **adequate** | **limited or no** |
    |---|---|---|
    | support | support | support |

# Case Study/Assignment E

# RICA Practice Case Study Evaluation Form

Use this checklist to evaluate your essay:

1. To what extent does this response reflect an **understanding of the relevant content** and academic knowledge from the applicable RICA domain?

| **thorough** | **adequate** | **limited** | **little or no** |
|---|---|---|---|
| understanding | understanding | understanding | understanding |

2. To what extent does this response **fulfill the purpose of the assignment?**

| **completely** | **adequately** | **partially** | **fails to fulfill** |
|---|---|---|---|
| fulfills | fulfills | fulfills | |

3. To what extent does this essay **respond to the given task(s)?**

| **fully** | **adequately** | **limited** | **inadequately** |
|---|---|---|---|
| responds | responds | responds | responds |

4. How **accurate** is the response?

| **very** | **generally** | **partially** | **inaccurate** |
|---|---|---|---|
| accurate | accurate | accurate | |

5. Does the response **demonstrate an effective application** of the relevant content and academic knowledge from the applicable RICA domain?

| **yes** | **reasonably** | **limited** | **no** |
|---|---|---|---|
| effective | effective | generally ineffective | inaccurate and ineffective |

6. To what extent does the response **provide supporting examples, evidence, and rationale** based on the relevant content and academic knowledge from the applicable RICA domain?

| **strong** | **adequate** | **limited** | **little or no** |
|---|---|---|---|
| support | support | support | support |

# Essay Review

Compare your essays to the ones given and review the Evaluation Forms, which you have had a reader complete, for each assignment. From this information, circle what you feel is the appropriate level of response for each assignment. This should help give you some general guidelines for your review.

| Open-Ended Questions | | |
|---|---|---|
| Level of Response | | |
| Assignment A (Domain 2) | good | average | poor |
| Assignment B (Domain 3) | good | average | poor |
| Assignment C (Domain 4) | good | average | poor |
| Assignment D (Domain 5) | good | average | poor |
| Assignment E (Case Study) | good | average | poor |

## Practice Test 2 Answer Document

### Multiple-Choice Answer Sheets

CUT HERE

| | |
|---|---|
| 1 Ⓐ Ⓑ Ⓒ Ⓓ | 36 Ⓐ Ⓑ Ⓒ Ⓓ |
| 2 Ⓐ Ⓑ Ⓒ Ⓓ | 37 Ⓐ Ⓑ Ⓒ Ⓓ |
| 3 Ⓐ Ⓑ Ⓒ Ⓓ | 38 Ⓐ Ⓑ Ⓒ Ⓓ |
| 4 Ⓐ Ⓑ Ⓒ Ⓓ | 39 Ⓐ Ⓑ Ⓒ Ⓓ |
| 5 Ⓐ Ⓑ Ⓒ Ⓓ | 40 Ⓐ Ⓑ Ⓒ Ⓓ |
| 6 Ⓐ Ⓑ Ⓒ Ⓓ | 41 Ⓐ Ⓑ Ⓒ Ⓓ |
| 7 Ⓐ Ⓑ Ⓒ Ⓓ | 42 Ⓐ Ⓑ Ⓒ Ⓓ |
| 8 Ⓐ Ⓑ Ⓒ Ⓓ | 43 Ⓐ Ⓑ Ⓒ Ⓓ |
| 9 Ⓐ Ⓑ Ⓒ Ⓓ | 44 Ⓐ Ⓑ Ⓒ Ⓓ |
| 10 Ⓐ Ⓑ Ⓒ Ⓓ | 45 Ⓐ Ⓑ Ⓒ Ⓓ |
| 11 Ⓐ Ⓑ Ⓒ Ⓓ | 46 Ⓐ Ⓑ Ⓒ Ⓓ |
| 12 Ⓐ Ⓑ Ⓒ Ⓓ | 47 Ⓐ Ⓑ Ⓒ Ⓓ |
| 13 Ⓐ Ⓑ Ⓒ Ⓓ | 48 Ⓐ Ⓑ Ⓒ Ⓓ |
| 14 Ⓐ Ⓑ Ⓒ Ⓓ | 49 Ⓐ Ⓑ Ⓒ Ⓓ |
| 15 Ⓐ Ⓑ Ⓒ Ⓓ | 50 Ⓐ Ⓑ Ⓒ Ⓓ |
| 16 Ⓐ Ⓑ Ⓒ Ⓓ | 51 Ⓐ Ⓑ Ⓒ Ⓓ |
| 17 Ⓐ Ⓑ Ⓒ Ⓓ | 52 Ⓐ Ⓑ Ⓒ Ⓓ |
| 18 Ⓐ Ⓑ Ⓒ Ⓓ | 53 Ⓐ Ⓑ Ⓒ Ⓓ |
| 19 Ⓐ Ⓑ Ⓒ Ⓓ | 54 Ⓐ Ⓑ Ⓒ Ⓓ |
| 20 Ⓐ Ⓑ Ⓒ Ⓓ | 55 Ⓐ Ⓑ Ⓒ Ⓓ |
| 21 Ⓐ Ⓑ Ⓒ Ⓓ | 56 Ⓐ Ⓑ Ⓒ Ⓓ |
| 22 Ⓐ Ⓑ Ⓒ Ⓓ | 57 Ⓐ Ⓑ Ⓒ Ⓓ |
| 23 Ⓐ Ⓑ Ⓒ Ⓓ | 58 Ⓐ Ⓑ Ⓒ Ⓓ |
| 24 Ⓐ Ⓑ Ⓒ Ⓓ | 59 Ⓐ Ⓑ Ⓒ Ⓓ |
| 25 Ⓐ Ⓑ Ⓒ Ⓓ | 60 Ⓐ Ⓑ Ⓒ Ⓓ |
| 26 Ⓐ Ⓑ Ⓒ Ⓓ | 61 Ⓐ Ⓑ Ⓒ Ⓓ |
| 27 Ⓐ Ⓑ Ⓒ Ⓓ | 62 Ⓐ Ⓑ Ⓒ Ⓓ |
| 28 Ⓐ Ⓑ Ⓒ Ⓓ | 63 Ⓐ Ⓑ Ⓒ Ⓓ |
| 29 Ⓐ Ⓑ Ⓒ Ⓓ | 64 Ⓐ Ⓑ Ⓒ Ⓓ |
| 30 Ⓐ Ⓑ Ⓒ Ⓓ | 65 Ⓐ Ⓑ Ⓒ Ⓓ |
| 31 Ⓐ Ⓑ Ⓒ Ⓓ | 66 Ⓐ Ⓑ Ⓒ Ⓓ |
| 32 Ⓐ Ⓑ Ⓒ Ⓓ | 67 Ⓐ Ⓑ Ⓒ Ⓓ |
| 33 Ⓐ Ⓑ Ⓒ Ⓓ | 68 Ⓐ Ⓑ Ⓒ Ⓓ |
| 34 Ⓐ Ⓑ Ⓒ Ⓓ | 69 Ⓐ Ⓑ Ⓒ Ⓓ |
| 35 Ⓐ Ⓑ Ⓒ Ⓓ | 70 Ⓐ Ⓑ Ⓒ Ⓓ |

**Note:** On the actual RICA you will NOT be tearing out any pages as your answers and essay will be written in separate documents or booklets.

## Assignment A

_____

CUT HERE

## Assignment B

CUT HERE

_____

_____

_____

_____

_____

_____

_____

_____

_____

_____

_____

_____

_____

_____

_____

_____

_____

_____

_____

_____

_____

_____

_____

_____

_____

_____

_____

_____

_____

_____

_____

_____

CUT HERE

## Assignment C

CUT HERE

## Assignment D

CUT HERE

# Practice Test 2 Case Study Response Booklet

## Assignment E

CUT HERE

# General Directions

The RICA test is composed of two sections: a multiple-choice question section, which contains 70 multiple-choice questions, and an open-ended assignment section. This assignment section contains five assignments, A to E, requiring written responses. The weight of each section toward the total examination score is approximately 50 percent. Therefore, your performance on both sections is equally important.

The directions for each section appear immediately before that section. The multiple-choice questions and the open-ended assignments may be worked on or completed in any order that you choose. On the actual RICA test you will be given a checklist to help you keep track of the sections you have completed. Plan your time carefully to make sure that you can complete the entire test within the time allotted.

**For security reasons, you may not take notes or remove any of the test materials from the room.** Since no scratch paper is allowed, you may use the margins of this test booklet for your notes. Keep in mind that only the responses recorded in your Answer Document and your Case Study Response Booklet will be scored.

Following the last open-ended assignment (E) you will see the words "End of Test." You may go back and review your answers at any time during the testing session if time permits. When you are sure you have answered all the multiple-choice questions, completed all the assignments, and properly recorded all of your responses in your Answer Document and Case Study Response Booklet, alert the proctor by raising your hand. At that time, your test materials will be collected, and you will be allowed to leave.

If you have any questions when you are taking the actual RICA test, be sure to ask them before beginning the test.

GO ON TO THE NEXT PAGE

# Directions for Section I: Multiple-Choice Questions

**Questions 1 to 70**

This section is composed of 70 multiple-choice questions. Each question is followed by four answer choices. Carefully read each question and choose the **one** best answer. Make sure that you record each answer on page 1 or 2 of the Answer Document in the space that corresponds to the question number. Completely fill in the circle having the same letter as the answer you have chosen. *Use only a No. 2 lead pencil.*

Sample Question:

---

**1.** Which of the following cities is farthest south?

    **A.** Los Angeles

    **B.** Sacramento

    **C.** San Diego

    **D.** San Francisco

---

The correct answer to this question is C. You would indicate that on the Answer Document as follows:

1

You should try to answer all the questions. If you have some knowledge about the subject of a question, you should try to use that knowledge to help answer it. You will not be penalized for guessing, because no points are deducted for incorrect answers.

DO NOT GO ON UNTIL YOU ARE TOLD TO DO SO.

1. A second-grade teacher assesses reading development by listening to her students read aloud. The teacher observes Shaniqua reading quickly with much expression. She notes that she is reading *home* for *house, child* for *kid,* and *puppy* for *dog.* The teacher analyzes her assessment and decides that Shaniqua is:

   A. reading at instructional level and needs direct instruction in phrasing and fluency.
   B. reading a story that is too difficult for her and that she should be given instruction in using structure cues.
   C. relying on meaning and structure cues and needs practice using visual cues so she can rely less on context clues.
   D. reading a story at her instructional level, so she focuses on other reading errors because it is clear that Shaniqua understands the meaning of the text.

2. Mrs. O'Malley would like to get parents more involved in her students' reading process. She is *least* likely to make an impact on student learning by:

   A. encouraging parents to accumulate books for home use and at the same time earn literacy materials for the classroom library by making purchases from recommended book club lists.
   B. sending home books that children are to read with their families.
   C. organizing a family reading night at school, where children come with their families and engage in a variety of literacy activities.
   D. planning a parent education night, at which parents participate in activities to develop their knowledge of how to read with children.

3. When planning differentiated guided-reading instruction so student reading development is supported, a teacher should be aware of the importance of:

   A. creating well-balanced and diverse groups.
   B. providing high-interest, grade-level reading material.
   C. meeting with each student an equal amount of time per week.
   D. planning flexible groups in which students read at approximately the same level.

4. Mr. Forester's class is composed of children from varied economic backgrounds, including families of low socioeconomic status. He knows it is important to be sensitive to the needs of students and their families. As a result, he can have the most impact on his families by:

   A. differentiating instruction for the children from the poorest families by meeting with them frequently in a small group, modeling the reading behaviors they may not observe at home.
   B. recognizing that children from low socioeconomic status have a limited number of books at home and sending home books for those students.
   C. working to involve all of his parents in literacy activities, both at home and school.
   D. becoming partners with the children from homes with low socioeconomic status.

5. Ms. Chu is a sixth-grade teacher. She frequently asks students to respond to literature through purposeful writing opportunities. When creating writing lessons, it is most important that Ms. Chu's lessons and activities:

   A. address at least two writing skills specified in the California reading and writing standards.
   B. involve different learning modalities and connect reading, listening, speaking, and writing.
   C. reflect the state, district, and grade-level norms.
   D. relate to the specific instructional needs of her students.

6. Ms. Jackson regularly listens to her students read, frequently administers running records, and follows up with comprehension questions related to the passage. The best reason for using this type of assessment is to:

   A. generate ongoing data for use in communicating with parents and for planning at-home reading interventions.
   B. analyze data to determine student strengths and weaknesses and use data to guide instruction.
   C. rank students according to grade level and help teachers plan classes for the next school year.
   D. plan phonics interventions and design appropriate groupings for her learners.

GO ON TO THE NEXT PAGE

7. A second-grade teacher conducts reading assessments of her lower-performing students more frequently than she does of her students who are achieving at grade level. The best reason for doing this is:

   A. frequent informative assessments help her guide instruction and make decisions for providing any intervention for the lower-performing students.

   B. she can more easily help the lower-performing students make informed decisions about choosing independent reading material.

   C. more frequent assessment of lower-performing students is often required by school districts and is sent to the state education department to better evaluate how schools are performing.

   D. frequent assessments are necessary for reporting to parents.

8. Elijah is a sixth grader who struggles with reading and has an Individualized Education Program (IEP). His teacher asks him to practice reading a nonfiction passage along with a tape-assisted reading. Elijah then uses an individual timer and times himself as he reads the same passage aloud two more times. He uses two different colored pencils to record the words correct per minute (WCPM) on a graph. What is the best reason for assigning this task?

   A. The use of timers is a powerful tool for motivating reluctant readers.

   B. The use of different colors helps students visually highlight different reading rates and WCPM.

   C. Rereading and plotting reading rates on a graph enables students and teachers to see improvements in WCPM.

   D. Rereading and plotting reading rates on a graph help develop automaticity, orthography, phonology, and enhancement of student ability to use meaningful phrasing.

9. The 2007 California Reading Language Arts Framework (RLA) recommends using a balanced, comprehensive literacy program that includes:

   A. a systematic phonics-based program that builds from simple to complex in a logical manner. It may also include guided reading.

   B. a well-balanced literature program, which includes fiction and nonfiction texts as well as books from all the major literature genres.

   C. comprehensive differentiated instruction based on content and performance standards in all the subject areas.

   D. direct, explicit instruction of reading skills and strategies based on content and performance standards in all the major language arts areas. It may also include content-area reading.

10. Mrs. Fung is a beginning fourth-grade teacher setting up her classroom for the first time. Her class comprises students from many different linguistic and ethnic backgrounds. She wants to create an environment that supports literacy. A portion of her room will be devoted to a class library. Included in her daily instructional plan will be time for sustained, silent reading time. She is eagerly acquiring books for her classroom library. She should be most concerned with finding books that are:

   A. at her students' instructional level and that reflect the cultures of her diverse group of students.

   B. at a fourth-grade reading level and considered to be literature.

   C. at various reading levels and include a variety of topics and genres as well as reference books.

   D. from the school-adopted literature series or reflect the appropriate content areas.

11. A fifth-grade teacher is trying to improve the prosody of Boris and Juanita, both second-language learners. How could the teacher best address their needs?

    A. by using timers to record repeated silent readings and plotting reading rates on a graph

    B. by providing differentiated instruction in prosody during English Language Learner time

    C. by practicing automaticity and reading rate at a fluency station during Universal Access time

    D. by modeling reading with appropriate phrasing and expression

12. At the beginning of each school year, Ms. Ohuru, a first-grade teacher, creates a general plan for reading and writing instruction. She develops long-range goals related to first-grade academic content standards and the district-adopted reading language arts text and materials. In addition, on a weekly basis, she regularly assesses her students and adjusts her teaching according to student needs. Ms. Ohuru is most likely to make changes to her weekly and daily plans based on:

    A. covering a large amount of material in a short amount of time.

    B. considering California and district standards as well as grade-level guidelines.

    C. developing curriculum based on student interest.

    D. examining results of ongoing assessments, developmental level of students, and individual student needs.

13. Which of the following can be used by teachers to inform instruction and determine a student's reading level?

    A. informal reading inventories

    B. criterion-referenced and reading fluency tests

    C. high-frequency word tests and phonemic awareness inventories

    D. interest inventories and phonic tests

14. Following analysis of a series of mid-year assessments, a primary teacher determines that Miya is not making adequate progress toward the benchmarks set by the school district. The teacher decides to hold a Student Success Team (SST) meeting. She invites the student's parents, previous teacher, guidance counselor, and the school principal. When planning strategic interventions for the child, which is the most important information to consider?

    A. results from the previous year's State of California Standardized Assessment Test

    B. analysis of the student's strengths and weaknesses

    C. awareness of how the child's low performance may impact her self-esteem

    D. examination of the student's performance compared with her grade-level peers

15. A first-grade teacher notices that Jack, one of her students, is having difficulty during a variety of phonological awareness activities. Although her assessment is made through informal observation, she does have an indication of his general weaknesses. Which of the following strategies is likely to be most effective in addressing his phonemic awareness weaknesses?

    A. practicing alliteration, rhyming, blending, and segmentation

    B. brainstorming lists that start with particular letters

    C. sorting word cards by sounds and developing automaticity

    D. practicing letter identification, and hearing sounds in words

16. A second-grade student often writes *rane* for *rain, nite* for *night,* and *fead* for *feed.* To correct this, the teacher should implement:

    A. weekly spelling tests focusing on long vowel patterns.

    B. systematic, explicit phonemic awareness instruction focusing on long vowel sounds.

    C. direct instruction in long vowel patterns that includes word sorts and word study notebooks.

    D. systematic spelling instruction that emphasizes morphology, etymology, and long vowel patterns.

GO ON TO THE NEXT PAGE

17. Mr. McDonald, a fifth-grade teacher, notes that Yusef is in the syllable and affixes stage of spelling. Mr. McDonald can help Yusef further develop his spelling in a systematic manner by teaching:

   A. words for specific content areas, highly irregular words, and spelling patterns for multisyllabic words.

   B. inflectional endings, syllabication, and homophones.

   C. long-vowel patterns, r-controlled vowels, complex consonant patterns, and dipthongs.

   D. consonant and vowel alternations, affixes and root words, and etymologies.

18. What intervention technique would be the most effective for a teacher to use with a student who is having difficulty becoming a fluent reader?

   A. The teacher can read many books with the student on an individual basis.

   B. The teacher needs to group the student by ability with readers on his level.

   C. The teacher needs to give the student additional practice worksheets that are related to his reading difficulty.

   D. The teacher can give the student many opportunities to reread books while providing books on the student's independent reading level.

19. The students in Ms. Tyler's class individually read a chapter on insects from their science books. During a follow-up discussion about ants, one sixth grader continually contributes incorrect information. Ms. Tyler is uncertain whether the misunderstanding stems from an inability to comprehend this particular grade-level text or a different reason. Which of the following assessments is the best to help Mrs. Tyler understand her student's difficulty?

   A. Use teacher observation to build anecdotal records of his reading behaviors. She notes when he has difficulty decoding grade-level material.

   B. Administer a cloze test from a chapter in his sixth-grade science book. She chooses an unread passage and omits every fifth word. The child is told to read the passage and try to fill in the missing words.

   C. Examine his science journal. She notes how he responded to previous science textbook passages and which pages have the best examples of six-trait writing based on the sixth-grade rubric.

   D. Give the sixth-grade Informal Reading Inventory. She registers how many words he is able to read correctly from the grade-level reading list. Subsequently, she gives the student a passage, asks him to read silently, and then asks him to retell the passage in his own words.

20. At the beginning of the school year, Mrs. Wilkerson administers the Observational Survey by Marie Clay. It becomes clear that Talia, a kindergartner, does not understand that print conveys meaning. Talia is most likely to benefit from:

   A. practicing printing while writing about meaningful experiences such as a class field trip.

   B. dictating an account of a particular experience to an adult who records it word for word. Then the child and adult can read the story aloud.

   C. retelling stories, sequencing, and other comprehension skills in order to become more aware of text meaning.

   D. using both tactile and kinesthetic methods in order to understand that print carries meaning.

21. Ms. Haupeakui knows that the development of vocabulary, reading, writing, and spelling are interrelated. During a unit on geology, Ms. Haupeakui creates a geology word wall. On the word wall, she alphabetically lists some geology words taken from texts her students are studying. Later on in the unit, students will find additional geology words from their readings and record them on this wall. Students will refer to these words when writing geology reports. The instructional strategy that is most likely to develop spelling is the:

   A. memorization of difficult content-area words such a *metamorphic.*

   B. practice of spelling content-area words in context and accurately spelling words when writing.

   C. development of spelling fluency by quickly reading alphabetical thematic word lists and recording words in a word journal.

   D. spelling of content-area words using the look-see-say method as part of a systematic program of spelling instruction.

22. At the beginning of each year, Mr. Carrington administers the Yopp-Singer phonological awareness exam to his first grade class. He determines that many students are having difficulty segmenting the sounds in words. One appropriate instructional strategy would be to:

   A. write words on the board and then ask the children to segment the words into letters and letter sounds.

   B. say words aloud and then break them up into sounds. For example, after hearing "chat," students would say /ch/-/a/-/t/.

   C. ask students to move magnetic letters as they say the sounds in words. For example, after hearing /bl/-/a/-/ck/, students would move the matching letters with their sounds to form *black.*

   D. say words aloud and then break them into syllables. For example, after hearing "computer," students would say /com/-/pu/-/ter/.

23. Mrs. Samir is planning her phonological awareness instruction. Her lesson plans might include:

   A. rhyming, blending sounds, alliteration, deleting sounds, syllable awareness, and word awareness.

   B. identifying and letter clusters, segmentation, and sound substitution.

   C. blending sounds, syllabication, phoneme deletion and addition, and alphabet recognition.

   D. using onsets, rimes, alliteration, rhyming, word boundaries, morphemes, and graphemes.

24. Hien, a first-grade English Language Learner, can identify the letters of the alphabet. She can automatically read some words, such as *cat* and *dog.* However, when asked to read similar words, such as *hat* and *fog,* she responds, "I don't know that word." One instructional strategy would be to provide:

   A. activities that help her develop listening comprehension.

   B. systematic, explicit instruction in research-based word strategies.

   C. direct instruction in rhyming and sound substitution.

   D. audio cassettes for her to listen to in the class listening center in order to increase vocabulary.

GO ON TO THE NEXT PAGE

25. In the following conversation, a kindergarten teacher is preparing a special-needs student for a phonemic awareness test. After reading, answer the question that follows.

    **Teacher:** I'm going to say the sounds in a word. The sounds are /k/-/i/-/t/. When I put those sounds together, they say *kit*. Now I'm going to say some more sounds, and I want you to put them together to make a word. This time, the sounds are /f/-/i/-/t/. Can you put those sounds together to make a word?"

    **Student:** /f/-/i/-/t/. That says *fit!*

    **Teacher:** That's right, fit. Now, I'd like you to do this for some more words.

    This assessment would be an appropriate way to measure which of the following phonemic awareness tasks?

    A. identifying phonemes and their letters
    B. blending the phonemes in a given word
    C. matching phonemes in rhyming words
    D. segmenting the phonemes in a given word

26. A first-grade teacher plays the song "Willaby Wallaby." One verse says, "Willaby, Wallaby, Wustin, an elephant sat on Justin." Next she uses this to introduce a game to her students. She looks at Tammy and sings, "Willaby, Wallaby, Wammy, an elephant sat on Tammy." She then encourages the class to sing along as she looks at Pedro and sings, "Willaby, Wallaby, Wedro, an elephant sat on Pedro." The next day she sings "Zippedy Doo Dah," and then asks students to sing along when she sings "Pippedy Poo Pah, Rippedy Roo Rah," etc. This activity is most likely to promote the reading development of students primarily by helping them:

    A. understand the principles of spoken words.
    B. develop the /w/ sound while studying the letter *W.*
    C. be motivated during transitions between literacy activities.
    D. manipulate the initial sounds in words.

27. A first-grade teacher is organizing her phonological awareness instruction. She should make sure to do all of the following *except:*

    A. create flexible phonemic awareness groups.
    B. prepare systematic, structured instruction based on the needs of her students.
    C. introduce Big Books and songs during phonemic awareness activities to make connections between oral language and print.
    D. assess students and provide systematic, direct instruction in word-identification strategies.

28. A first grader seems to have visual discrimination difficulties and often confuses similar letters. The student may best learn to distinguish between frequently confused letters by:

    A. writing capital and lowercase letters and recording them in a learning log.
    B. drawing letters in a salt tray and using her body to make the shape of the letters while saying their letter names.
    C. saying letters aloud while the teacher reads aloud from shared reading.
    D. working with a partner to find *b*'s, *d*'s, *p*'s, *q*'s, and other tricky letters "hidden" in books.

29. Mrs. Rashid is teaching her students to read words such as *do, through,* and *goes.* The most helpful strategy for identification of these words would be to directly teach students:

    A. selected words as sight vocabulary.
    B. to decode such words phonetically.
    C. selected words as part of an organized context-clue program.
    D. to unlock unknown words using syntax.

30. A first-grade teacher is working with her class during morning circle time. She is teaching a mini-lesson on onsets and rimes. The teacher uses the word *hair* as an example. Which of the following best represents an understanding of onsets and rimes?

    A. hare and hair
    B. hair and care
    C. /h/ and /air/
    D. hair and chair

31. A third-grade teacher wants to informally assess an individual child's knowledge of orthography in context. Which of the following assessments would be most appropriate?

    A. examining writing taken from the child's journal

    B. asking the student to identify the beginning, middle, and end sounds from a series of dictated words

    C. examining spelling tests from the beginning and middle of the year

    D. giving the student a list of words with related patterns that the student can organize and record in a word study notebook

32. Which of the following strategies would a first-grade teacher instruct her students to use when figuring out unknown words?

    A. use phonetic clues, find parts of words you can read, use picture clues

    B. skip the word you don't know, ask the teacher for help, ask a peer

    C. spell the word aloud, use the sentence context to figure out the word, use onsets and rimes

    D. use a word wall, reread the story, use phonemic awareness

33. A second-grade teacher notes that Jonah is having difficulty with reversals. In particular, he mixes up *p*'s and *q*'s and *b*'s and *d*'s when reading aloud. Which of the following strategies is likely to have the greatest impact on Jonah?

    A. referring Jonah to the Student Success Team. The team can pinpoint best practices for dyslexia intervention.

    B. giving Jonah sets of similar letters (such as *b*'s and *d*'s) printed in different fonts. Jonah then sorts them into piles next to icons representing their sound, such as butterfly (*b*) and dog (*d*).

    C. practicing writing words beginning with target letters (such as *b*'s and *d*'s).

    D. listening to a series of words beginning with target letters. Jonah then says the initial sounds out loud and forms the shape with his body.

34. Leah is an eighth-grade student who reads very slowly. During a parent-teacher conference, Leah's mother expresses her wish that Leah could read "more smoothly." Leah's teacher gives her direct instruction and guided practice in reading fluently. Leah is likely to make the greatest gains in overall fluency by:

    A. participating in activities such as Readers' Theatre, reading into a tape recorder, partner reading, and choral reading.

    B. studying organized word lists and flash cards to develop automatic word recognition.

    C. having multiple opportunities for silent, independent reading at her independent level in the classroom.

    D. being timed and calculating words per minute as she reads from grade-level reading lists.

35. In the word *blustery,* which of the following pairs of letters is a consonant blend?

    A. *st*

    B. *er*

    C. *bl*

    D. *ry*

36. A second-grade teacher is teaching her students different ways of spelling the long *e* sound. She gives her students flash cards with long *e* words printed on them and asks her students to sort them by spelling patterns. The flash cards include the following words: *key, leaf, bee, sheep, we, beast, me, believe, cheese, cede, see,* and *tea.* After the sorting activity, the teacher asks her students to complete a follow-up activity. The greatest benefit to her students would result from promoting:

    A. growth across the content areas by writing and illustrating a story in their learning logs using mostly long *e* words.

    B. application of spelling strategies and knowledge transfer by giving students a long *e* spelling test.

    C. vocabulary development by asking students to look up unknown words and record long *e* words in a word study notebook complete with illustrations.

    D. spelling patterns and generalizations by asking students to read results aloud and record categorized words in a word study notebook.

GO ON TO THE NEXT PAGE

37. Teachers often ask students to predict what will happen in a text they are about to read. Which of the following is the best explanation of why this is a valuable technique?

   A. Students' ability to predict story happenings often is a predictor of reading success.

   B. The teacher's ability to ask thought-provoking questions will lead the students to become more proficient readers.

   C. Prediction questions often stimulate students' interest in a text, encourage thinking, and give opportunities to share background knowledge.

   D. This technique encourages the student to take risks.

38. Mrs. Cervantes places a word wall on a large sheet of colored butcher paper posted in her first-grade classroom. On this wall she lists high-frequency words such as *said, was, because,* and *have.* They are arranged on word cards placed under the initial letter of the word and in alphabetical order. This strategy is most likely to be effective because students can:

   A. see the words placed on the walls and use them when writing to develop the spelling of sight words.

   B. practice reading sight words and develop their alphabetization skills.

   C. read the environmental print and then use structural analysis skills when decoding those words in other texts.

   D. improve their phonics skills by practicing decoding sight words.

39. On Monday Mrs. Valdez notices that many of her seventh-grade students have difficulty comprehending nonfiction texts. The next day, Mrs. Valdez introduces an unseen expository text. The following instructional strategy would be most effective in facilitating comprehension of expository text:

   A. using cooperative learning so a greater number of students will understand the text.

   B. using graphic organizers for students to complete using information from the text.

   C. teaching comprehension strategies such as note taking and outlining for understanding nonfiction text.

   D. asking students to complete nonfiction book reports.

40. A majority of the students in Ms. Sobhani's third-grade class are second language learners. After reviewing their entry-level assessments, it is clear to Ms. Sobhani that many of her students struggle with prosody. She can best address the fluency needs of her English Language Learner students by:

   A. explicitly teaching English intonation patterns, punctuation, phrasing, and syntax followed by guided practice.

   B. providing differentiated instruction in fluency during a teacher read-aloud. Students then silently read the same text.

   C. systematically teaching English decoding skills during shared reading. Students then practice newly learned fluency skills with a partner.

   D. developing fluency by helping build reading competency in English and in the home language.

41. Ms. Hidalgo is teaching a unit on fairy tales to her diverse fourth-grade class. To begin with, students read and discuss *Cinderella.* The teacher then assigns *The Golden Slipper,* a Vietnamese version of the classic Cinderella story. Following the two stories, students are asked to complete a Venn diagram and include as many aspects of the stories as possible. This instructional strategy is most likely to promote student reading proficiency by:

   A. guiding students in comparing and contrasting several aspects shared by the two stories.

   B. fostering an understanding of cultural relativism and diversity.

   C. supporting the needs of the Vietnamese students in the classroom.

   D. helping students diagram the relationships between characters in both stories.

42. Which of the following pairs of words are homophones?

   A. *wood* and *would*

   B. *up* and *down*

   C. *came* and *flame*

   D. *prewrite* and *writing*

43. Of the following, the most effective "before reading" practices for a primary teacher to use are:

   A. brainstorming, connecting prior knowledge, and predicting what the book will be about.

   B. previewing new vocabulary, discussing the author's background, and naming other books by the same author.

   C. listing words by phonic elements, comparing similar books, and sequencing pictures.

   D. dramatizing story elements, labeling favorite parts, and asking questions.

44. The students in a second-grade classroom are asked to retell a story they have just heard. The teacher asks them to tell the story events in sequence and discuss the characters. The teacher is trying to gain information about:

   A. the children's understanding of the text and their developing comprehension.

   B. the children's use of story vocabulary and whether they recall phrases from the text.

   C. whether the students liked the story.

   D. finding the appropriate reading level for independent reading.

45. In choosing books for fourth graders to read independently, the teacher finds stories with similar themes. Why would a teacher do this?

   A. The students can compare and contrast the books, providing links for dialogue and topics for discussion.

   B. This technique enables the teachers to save planning time by researching only one theme.

   C. This technique opens the door to many interaction opportunities for students.

   D. The teacher can connect the independent literature to themes that the students dislike studying in their classrooms.

Use the information below to answer the two questions that follow.

Ms. Chang's fourth-grade class has been studying amphibians. Her class includes a large number of English Language Learners. Ms. Chang designs and implements the activity described below.

Before she gives directions to the students, the teacher leads a whole-class discussion on the life cycle of a frog. Next, the teacher creates mixed-ability cooperative learning groups with four students in each group.

---

**Student Directions**

1. The students in each group continue discussing the subject.

2. Students take turns writing what happens first, second, third, or fourth in the life cycle on sentence strips.

3. Each group then sequences the sentences to form a proper paragraph. At the same time, they correct any errors.

---

46. When planning whole-class activities, it is important to consider the needs of second language learners. During this activity, Ms. Chang should be most concerned with:

   A. helping second language learners gain a solid understanding of the text.

   B. covering the most material in the shortest amount of time.

   C. meeting the instructional needs of all her students.

   D. providing motivating assignments for her learners.

47. Ms. Chang's organizing and writing activity is most likely to develop student reading by helping students:

   A. build knowledge in a systematic manner.
   B. improve reading comprehension skills.
   C. increase automaticity and fluency.
   D. transfer oral language skills to written language.

GO ON TO THE NEXT PAGE

48. Several students have been reading *Nate the Great* books during guided reading. In the books, the main character and his friends use detective skills to solve mysteries. Which of the following activities would allow the teacher to informally evaluate each student's ability to make a text-to-self connection?

    A. Each student cites passages from one of the stories that show suspense.

    B. Students use graphic organizers to retell one of the mysteries in their own words.

    C. Students create a class web and brainstorm traits commonly found in *Nate the Great* mystery stories.

    D. Each student describes which character from *Nate the Great* book is most like himself.

49. Which of the following is *not* a true statement?

    A. Effective fluency instruction is ongoing, organized, targeted, and direct.

    B. Fluency instruction needs to use progressively difficult text as well as provide opportunities for rereading familiar text.

    C. Fluent readers can focus attention on ideas and background knowledge, which will help their comprehension.

    D. Fluency occurs automatically when students are able to decode all words in their oral vocabulary.

**Use the information below to answer the two questions that follow.**

Students in a middle-school class frequently use K-W-L charts when reading expository texts. Before beginning a unit on the Periodic Table, students are asked to form small groups and list everything known about the Periodic Table. Then the whole class meets to share the groups' lists on a class K-W-L chart.

| K | W | L |
|---|---|---|
|   |   |   |

50. This strategy is likely to be particularly useful in helping the teacher evaluate her class's ability to:

    A. organize textual information by analyzing similarities and differences.

    B. activate, think about, and organize background knowledge.

    C. clarify known and unknown vocabulary.

    D. use QARs to teach inferential and evaluative comprehension.

51. The middle school students are then told to read a passage on atoms from their science text. The teacher distributes to each student a copy of the K-W-L chart that was previously filled out by the class. She could best help students use the chart to learn and retain facts from their reading by asking them to:

    A. memorize all the known information before starting the passage.

    B. complete the L (learned) section of the chart. Students can use the Internet or search other reference materials to find all unanswered questions from the W (want to learn) category.

    C. add continuously to the K-W-L chart as they absorb new information from the passage.

    D. work with a partner to form known fact categories.

52. Which of the following is *not* a component of Reciprocal Teaching?

    A. The teacher explains how a particular reading strategy should be used, models its use, and helps children use the strategy independently.

    B. Students participate in questioning, summarizing, clarifying, and predicting.

    C. Students self-monitor their own reading and understanding in a passage.

    D. The teacher helps students reflect on passages and develop a sense of how the written word is formed.

53. A fourth-grade class is studying California Missions. Students are told to open to a chapter that discusses Missions in their social studies books and locate all references to Native Americans. They are explicitly being taught:

    A. skimming.

    B. scanning.

    C. in-depth reading.

    D. structured reading.

54. Which of the following is the *least* effective strategy a teacher should model for using context clues to derive the meaning of an unknown word?

    A. unlock the meaning by reading a definition in a sentence from their text

    B. understand the definition of the word because it is contrasted with another word in the sentence

    C. utilize their knowledge of root words, prefixes, and suffixes to discover the meaning

    D. use word attack skills to alphabetically decode the meaning

55. As part of a Dr. Seuss author study, Mrs. Miyashta begins to read aloud *The Butter Battle* book. Halfway through the book, she stops reading. The teacher wants to facilitate comprehension while encouraging students to connect elements in the text to their background knowledge. They complete one of the following activities before Mrs. Miyashta finishes the end of the story. Which activity is likely to be most effective?

    A. Students are asked to confirm whether or not they correctly predicted the book's outcome.

    B. Students write what they think might happen next in the story and are encouraged to justify their predictions to the class.

    C. The students preview a set of comprehension questions that they will answer at the end of the book.

    D. The students rewrite the first part of the story and then record all their background knowledge about Dr. Seuss.

56. Chad is a behaviorally challenged seventh grader who performs significantly below average in reading. A teacher plans to assess his comprehension of a short story through oral retelling. After Chad silently reads the short story, his teacher prompts his retelling and understanding by asking open-ended questions. Chad behaves well and answers the questions thoughtfully. The best use of this assessment is to inform:

    A. other seventh-grade teachers, resource specialists, and the principal about the need for a Student Study Team and the possibility of developing a 504 plan.

    B. parents about his academic performance on the school standards-based report card.

    C. his teacher about his comprehension needs so that she can provide effective individualized reading interventions.

    D. his teacher about his reading so she can group Chad with others who need assistance accessing components of the core California State Board of Education–adopted materials.

GO ON TO THE NEXT PAGE

57. Before beginning a writing assignment, a fifth-grade teacher asks her students to share orally with their neighbors about the suggested topic. Students are instructed to discuss their ideas for writing with their group. Which of the following reasons is *least* likely to explain why she uses this strategy?

   A. The discussion helps students make connections between their oral language and writing.

   B. Students may become more interested in writing about the topic following discussion with partners.

   C. Student writing tends to be more detailed following discussion.

   D. Oral language helps second language learners develop spelling skills.

58. Michael and Yael are eighth graders working on developing "masterpiece sentences." After their teacher reads aloud several poems and invites discussion of the poetry's descriptive language, the teacher writes on the board, "The frog jumped in the water." She then asks the two students "who, what, where, when, and how" questions and has them brainstorm additional descriptive language to expand the sentence. In the end, the final sentence reads, "The bumpy amphibian leaped through the reeds into the frigid river."

   The teacher models this with several additional sentences and then Michael and Yael expand several sentences on their own. This "masterpiece sentence" activity is likely to be most effective in helping students:

   A. develop their evaluative comprehension skills when reading similar types of poetry.

   B. enhance their understanding of figurative language.

   C. improve their ability to write and comprehend complex sentences by using their existing oral vocabulary.

   D. increase sentence-writing capability by focusing on inferencing and concepts of print.

59. An eighth-grade teacher designs the following instructional activity. Students are given the word *sweltering*. Students brainstorm the definition, synonyms, an antonym, and create a sentence using the word *sweltering*. The teacher uses their suggestions to complete the following diagram on the board.

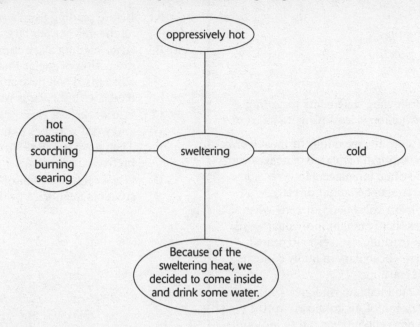

This activity is most accurately called a:

A.  concept diagram.
B.  syntactic structure.
C.  graphic organizer.
D.  semantic map.

GO ON TO THE NEXT PAGE

60. Structural analysis would be an especially appropriate strategy for determining meaning in which of the following words?

   A. pigeon
   B. misinformation
   C. lethal
   D. guava

61. Which of the following statements regarding vocabulary instruction is least likely to be true?

   A. Children learn the meanings of most words indirectly, through regular experiences with oral and written language. However, some vocabulary must be taught directly.
   B. Students learn vocabulary directly when they are explicitly taught individual words and word-learning strategies. Repeated exposure to vocabulary in many contexts aids word learning.
   C. Teachers can facilitate student comprehension of all unknown words. Children need encouragement to look up each word in the dictionary when reading an unknown word.
   D. Teachers can encourage indirect learning of new vocabulary by reading aloud to students. Reading aloud is especially helpful when teachers help students relate new words to prior knowledge and experiences.

62. Which of the following is the most effective way to teach students to learn unfamiliar word meanings?

   A. Before reading from a passage, introduce all the new vocabulary.
   B. After reading a selection, facilitate a discussion of the academic content and concepts. Then have students create word banks with the focus words.
   C. Use worksheet exercises, matching words, and word searches to teach root words. Then have students sort and record bases, prefixes, and suffixes.
   D. Use weekly vocabulary lists in which students memorize word meanings.

**63.** Mr. Gandin, a fourth-grade teacher, displays the following sentences on a piece of chart paper:

- Even though he had been *reminded,* D'Andre still forgot to call his mother.
- The electrician *rewired* the ceiling lights so they would stop blinking off and on.
- Harrison *retold* the story to his teacher after recess.
- Kristof *rewrote* his essay when he had finished editing it.
- The weaver *rewove* the loose piece of yarn into the rug.

Students are told to read the sentences and reread the italicized words. Individual children are chosen to come to the white board and highlight the common element. Mr. Gandin facilitates the class working together to arrive at the meaning of the *underlined* words.

To provide continued vocabulary development, Mr. Gandin could best follow up by:

**A.** continuing to study the origin and development of common Greek words. Students are asked to print words on index cards, use guide words to find their meanings in the dictionary, and share findings with partners.

**B.** providing direct instruction in breaking down words into word parts. Students then look for other examples of *re–* words in their independent reading, record them on a class list, and discuss their meanings.

**C.** continuing teaching prefixes, root words, and antonyms. Antonyms are added to the prefixes and root words to form new words. Students record new words in a word study notebook.

**D.** brainstorming additional words that have the letters *re–* as a prefix and/or end with the same letters in the suffix *–er.* Students then sort the words into alphabetical order.

GO ON TO THE NEXT PAGE

**Use the following passage to answer the three questions that follow.**

Mrs. Feinberg, a first-grade teacher, engages with students about the stories they are reading. Printed below is an excerpt from a conversation with Rosa, an ELL student. After this conversation, Rosa will write a story about her bike.

**Mrs. Feinberg:** What did you like about the bikes in this book?

**Rosa:** The colors bikes are pretty.

**Mrs. Feinberg:** Oh. You liked the pretty colors on the bikes. What else did you like about the bikes?

**Rosa:** I like the bikes big and the bikes fast.

**Mrs. Feinberg:** I also liked the big bikes and the fast bikes. Do you know anybody who has a bike?

**Rosa:** I have a new bike. It is pretty.

**Mrs. Feinberg:** I would love to hear more about your bike. I want you to write in your journal about your *fast, new* bike.

64. After reading this conversation, it is likely that Mrs. Feinberg knows the importance of:

    A. using metacognitive strategies to clarify meaning during reading and writing.
    B. drawing on a variety of cues to help English Language Learners identify unfamiliar English words.
    C. supporting English Language Learners in learning grammar and syntax through modeling.
    D. helping beginning readers who have difficulty with words that are not already part of their oral vocabulary.

65. The most appropriate follow-up activity for Rosa would be:

    A. a grammar mini-lesson followed by a worksheet filled with nouns and adjectives.
    B. direct, explicit instruction in grammar, syntax, and prepositional order.
    C. a pile of index cards with adjectives and the words *car, skateboard,* and *bus* written on them. An English-only student places them on a pocket chart and uses them to describe the vehicles with proper English grammar.
    D. direct, explicit instruction during a mini-lesson in use of adjectives and their placement in relation to nouns.

66. Which assessment is likely to be most helpful to Mrs. Feinberg in evaluating Rosa's ability to use appropriate English grammar in the classroom?

    A. qualitative assessment based on Rosa's written and oral language
    B. six-trait writing rubric evaluating Rosa's language skills
    C. CELDT test
    D. analytic summative assessment based on Rosa's journal entry about her bike

67. Ms. Palacios has her kindergarten class regularly participate in Language Experience Approach (LEA) activities. LEA instruction is *least likely* to promote student understanding of:

   A. sentence, word, and letter representation.
   B. directionality and tracking of print.
   C. print conveying meaning.
   D. sound/symbol correspondence.

68. At the beginning of the school year, a kindergarten teacher notices a child reading aloud fluently during silent reading time. Which is likely to be most effective in developing her reading ability?

   A. communicating with the student's parents about her advanced reading ability and suggesting possible enrichment activities
   B. sending home chapter books so the child can discuss complex ideas and further advance at home
   C. formally assessing the child to determine independent reading level and planning individualized instruction
   D. differentiating instruction for the student throughout the language arts block

69. Mr. Kassisseah is helping his seventh graders understand the similarities and differences between language structures used in spoken and written English. He can best help students master academic language by providing:

   A. direct instruction in systematic oral and written language development.
   B. direct instruction in academic language used in literature texts.
   C. a balanced language approach when speaking and writing across the curriculum.
   D. modeling and guided practice to teach oral and written language structures.

70. A seventh-grade teacher decides to introduce the following words during an instructional activity: *cyclone, cyclical, tricycle,* and *encyclopedia.* She explains that *cycl* comes from the Latin meaning circle or wheel. The teacher then asks students if they can think of other English words that include *cycl.* She lists their answers on the board. This brainstorm activity is likely to promote vocabulary development primarily by helping students:

   A. build word banks and semantic maps and sort words into categories.
   B. break down the components of a word to derive its meaning.
   C. use morphemic analysis to determine word history and origin.
   D. identify prefixes and suffixes for comprehension.

**END OF SECTION I**

Proceed to Section II of the test.

# Directions for Section II: Open-Ended Assignments

## Assignments A to E

This section of the test consists of four focused educational problems and instructional tasks and one case study. You are required to prepare a written response for each of these assignments and record each in the appropriate area provided in the Written Response Sheet in the Answer Document or, for the case study, in the Case Study Response Booklet.

Before you begin to write your response to an assignment, read the assignment carefully. Take some time to plan and organize your response. Blank space is provided in this test booklet following each assignment so that you can make notes, write an outline, or do any prewriting necessary. *Your final responses, however, must be written on the appropriate page(s) of the Answer Document. The case study must be written in the Case Study Response Booklet.*

The evaluation of your written responses will be based on how well the responses demonstrate knowledge and skills important for effective delivery of a balanced, comprehensive reading program. Make sure that you address all aspects of each given assignment and demonstrate your understanding of relevant content and pedagogical knowledge. Your responses will be evaluated on the following criteria: (1) fulfilling the purpose of the assignment; (2) effectively applying relevant content and academic knowledge; and (3) supporting your responses with appropriate evidence, examples, and rationales.

Considering that the multiple-choice section is weighted 50% of the total RICA score, each of the individual assignments will be weighted approximately as follows:

| | |
|---|---|
| Assignment A | 10% |
| Assignment B | 5% |
| Assignment C | 5% |
| Assignment D | 10% |
| Assignment E | 20% |
| Total | 50% |

The assignments are intended to assess knowledge and skills of reading instruction and, although writing ability is not directly assessed, your responses must be written clearly enough to allow for a valid judgment of your knowledge and skills. As you plan your responses, keep in mind that the audience is composed of educators knowledgeable about reading instruction. Each written response should conform to the conventions of edited American English.

Your responses to the assignments should be your original work. They should be written in your own words and not copied or paraphrased from some other work. Citations, however, may be used when appropriate.

To maintain your anonymity during the scoring process of the written assignments, the multiple-choice section of the Answer Document containing your name will be removed from your written responses. Do not write your name on any other portion of the Answer Document, and do not separate any of the sheets from the document.

You may work on the assignments in any order you choose, but be sure to record your final responses in the appropriate locations, as listed in the directions for each individual assignment.

# Assignment A

**Record your written response to Assignment A on the Assignment A Response Sheet** on page 3 of the Answer Document. The length of your response is limited to the lined space available on the Assignment A Response Sheet.

---

**Use the information here to complete the exercise that follows.**

It is important to have an implementation plan when teaching specific skills—for example, phonemic awareness. Study the Curriculum Implementation Plan that follows.

## Curriculum Implementation Plan

**1. ASSESS**
   **Informal / Formal:**
   • Fluency
   • Sight Word Check Off
   • Decoding Test (BPST)
   • Other Assessments

**2. PLAN**
   **Data Use:**
   • Standards & Framework
   • Grouping
   • Scheduling
   • Instructional Strategies
   • Student Tasks
   • Technology
   • Individual Needs

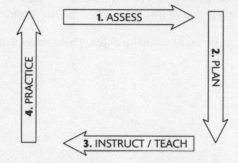

**4. MEANINGFUL PRACTICE**
   **Instructional Tasks:**
   • Highly Structured Practice
   • Guided Practice
   • Independent Practice
   • Decodable Text
   • Leveled Readers

**3. INSTRUCT / TEACH**
   **Direct & Explicit Instruction:**
   • Decoding
   • Sight Word Mastery
   • Comprehension Strategies
   • Comprehension Skills
   • Writing Skills
   • Other Instructional Strategies

### Examinee Task

Based on the information given and your knowledge of reading, write a response in which you: (1) explain how phonemic awareness is related to reading achievement and (2) describe the steps or instructional process a teacher must take to teach phonemic awareness to his/her kindergarten class.

---

Remember to record your final response on the **ASSIGNMENT A RESPONSE SHEET**
on page 3 of the Answer Document.

**(On the actual RICA test you will be warned NOT TO REMOVE THIS OR ANY OTHER PAGE,
or any portion of any page, from the test booklet.)**

**You may use the space on this page to make notes. These notes will not be scored.**

GO ON TO THE NEXT PAGE

# Assignment B

**Record your written response to Assignment B on the Assignment B Response Sheet** on page 5 of the Answer Document. The length of your response is limited to the lined space available on the Assignment B Response Sheet.

---

**Use the information here to complete the exercise that follows.**

In analyzing a fluency assessment and retelling, which she had administered to her third-grade students, a teacher notes that Jane is carelessly reading the words and not applying knowledge of prefixes and suffixes when encountering multisyllabic words.

**Examinee Task**

Using your knowledge of reading comprehension and the need for understanding multisyllabic words, write a response in which you: (1) discuss one reading comprehension need identified by the teacher; (2) describe one instructional strategy and one student activity to address the student need; and (3) explain why the instructional strategy and student activity you describe would be effective for this purpose.

---

Remember to record your final response on the **ASSIGNMENT B RESPONSE SHEET**
on page 5 of the Answer Document.

**(On the actual RICA test you will be warned NOT TO REMOVE THIS OR ANY OTHER PAGE,
or any portion of any page, from the test booklet.)**

**You may use the space below to make notes. These notes will not be scored.**

# Assignment C

**Record your written response to Assignment C on the Assignment C Response Sheet** on pages 7 and 8 of the Answer Document. The length of your response is limited to the lined space available on the Assignment C Response Sheet.

---

**Use the information here to complete the exercise that follows.**

A fifth-grade teacher plans to have her class read E.B. White's *Charlotte's Web* at the beginning of the school year. This novel is about a pig named Wilbur who develops a friendship with an intelligent barnyard spider, Charlotte. The teacher would like the students to understand the concept of "injustice" before starting their reading assignment. What should the teacher do to prepare for teaching this concept to her to her fifth graders?

**<u>Examinee Task</u>**

Write a response in which you describe strategies and resources the teacher should use to prepare for teaching.

---

Remember to record your final response on the **ASSIGNMENT C RESPONSE SHEET**
on pages 7 and 8 of the Answer Document.

**(On the actual RICA you will be warned NOT TO REMOVE THIS OR ANY OTHER PAGE,
or any portion of any page, from the test booklet.)**

**You may use the space below to make notes. These notes will not be scored.**

GO ON TO THE NEXT PAGE

# Assignment D

**Record your written response to Assignment D on the Assignment D Response Sheet** on pages 9 and 10 of the Answer Document. The length of your response is limited to the lined space available on the Assignment D Response Sheet.

---

**Use the information here to complete the exercise that follows.**

There are three levels of comprehension skills—literal, inferential, and evaluative comprehension. A number of comprehension strategies are appropriate to teach each level of comprehension.

**<u>Examinee Task</u>**

Using your knowledge of reading comprehension, write a response in which you: (1) describe the three levels of comprehension skills and (2) describe two comprehension strategies that would be appropriate to teach each level.

---

Remember to record your final response on the **ASSIGNMENT D RESPONSE SHEET**
on pages 9 and 10 of the Answer Document.

**(On the actual RICA test you will be warned NOT TO REMOVE THIS OR ANY OTHER PAGE,
or any portion of any page, from the test booklet.)**

**You may use the space below to make notes. These notes will not be scored.**

# Assignment E

## Case Study

**Record your written response to the case study in the Case Study Response Booklet.** Your response is limited to the lined space available in the Case Study Response Booklet.

---

This case study focuses on a student named Tara, who is 11 years old and in the sixth grade. The information and data on the following pages describe Tara's performance on assessments and observations. Using these materials, write a response in which you apply your knowledge of language arts assessment and instruction to analyze this case study. Your response should include three parts:

1. identify three of Tara's important reading strengths and/or needs at this point, citing evidence from the documents to support your observations;

2. describe two specific instructional strategies and/or activities designed to enhance Tara's skills; and

3. discuss Tara's literacy development by addressing the needs and/or building on the strengths you identified, and explain how each strategy/activity you describe would promote Tara's reading proficiency.

---

Remember to record your final response in the **CASE STUDY RESPONSE BOOKLET.**

**(On the actual RICA you will be warned NOT TO REMOVE THIS OR ANY OTHER PAGE, or any portion of any page, from the test booklet.)**

**You may use the space below to make notes. These notes will not be scored.**

GO ON TO THE NEXT PAGE

## Interest Survey

Tara's teacher created an interest survey for her students to complete at the beginning of the year. Printed on the following page are Tara's responses to the survey.

## Interest Survey

1. What do you like to do? _Cheerleading, play basketball and softball_

2. What is your favorite subject in school? _History and science_

3. What is your least favorite subject in school? _Math_

4. What are you good at doing? _Drawing cartoons_

5. What would you like to do better? _Write and spell_

6. Do you like to read? Why? Or Why not? _Yes. When the book is interesting._

7. Are you a good reader? _I'm ok_

8. What kinds of things do you like to read? _Mysteries and instructional books._

9. Are you a good writer? _Yes_

10. What do you like to write about? _Me and my hobbies_

11. What do you want to be when you grow up? _A designer_

12. What will you need to do to prepare yourself for your future career? _Learn a lot of math, and be a better writer and speller_

GO ON TO THE NEXT PAGE

## Phonics Test

Tara's teacher gave her a phonics inventory in which she tried to decode nonsense words containing the most common spelling patterns. The purpose was to determine which phonics elements she could read, and on which ones she needed to work. She was able to recognize consonant blends and digraphs; she was able to identify the short vowels and the sounds they make, but she had difficulty with the following short vowel nonsense words: *fis, gud,* and *hin.* She also read *nail* for *nel,* and *doke* for *dook.* She could read some nonsense words with prefixes and suffixes, although the words with suffixes were more difficult for her. She could read the nonsense compound words correctly, but had some problems with words with silent letters and r-controlled vowels. She could correctly divide multisyllabic words into syllables four out of seven times. On all the tasks she did not read the words with automaticity.

On another phonics assessment, Tara had difficulty with vowel diphthongs saying:

> "mail" for maul
> "coal" for cowl
> "owl" for awl
> "rock" for rook

She did not read the words on this assessment with automaticity.

## Running Record

Tara's teacher took a running record of her reading various grade-level passages. A running record is an informal assessment of reading performance to assess the rate and accuracy with which a student reads aloud. Self-corrections are also noted. For this assessment, Tara read aloud short, graded selections, and the teacher made notes about her performance. Following are the results of the fourth-grade passage she read. After reading each passage, Tara was asked to retell what the selection was about, to check for comprehension, and she was able to retell this passage with great accuracy, although she had to be prompted to supply details.

GO ON TO THE NEXT PAGE

## RECORD OF READING BEHAVIOUR

| | |
|---|---|
| Name: **Tara** | Title: **My Favorite Lunch** |
| Age: **11**  Grade: **6** | Running Words: **99**  Seen |
| Date: **10/01/2009** | Grade Level: **4**  (Unseen) |

### Calculations

Error Rate $\frac{SC}{E}$ = 1:**42**

Accuracy % **92**

S/C Rate $\frac{E - SC}{SC}$ = 1:**5**

Level:   Easy   (Instr)   Hard

### Understanding from Retelling/Questioning

| | | |
|---|---|---|
| Characters | (Yes) ............... | No |
| Setting | (Yes) ............... | No |
| Plot | (Yes) ............... | No |
| Inferences | (Yes) ............... | No |

### Competencies (circle predominant behaviors)

(1 on 1 matching)   (Directionality)   Fluent Reading
**No-reads
very slowly**

**At an unknown word**

Makes no attempt   Seeks help   Reruns   (Reads on)

Attempts using   (Letter/sound knowledge)   Meaning   Syntax

**After an error**

(Ignores)   Seeks help   Reruns   Attempts s/c

Self-corrects using   Letter/sound knowledge   (Meaning)   Syntax

| | | E | SC | E msv | SC msv |
|---|---|---|---|---|---|
| ✓ ✓  ✓ ✓ ↓ ✓ ✓R ✓ | | | | | |
| ✓ ✓ ✓  ✓ ✓ ✓  ✓ ✓ | | | | | |
| ✓ $\frac{can}{can't}$ ✓ ✓ $\frac{wait/sc}{want}$ ✓ ✓ ✓R | | 1 | 1 | M S Ⓥ | Ⓜ S V |
| ✓ ✓ ✓ ✓ $\frac{everywhere}{everything}$ ✓ ✓ | | 1 | | M S Ⓥ | |
| ✓ ✓ ✓ ✓ ✓ ✓ ✓ ✓ ✓ | | | | | |
| ✓ ✓ ✓ $\frac{hummingbird}{hamburger}$ ✓ $\frac{search}{scratch}$ | | 2 | | M S Ⓥ | |
| ✓ ✓ $\frac{pull}{put}$ ✓ ✓ ✓ ✓ | | 1 | | M S Ⓥ | |
| ✓ ✓ ✓ $\frac{double/sc}{doorbell}$ ✓ $\frac{granted}{greeted}$ ✓ ✓ | | 1 | 1 | M S Ⓥ | Ⓜ S V |
| ✓ ✓ $\frac{concentrated}{concerned}$ ✓ ✓ ✓ ✓ | | 1 | | M ⓈⓋ | |
| ✓ ✓ ✓ ✓ ✓  ✓ ✓ ✓ | | 1 | | M Ⓢ Ⓥ | |
| ✓  ✓ ✓R ✓  ✓ ✓ $\underset{-}{very}$ ✓ | | | | | |
| ✓ ✓ ✓ ✓ ✓  ✓ ✓ ✓  ✓ | | | | Ⓜ S V | |

## Qualitative Spelling Inventory

Tara's teacher gave her a qualitative spelling inventory to find out where she is making spelling errors and what spelling features she already has in place. When Tara missed five out of the first seven words on the Upper Elementary Spelling Inventory, her teacher administered Bear's Elementary Qualitative Spelling Inventory to her to determine her spelling stage. Tara's spelling test and analysis of errors on the Feature Guide are on the two following pages.

GO ON TO THE NEXT PAGE

# Qualitative Spelling Checklist

Student **Tara**        Observer **Ms. Mellon**

Use this checklist to help you find what stages of spelling development your students are in. There are three gradations within each stage—early, middle, and late. The words in parentheses refer to spelling words on the first Qualitative Spelling Inventory.

This form can be used to follow students' progress. Check when certain features are observed in students' spelling. When a feature is always present check "Yes." The last place where you check "Often" corresponds to the student's stage of spelling development.

**Emergent Stage**        Dates:____ ____ ____

*Early*
- Does the child scribble on the page?    Yes ✓   Often___   No___
- Do the scribbles follow the conventional direction? *(left to right in English)*    Yes ✓   Often___   No___

*Middle*
- Are there letters and numbers used in pretend writing? *(4BT for ship)*    Yes ✓   Often___   No___

*Late*
- Are key sounds used in syllabic writing *(P for ship)*    Yes ✓   Often___   No___

**Letter Name—Alphabetic**

*Early*
- Are beginning consonants included *(B for bed, S for ship)*    Yes ✓   Often___   No___
- Is there a vowel in each word?    Yes ✓   Often___   No___

*Middle*
- Are some consonant blends and digraphs spelled correctly? *(ship, when, float)*    Yes ✓   Often___   No___

*Late*
- Are short vowels spelled correctly? *(bed, ship when, lump)*    Yes ✓   Often___   No___
- Is the *m* included in front of other consonants? *(lump)*    Yes ✓   Often___   No___

**Within Word Pattern**

*Early*
- Are long vowels in single-syllable words "used but confused"? (FLOT for *float*, TRANE for *train*)    Yes___   Often ✓   No___

*Middle*
- Are most long vowels in single-syllable words spelled correctly but some long vowel spelling and other vowel patterns "used but confused"? *(COTE for caught)*    Yes___   Often___   No ✓
- Are most consonant blends and digraphs spelled correctly?    Yes ✓   Often___   No___
- Are most other vowel patterns spelled correctly? *(caught, chased, preparing)*    Yes___   Often ✓   No___

**Syllables and Affixes**

*Early*
- Are inflectional endings added correctly to base vowel patterns with short vowel patterns? *(popping, beaches)*    Yes ✓   Often___   No___
- Are consonant doublets spelled correctly? *(cattle, cellar)*    Yes ✓   Often___   No___

*Middle*
- Are inflectional endings added correctly to base words? *(inspection, cellar)*    Yes___   Often ✓   No___

*Late*
- Are less frequent prefixes and suffixes spelled correctly? *(confident, ripen, cellar, opposition, puncture)*    Yes___   Often___   No ✓

**Derivational Relations**

*Early*
- Are most polysyllabic words spelled correctly? *(fortunate, confident)*    Yes___   Often___   No ✓

*Middle*
- Are unaccented vowels in derived words spelled correctly? *(confident, civilize, opposition)*    Yes___   Often ✓   No___

*Late*
- Are words from derived forms spelled correctly? *(pleasure, civilize)*    Yes___   Often___   No ✓

Words Their Way Appendix © 2000 by Prentice-Hall, Inc.

# Spelling Test

Name <u>Tara</u>

1. bed
2. ship
3. drive
4. bump
5. when
6. trane ✓
7. closet
8. chase
9. flot ✓
10. beaches
11. prepairing ✓
12. popping
13. cattle
14. cote ✓
15. inspecsion ✓
16. pouchser ✓
17. seller ✓
18. pleasher ✓
19. squirrel
20. forcanet ✓
21. confident
22. civilize
23. flexible
24. oposelon ✓
25. enfasize ✓

GO ON TO THE NEXT PAGE

## Writing Samples

Tara's teacher examined three writing samples. Tara had been instructed to choose any topic about which she wanted to write. She wrote about her cheerleading competition, her family, and sports. Her writing did not include many details and was incomplete because she ran out of time. Her sentence structure was simple and to the point. She misspelled words with common long vowel spelling patterns.

## Elementary Inventory Error Guide

| Stages | Early Letter Name | Letter Name | Within Word Pattern | Syllable Juncture | Derivational Constancy |
|---|---|---|---|---|---|
| 1. bed | b bd | bad | (bed) | | |
| 2. ship | s sp shp | sep shep | sip (ship) | | |
| 3. drive | irv drv | griv driv | drieve draive (drive) | | |
| 4. bump | b bp bmp | bop bomp bup | (bump) | | |
| 5. when | w yn wn | wan whan | wen (when) | | |
| 6. train | j t trn | jran chran tan tran | teran traen (trane) train | | |
| 7. closet | k cs kt clst | clast closet clozt | clozit closet (closed) | | |
| 8. chase | j jass cs | tas cas chas chass | case chais (chase) | | |
| 9. float | f vt ft flt | for (flot) flort | flowt flount floate | | |
| 10. beaches | b bs bcs | bechs becis behis | bechise beches beeches (beaches) | | |
| 11. preparing | | | preparng preypering | preparing (preparing) preparing | |
| 12. popping | | | popin poping | (popping) | |
| 13. cattle | | | catl cadol | catl cattle cattle (cattle) | |
| 14. caught | | | cot (cote) cour cought caught | | |
| 15. inspection | | | inspshn, inspectin | inspecshum (inspecsion) inspection | |
| 16. puncture | | | (Pouchser) pucshre pungchr puncker | punksher punture puncture | |
| 17. cellar | | | sulr selr celr seler | (seller) cellar celler cellar | |
| 18. pleasure | | | plasr plager plejer pleser plesher (Pleasher) | plesour plesure | pleasure |
| 19. squirrel | | | scrl skwel skwrel | scqori sqrurel squirrel (squirrel) | |
| 20. fortunate | | | furhnat frehnit foohinit (forcanet) | forchenut fochininte forchenut | fortunate |
| 21. confident | | | | confedent confedint confedent confadent, conphident (confident), sivils sevelies sivillicse cifillazas sivelize | confident confedint confedent confadent, conphident (confident) |
| 22. civilize | | | | sivalize civalise (civilize) sivilize | sivils sevelies sivillicse cifillazas sivelize, sivalize civalise sivilize (civilize) |
| 23. flexible | | | | flecksibl flexobil fleckuble flecible, flexeble flaxable flexibal flexable | (flexible) |
| 24. opposition | | | (oposeion) opasion opasishan opozcison opishien, opssition | opasition oppasishion oppsition | opposition opusition |
| 25. emphasize | | | | (emfasize) infaxize imfacize emphasize, emphasise | emphasize |

Words Their Way, 1996

## Teacher Comments

Tara's teacher made the following notes about her:

Tara is a positive and enthusiastic learner with a great sense of humor.

Frequently aware of mistakes she is making in reading and spelling, but lacks the strategies to correct them.

A one-to-one learning situation helps her to learn.

Is open about her feelings.

Is willing to try new learning methods and strategies and tries to apply them.

Tara is able to work independently and is able to concentrate on a task for a long period of time without losing interest.

**End of Test**

# Answers and Explanations for Practice Test 2

## Section I: Multiple-Choice Questions

### Answer Key

1. C (Domain 2, Content Specification 006)
2. A (Domain 1, Content Specification 001)
3. D (Domain 1, Content Specification 001)
4. C (Domain 1, Content Specification 001)
5. D (Domain 5, Content Specification 012)
6. B (Domain 1, Content Specification 002)
7. A (Domain 1, Content Specification 002)
8. C (Domain 3, Content Specification 009)
9. D (Domain 1, Content Specification 001)
10. C (Domain 1, Content Specification 001)
11. D (Domain 3, Content Specification 009)
12. D (Domain 1, Content Specification 002)
13. A (Domain 1, Content Specification 002)
14. B (Domain 1, Content Specification 002)
15. A (Domain 2, Content Specification 003)
16. C (Domain 2, Content Specification 006)
17. B (Domain 2, Content Specification 006)
18. D (Domain 3, Content Specification 009)
19. B (Domain 5, Content Specification 013)
20. B (Domain 2, Content Specification 004)
21. B (Domain 2, Content Specification 007)
22. B (Domain 2, Content Specification 003)
23. A (Domain 2, Content Specification 003)
24. C (Domain 2, Content Specification 003)
25. B (Domain 2, Content Specification 003)
26. D (Domain 2, Content Specification 003)
27. D (Domain 2, Content Specification 003)
28. B (Domain 2, Content Specification 004)
29. A (Domain 2, Content Specification 005)
30. C (Domain 2, Content Specification 003)
31. A (Domain 2, Content Specification 007)
32. A (Domain 2, Content Specification 005)
33. B (Domain 2, Content Specification 004)
34. A (Domain 3, Content Specification 009)
35. C (Domain 2, Content Specification 005)
36. D (Domain 2, Content Specification 006)
37. C (Domain 5, Content Specification 013)
38. A (Domain 2, Content Specification 005)
39. C (Domain 5, Content Specification 015)
40. A (Domain 3, Content Specification 009)
41. A (Domain 5, Content Specification 014)
42. A (Domain 2, Content Specification 007)
43. A (Domain 4, Content Specification 011)
44. A (Domain 5, Content Specification 014)
45. A (Domain 5, Content Specification 014)
46. C (Domain 4, Content Specification 011)
47. D (Domain 4, Content Specification 011)
48. D (Domain 5, Content Specification 014)
49. D (Domain 3, Content Specification 008)
50. B (Domain 4, Content Specification 011)
51. C (Domain 5, Content Specification 015)
52. D (Domain 5, Content Specification 013)
53. B (Domain 5, Content Specification 015)
54. D (Domain 4, Content Specification 011)
55. B (Domain 5, Content Specification 013)
56. C (Domain 5, Content Specification 013)
57. D (Domain 4, Content Specification 011)
58. C (Domain 4, Content Specification 011)
59. D (Domain 4, Content Specification 011)
60. B (Domain 4, Content Specification 010)
61. C (Domain 4, Content Specification 011)
62. B (Domain 4, Content Specification 010)
63. B (Domain 4, Content Specification 011)
64. C (Domain 4, Content Specification 010)
65. D (Domain 4, Content Specification 011)
66. A (Domain 4, Content Specification 011)
67. D (Domain 4, Content Specification 010)
68. C (Domain 1, Content Specification 002)
69. D (Domain 4, Content Specification 011)
70. B (Domain 4, Content Specification 011)

# Explanations

1. **C.** All of Shaniqua's known errors involved reading a synonym for the correct word. Therefore, she is using her meaning and structure cueing systems. She is relying on context rather than using decoding skills to "unlock" an unknown word. Choice A is incorrect because Shaniqua is already reading with expression. Choice B is incorrect because the story is not too difficult for her and she doesn't need structure cue (syntax) instruction. Although her mistakes imply an understanding of the text, the goal must be to have students reading all words accurately. Additionally the responses are counted as errors in the student's accuracy score on the running record. Therefore, Choice D is also incorrect. It is impossible to make assumptions about her instructional level without more data. (Domain 2, Content Specification 006)

2. **A.** While students and their families often love student book clubs, this is not a way to reach the majority of parents. Choices B, C, and D are likely to widely benefit the greatest number of families. Recruiting volunteers, conferences, support groups, and parent workshops are effective ways to increase parent involvement. (Domain 1, Content Specification 001)

3. **D.** In organizing reading groups for Universal Access, the teacher must target her plan to meet the identified instructional levels of all her students. To accomplish this goal, she should form flexible groups according to students' instructional reading level and then provide individual and/or differentiated instruction. Reading groups should be leveled according to ability yet remain flexible to accommodate the constantly shifting abilities of the students. Historically, some teachers have chosen to place students according to levels at the beginning of the year and seldom waiver from those leveled groups. By continually assessing student ability with entry-level, monitored, and summative assessments, the teacher can be certain that each child is placed in the group that best matches his or her instructional reading level. Choice B is incorrect because during guided reading, it is important to provide materials at the instructional level, which is not necessarily grade level. Choice C is incorrect because a teacher might meet with lower-performing students more often than other children. Although classrooms comprise diverse learners and their reading levels, guided reading groups should be based on student instructional reading level. Therefore, Choice A is not appropriate. (Domain 1, Content Specification 001)

4. **C.** Effective teachers must work to involve *all* of their students' families. While choices A, C, and D may indeed benefit some of his students, only choice C applies to all of the children. Although a child from a poor family is less likely to be involved in literacy in the home, a teacher needs to look at each individual student and not make generalizations about students based on their socioeconomic backgrounds. (Domain 1, Content Specification 001)

5. **D.** Choices A, B, and C are all good things to keep in mind when lesson planning. However, only choice D refers specifically to planning according to the needs of the individual and class. The goal of reading instruction is to develop reading competence in all students. Writing activities such as responding and summarizing help reinforce student understanding of texts and the development of their comprehension skills. (Domain 5, Content Specification 012)

6. **B.** Although running records can be used to communicate with parents and rank students in a grade level as indicated in choices A and C, choice B is nevertheless the best answer. The main reason for conducting an assessment is to provide specific information about what students know. The teacher can then consistently use assessment data to plan her reading interventions based on student strengths and identified needs. This idea of assessment analysis and using data to differentiate instruction should be kept in mind throughout the RICA exam. Running records can also be used to determine instructional reading level and provide information on student decoding strategies. Choice D is incorrect because it focuses only on phonics rather than on all the skills necessary for reading. (Domain 1, Content Specification 002)

7. **A.** While choices B, C, and D may be true, choice A is the best answer. The purposes of frequently monitoring lower-performing students are to collect information to inform instruction, identify at-risk students, and influence decisions regarding early interventions. Schools and school districts should provide

all teachers with a variety of assessment tools and research-based strategies necessary for daily instruction. (Domain 1, Content Specification 002)

The following are some of the literacy assessments used to screen and monitor students:

- developmental checklists
- running records
- writing rubrics
- reading logs
- collections of student work
- spelling inventories
- fluency tests
- oral reading inventories
- phonics surveys
- phonological awareness surveys
- high-frequency word recognition assessments
- observational survey or concepts about print test
- alphabetic knowledge assessments
- comprehension assessments
- vocabulary assessments

8. **C.** Although both choice A and choice B may be useful with students, only choice C provides the best reason for this activity. Rereading is one of the best ways to increase reading speed. Noting times on a graph can be particularly helpful when trying to increase rate. Repeated reading often increases automaticity, prosody, vocabulary, and comprehension. Choice D is incorrect because it mentions phonology and orthography, which are not the primary purposes of this task. (Domain 3, Content Specification 009)

9. **D.** Choices A and B are important components of a balanced, comprehensive literacy program but are not complete on their own. Choice C is too broad an answer, because it refers to all subject areas rather than just literacy. Choice D is more specific and therefore more accurate than choice C because it includes direct, explicit instruction, which is a necessary part of a balanced literacy program. (Domain 1, Content Specification 001)

10. **C.** The teacher should know how to select instructional materials and create a learning environment that promotes student reading. When creating a library, it is important to have varied, motivating texts at students' independent and instructional reading levels, regardless of grade level. Choices A, B, and D are incorrect answers because they are too specific; they limit the types of books to be found in the classroom library. (Domain 1, Content Specification 001)

11. **D.** Choice D is correct because an effective teacher knows that explicit, systematic strategies for building prosody include modeling and phrase-cued reading. Choice A is incorrect because the students are reading silently rather than aloud. Silent reading is less likely to have an impact on fluent reading than oral reading. Choice B is incorrect because the students are practicing prosody during English Language Learner (ELL) instruction, a time that should be devoted to developing vocabulary, grammar, syntax, and overall oral language. Choice B is also incorrect because it suggests that all ELL students would benefit from fluency instruction, which is not necessarily true. Choice C is incorrect because automaticity and rate are not the main components of prosody. (Domain 3, Content Specification 009)

12. **D.** When planning long-term instruction, the beginning teacher should indeed follow California and district standards as well as text and grade-level guidelines as mentioned in choice B. However, the question specifically asks about weekly and daily planning, which makes choice D the correct answer. Although a teacher does want to use time efficiently (choice A) and also consider student interests (choice C), it is the assessment and student needs that should guide the teacher's weekly and daily plans. (Domain 1, Content Specification 002)

13. **A.** Although the choices include assessments that can help teachers plan their instruction, only choice A includes an Informal Reading Inventory (IRI), a test that can help determine a student's reading level. The IRI is individually administered and generally comprises graded word lists, graded passages, and comprehension questions. Scores from an IRI can be used to calculate independent, instructional, and frustration reading levels. (Domain 1, Content Specification 002)

14. **B.** While it is important to bring many types of information to an SST meeting, choice B is the best answer. It is important to analyze the student's individual strengths and weaknesses, and then use the data to drive individualized instruction. Choices A, C, and D are not as relevant for strategic intervention. (Domain 1, Content Specification 002)

15. **A.** Students must develop an awareness that words are made of individual speech sounds. The teacher must provide direct instruction in phonemic awareness. This instruction should be both implicit and explicit. Alliteration, rhyming, blending, and segmenting are all examples of phonemic awareness activities. Although choice D is partially correct because it mentions "hearing sounds in words," letter identification is a phonics rather than phonemic awareness activity. Choices B and C, also phonics activities, rely on visual skills rather than a primary emphasis on hearing or articulating sounds. (Domain 2, Content Specification 003)

16. **C.** Systematic spelling instruction should be related to students' spelling development. A good assessment to determine a student's spelling development level is the Qualitative Spelling Inventory by Donald Bear. It is helpful for the teacher to use multisensory techniques to teach and reinforce spelling patterns. Word sorts and activities that involve long vowel sounds would be appropriate for this student. It is also important that the student works on skills that are at his or her spelling development level. While morphology and etymology (choice D) are important in a systematic spelling program, they don't address spelling long vowel patterns. Choice B is inappropriate because phonemic awareness refers to sounds that are articulated and heard rather than spelled. Choice A is incorrect because success on spelling tests doesn't necessarily translate to proper spelling in written work. (Domain 2, Content Specification 006)

17. **B.** Choice B refers to teaching in the syllable and affixes stage. Choice C would be appropriate for the within-word pattern spelling stage, and choice D would help develop skills in the derivational relations stage. Only part of choice A corresponds to developing spelling for the spellers in this stage. (Domain 2, Content Specification 006)

18. **D.** The more children read, the more likely they are to develop reading fluency. Lack of fluency has an impact on decoding, comprehension, and vocabulary acquisition. Choices A, B, and C do not address fluency instruction. (Domain 3, Content Specification 009)

19. **B.** All of the answers describe assessment tools. You can rule out choice A because it mentions decoding rather than overall comprehension. Although the student's difficulty in decoding may contribute to his or her problem, choice B is better because it specifically relates to comprehension of his grade-level science text. Choice C is incorrect because it is based on six-trait writing, which does not assess his comprehension. Choice D is an attractive distracter because an Informal Reading Inventory is an effective way of measuring grade-level reading. However, since the question specifically asks about student ability to comprehend the content-area science text, choice B is the best assessment tool mentioned. (Domain 5, Content Specification 013)

20. **B.** Simply put, print is oral language, or talking, recorded onto paper. Talia will most benefit from seeing her own words put into print. Choice D is too vague to be the best response; it does not specify how tactile and kinesthetic methods will lead to improved understanding of concepts about print. Choice A is incorrect because its emphasis is on handwriting rather than understanding that print carries meaning. Choice C addresses general comprehension but not the lack of understanding that print conveys meaning. (Domain 2, Content Specification 004)

21. **B.** The teacher should teach spelling in context, and students can apply their spelling skills across the curriculum. Choice A is incorrect because with memorization a teacher cannot know whether a child is actually learning to spell the word or whether the child would accurately spell when writing for a purpose. Choices C and D do not specifically address this question. (Domain 2, Content Specification 007)

22. **B.** Choice B is correct because it addresses "phonological awareness," the knowledge that oral language is made up of units, such as words, syllables, and phonemes (sounds). Choice A incorrectly addresses phonics, which is related to the written form of language, rather than phonemic awareness, which deals specifically with hearing, manipulating, and articulating sounds. Choice C involves the phonemic awareness task of blending rather than segmenting. Choice D focuses on syllabication—breaking words into syllables—instead of phonemes in words. (Domain 2, Content Specification 003)

23. **A.** Choice A provides the only answer that is limited to phonological awareness. In contrast, all the other choices address phonics or vocabulary concepts in addition to phonemic awareness tasks. (Domain 2, Content Specification 003)

24. **C.** Choice C is the only option that correctly addresses this student's instructional needs. Choice A refers to comprehension, which is not Hien's known area of need. Choice B sounds attractive, but "word strategies" is not a literacy phrase. Choice D could be an appropriate activity but would not target the specified problem. (Domain 2, Content Specification 003)

25. **B.** Blending phonemes is the only choice that matches the phonemic awareness task listed. Phoneme blending is the act of listening to a sequence of separately spoken phonemes and then combining them to form a word. Choice A is wrong because phonics, not phonemes, refers to letters and letters clusters. Choice C is not a phonemic awareness task. An example of segmenting, choice D, would be asking students to break a word into beginning, middle, and ending sounds, such as separating *hen* into /h/-/e/-/n/. (Domain 2, Content Specification 003)

26. **D.** In the described activity, the focus is primarily on manipulating the initial sounds in words. This is a phonemic awareness element that helps promote reading development. Choice A is incorrect because this activity will not help students understand the principles of spoken words. Choice B is incorrect because the /w/ sound should not be taught in isolation. Choice C is irrelevant because it mentions being motivated during transitions. Although it is important to keep students motivated, this option is not the best answer. (Domain 2, Content Specification 003)

27. **D.** Choices A, B, and C should all be included in a systematic phonological awareness program. Word identification is a component of word analysis and is not a phonological awareness skill. (Domain 2, Content Specification 003)

28. **B.** The first-grade teacher should use engaging, multisensory techniques to assist children in recognizing letter shapes and names. Choice B is the best answer choice because the student will simultaneously engage visual, auditory, kinesthetic, and tactile modalities. Choices A, C, and D are limited learning experiences engaging one or two learning modalities. Choice D is a possible answer choice, but it is not the best answer for two reasons: (1) it engages only the visual modality and (2) although group work is often appropriate, in this case the first grader may rely on her partner to do the work for her. (Domain 2, Content Specification 004)

29. **A.** The words *do, through,* and *goes* are commonly used in the English language. However, they are irregular and do not follow typical phonetic rules. Since such words will never be decodable (choice B), it is important that students know these words automatically. Using syntax (choice D) and context clues (choice C) will not necessarily lead to automaticity. (Domain 2, Content Specification 005)

30. **C.** An *onset* is the initial consonant or consonant blend in a syllable, as /sh/ in shook. A *rime* is a vowel and any of the following consonants of a syllable, as /ook/ in shook. (Domain 2, Content Specification 003)

31. **A.** This question is asking about orthography, the spelling patterns of written language. Additionally, "in context" refers to an authentic writing experience rather than a spelling test. Therefore, choice A is correct because it is the only answer that mentions spelling during a real writing task. Choice B is incorrect because it refers to a phonological awareness task rather than spelling, or orthographic knowledge. (Domain 2, Content Specification 007)

32. **A.** A first-grade teacher could instruct her students to use phonetic clues, find parts of words that they can read, and use picture clues to figure out unknown words. All of these techniques are often used in the classroom and are successful strategies for word analysis. Choices B, C, and D are incorrect because they do not present strategies to address word analysis. (Domain 2, Content Specification 005)

33. **B.** Choice A is incorrect because it suggests convening a Student Success Team (SST) as the first course of action. It is possible that Jonah has dyslexia; however, letter reversal is a common problem in the primary grades and not necessarily a sign of a learning disability. An effective teacher works to differentiate within the classroom. Many problems like reversals can be remediated with repeated practice. Choices C and D are incorrect because Jonah is focusing on listening or writing without any visual cues to remind him of proper directionality. (Domain 2, Content Specification 004)

34. **A.** Although silent, independent reading (choice C) may increase fluency, direct instruction combined with oral reading practice is most likely to develop Leah's reading abilities (choice A). Choice B is incorrect because automaticity, or the ability to read a word quickly and accurately, is only one component of fluency. Likewise, timed reading from a word list, choice D, may not help her. Reading with speed and automaticity as well as components of prosody—such as meaningful phrasing, intonation, and expression—are necessary fluency skills. (Domain 3, Content Specification 009)

35. **C.** A consonant blend is a combination of sounds in one syllable made by blending two or more consonants together. (Domain 2, Content Specification 005)

36. **D.** All of the activities noted in Choice D could be part of an organized word study program, which helps the students improve decoding skills as well as spelling. Choice A is incorrect because it does not focus on orthographic patterns, and it limits writing by specifying long *e* words. Choice B is wrong because correct spelling on a test does not necessarily transfer to proper spelling in authentic writing situations. Choice C is inaccurate because it focuses on developing vocabulary for fairly basic words rather than paying attention to spelling patterns, a necessary component in an organized word study program. (Domain 2, Content Specification 006)

37. **C.** Prediction questions are among the best high-level thinking questions that teachers can use to engage students. Teachers can use them before they start reading a story or when students are already involved in a story. (Domain 5, Content Specification 013)

38. **A.** While students may improve their alphabetization skills as they read high-frequency words posted on the word wall (choice B), the main purpose for the activity is developing their spelling skills for the most commonly found words, which is addressed in choice A. Because many of these words are irregular sight words, they are not phonetically decodable, and therefore learning these words will not aid in the development of structural analysis (choice C) or phonics (choice D). A recommendation is that students learn to spell the 100 most frequently used words because these words represent more than 50 percent of all the words used in writing. (Domain 2, Content Specification 005)

39. **C.** The beginning teacher should model and teach various comprehension strategies that include but are not limited to self-monitoring, rereading, note taking, outlining, summarizing, mapping, and using learning logs. Note that the strategies in choice C apply to comprehending both fiction and nonfiction. Although choices A, B, and D all might help students understand the text, teaching actual comprehension strategies specifically for expository text would be most effective. (Domain 5, Content Specification 015)

40. **A.** Choice A is the best answer because it specifically addresses the prosodic skills that many English Language Learner students lack and adds guided practice. Choice B is incorrect because the focus is on students reading silently rather than reading aloud to develop fluency. While students are likely to benefit from instruction in decoding and partner reading (choice C), decoding should not be the focus of explicit instruction in prosody. Choice D is inaccurate because it only addresses reading competency, not prosody. (Domain 3, Content Specification 009)

41. **A.** Choice A is correct because a Venn diagram specifically helps students see comparisons and contrasts in any two works. Choices B and C are incorrect because they focus on culture rather than the best instructional strategy. Choice D is too narrow; it refers only to comparing characters rather than comparing and contrasting several aspects of the two stories. (Domain 5, Content Specification 014)

42. **A.** Homophones are words that sound alike but are spelled differently. Students often confuse the spellings of these words. To clarify meaning and increase recognition of common homophones, an effective teacher can use mini-lessons to directly teach specific word pairs. Teachers can post homophone charts, and students may make homophone lists or illustrate posters on which they record example sentences to contrast the homophones. (Domain 2, Content Specification 007)

43. **A.** Brainstorming, connecting prior knowledge, and predicting what the book will be about are all effective "before reading" practices. The teacher might also do a picture walk. (Domain 4, Content Specification 011)

44. **A.** Retelling, sequencing, and discussing characters are effective methods of informally assessing student comprehension. Choices B, C, and D do not address the question with sufficient specificity. (Domain 5, Content Specification 014)

45. **A.** Selecting stories with similar themes, such as courage and adventure, can provide wonderful opportunities for comparing and contrasting, which enhances reading comprehension. (Domain 5, Content Specification 014)

46. **C.** Although it is important to motivate students (choice D) and to help English Language Learners (choice A), choice C is the best answer because it addresses *all* of Mrs. Chang's students. Choice B is not an appropriate rationale for any classroom activity. (Domain 4, Content Specification 011)

47. **D.** The teacher should plan instruction in which reading, writing, and oral language are interrelated. It is important to provide meaningful writing opportunities in the content areas. Automaticity and fluency (choice C) are not likely to be developed during this activity. Although reading comprehension may increase as a result of this activity, choice B is not as complete as choice D. Choice A refers to scaffolding, a common English Language Learner strategy, but the knowledge acquired is not systematic; therefore, choice A is merely an attractive distracter. (Domain 4, Content Specification 011)

48. **D.** Choice D is the only answer that provides information about the individual students and how they make personal connections to the literature. Choices A, B, and C are all good activities that may help students understand features of mystery writing; however, they do not address making text-to-self personal connections. Choice C is incorrect because the work is done as a class rather than individually, so the teacher would not be able to accurately evaluate individual student understanding. (Domain 5, Content Specification 014)

49. **D.** Choice D is correct because it is not a true statement. Fluency development as well as comprehension and decoding require effective instruction within the reading classroom. Choices A, B, and C are components of effective fluency instruction. Readers who are not fluent must concentrate on decoding individual words. As a result, it is harder for them to focus attention on comprehension. (Domain 3, Content Specification 008)

50. **B.** The letters stand for *Know, Wonder* (or *Want* to know), and *Learned*. Choice B correctly focuses on prior knowledge, what the students already know. Choice D, QAR, "question-answer relationship" is a comprehension strategy that helps students learn how to ask better questions. This is an excellent strategy, but does not address the question about the K-W-L chart. Choice C may help to clarify vocabulary; however, a K-W-L chart does more than develop vocabulary. Choice A is not a true statement. (Domain 4, Content Specification 011)

51. **C.** The purpose of a K-W-L chart is to help students use prior knowledge, read with purpose, and clarify what they have learned. Choice A is wrong because it focuses only on rote memorization rather than facilitating understanding. Choice B is inaccurate; if the focus is to retain facts from the chosen passage, searching other reference materials will not necessarily transfer to learning the teacher-selected material. Choice D is not the best answer because merely making a list of facts with a partner does not necessarily equate to learning the content of the reading. (Domain 5, Content Specification 015)

52. **D.** Choice D is the correct answer since it is not a component of reciprocal teaching. The answer is vague, and reciprocal teaching has nothing to do with developing a sense of how the written word is formed. Reciprocal teaching is an instructional comprehension strategy for helping students approach reading in the same way successful readers do. It provides practice in the use of four comprehension strategies: questioning, summarizing, clarifying, and predicting. It also uses scaffolding to enable students to assume responsibility for understanding text. Choices A, B, and C are all components of reciprocal teaching. This technique works equally well for fiction and nonfiction texts. (Domain 5, Content Specification 013)

53. **B.** Choice B, scanning, is quickly seeking specific words or details from the passage; this is the skill the students will use as they search the text for references to Native Americans. Choice A, skimming, is usually done before or after reading a text. The reader quickly searches for key words, phrases, or sentences to gain a general overview. The reader may also focus on headings or areas printed in bold type. Choices C and D are skills that require a more lengthy comprehension task. (Domain 5, Content Specification 015)

54. **D.** Choice D is the correct answer since teachers would be least likely to encourage students to use word attack skills to alphabetically decode the meaning. The focus is on visually decoding rather than developing vocabulary. Choices A, B, and C are all types of context clues. In an effective vocabulary program, the teacher needs to teach students strategies for deriving meaning from context. Types of context clues include definition, example-illustration, grammar, logic, morphology, and contrast. It is important to note, however, that context clues are limited in their use because the clues rarely provide enough information to help students learn the meaning a new word. As a result, using context clues should be only one of many strategies used to develop vocabulary. (Domain 4, Content Specification 011)

55. **B.** Choice B is the best answer because it not only asks students to predict future action in the story but also to justify their choices; combining these steps is most effective. Choice A is wrong because it is impossible to completely confirm a prediction before the end of the story. Choice C prepares students to answer specific questions rather than a wider, more evaluative understanding of the text. Recording information about the author would not help achieve the teacher's comprehension goal, so choice D is also incorrect. (Domain 5, Content Specification 013)

56. **C.** Teachers should use both formal and informal assessment strategies to provide effective instruction in reading comprehension. Choices A and B are incorrect for the same reason: they do not address what the teacher should do to help the student. During the RICA exam, you should focus on what the teacher does to effect change, rather than communicating with parents (choice B) or a team of specialists (choice A). In addition, choice A suggests a 504 plan, which should not be influenced by this particular assessment. Although this type of communication is mentioned in Domain 1, the focus of the RICA exam tends to be on the teacher. Chad's challenging behavior is not as important as how he actually performs when reading. Although teachers should be using California State Board of Education–adopted materials, choice D does not mention a focus on comprehension and differentiating instruction. Therefore, choice C is the most thorough answer. (Domain 5, Content Specification 013)

57. **D.** Choice D is the correct answer; the statement is false, so it is least likely to explain the teacher's strategy. Reading, writing, speaking, and listening are interrelated, and students must connect their experiences to their reading and writing. Giving students meaningful opportunities to express their ideas orally and get peer feedback helps promote writing proficiency. (Domain 4, Content Specification 011)

58. **C.** Effective teachers must know explicit strategies for helping students make connections between their existing oral vocabulary and new written vocabulary. They also must help develop understanding of written language structures and conventions. Choice A is incorrect because it features evaluative comprehension, which is not a focus of this task. Although the poems may contain figurative language (choice B), it is not a focus of this writing exercise. Choice D is incorrect because neither making inferences nor concepts of print are main features of writing these complex sentences. (Domain 4, Content Specification 011)

59. **D.** Choice D specifies the precise name of the diagram for this assignment. Creating semantic and morphological maps is a way to provide students with meaningful exposure to new academic and content-area vocabulary. Choices A and C are not the most accurate answers because the terms concept diagram and graphic organizer are too broad and include more types of relationship-oriented diagrams than the one the teacher drew. Choice B, syntactic structure, is incorrect because this is a linguistic term that describes the grammatical structure of a sentence. (Domain 4, Content Specification 011)

60. **B.** A student can use structural analysis to break down the components of the word and derive its meaning. The remaining choices cannot be broken down structurally. (Domain 4, Content Specification 010)

61. **C.** Beware of any answer that says *all* or *every*. In addition to searching through the dictionary, students should be taught other strategies for gaining meaning from unknown words. Choices A, B, and D are all appropriate strategies. In a balanced literacy program, students can learn an average of 3,000 words a year through reading and direct instruction. (Domain 4, Content Specification 011)

62. **B.** Choice B is the only answer that provides an effective way to teach vocabulary. Choice A is incorrect because teachers should not introduce all new vocabulary but rather key vocabulary. Not all words should be given equal emphasis. Teachers need to evaluate the usefulness of a word and focus on giving students the opportunity to practice the most frequently found or most meaningful words. (Domain 4, Content Specification 010)

63. **B.** One of the goals of teaching common prefixes and suffixes is to help students learn the meanings of many new words. It is preferable that students be taught strategies for deriving meaning from unknown words in addition to dictionary analysis. Students must not be limited to studying only Greek word origins. For both of those reasons, choice A is wrong. Choice C is also wrong because antonyms are not word parts. Choice D is an attractive distracter. Although it would be appropriate to provide additional words that have *re–* as a prefix, sorting the words alphabetically would not necessarily help develop vocabulary. Although the affixes *–er* and *re–* contain the same letters, the meanings are entirely different. Such comparisons would only confuse students when taught at the same time. (Domain 4, Content Specification 011)

64. **C.** Although all the choices are important when working with students, Rosa's specific needs have to do with usage errors. Mrs. Feinberg is providing clear examples of English grammar through reading, writing, and oral language. (Domain 4, Content Specification 010)

65. **D.** Choice A, simply using a grammar lesson and worksheet with vague directions, is not the appropriate follow-up activity for Rosa. Choice B is wrong because it mentions prepositional order. Choice C would be an appropriate activity if Rosa completed the task, either alone or with a partner. However, the answer specifies that another student is responsible for executing the activity. (Domain 4, Content Specification 011)

66. **A.** Six-trait rubrics (choice B) focus only partially on grammar. Choice C is a second language assessment, but it is generally conducted by someone other than the teacher and based on student performance in a nonclassroom setting. Choice D focuses on many parts of writing rather than grammar only. It also analyzes only one piece of writing rather than making a broad assessment. In addition, despite inclusion of the term "summative," this option does not describe a summative assessment. (Domain 4, Content Specification 011)

67. **D.** Language Experience Approach (LEA) will teach most of the concepts about print. Although LEA can promote student understanding of sound/symbol correspondence, phonics is best learned when explicitly taught, choice D. This question is tricky because it asks for the *least likely* answer. (Domain 4, Content Specification 010)

68. **C.** Choices A and B are likely to benefit the child but are not effective strategies for classroom intervention. Choice D is incorrect because the teacher cannot assume that the student is advanced in all aspects of literacy (spelling, comprehension, written conventions, etc.). Although advanced fluency is likely to indicate high performance in related literacy areas, the teacher should not make this assumption without further assessment. (Domain 1, Content Specification 002)

69. **D.** Choice A is incorrect because oral and written language development would not necessarily address language similarities and differences. Choice B is incorrect because it refers only to academic language used in literature rather than in all the content areas. Although "a balanced language approach" (choice C) sounds right, it is not a recognized teaching term for specifically addressing academic language. (Domain 4, Content Specification 011)

70. **B.** Choice A lists excellent vocabulary activities; however, it does not correspond to the method introduced by the teacher. Determining word history and origin, choice C, should not be regarded as more important than the actual definition. Choice D is too vague to be correct. (Domain 4, Content Specification 011)

# Section II: Open-Ended Questions

## Sample Essays and Evaluations

### Domain 2/Assignment A

### Sample Essay

Phonemic awareness, as noted in Marilyn Adam's research, is one of the three predictors of success in early reading. Adams notes that if a student does not attain mastery of phonemic awareness, he/she will probably never be able to read on grade level. Keith Stanovich's research has shown that phonemic awareness is a core causal factor separating normal from disabled readers.

To teach phonemic awareness the teacher must first assess, using a phonemic awareness survey such as the Yopp-Singer Survey, to determine student skill needs in phonemic awareness. The teacher would use the results (data) from the assessment to plan and target instruction in such sub-skill areas as identifying phonemes, blending phonemes, or deleting/adding phonemes. Planning for instruction would address teaching one or two sub-skills at a time and would include a variety of variables such as grouping (small groups are best for PA Instruction), individual student needs, and resources. Students should have many opportunities to practice phonemic awareness skills, first with the teacher and then independently. The teacher monitors practice and provides intervention as needed. Skill mastery is noted in retesting with the original assessment tool, e.g., Yopp-Singer. Large group and individual practice in phonemic awareness is ongoing throughout the year in songs, games, and other activities.

### Evaluating the Essay

The essay must address the two tasks stated in the question. In the first paragraph the writer tells how phonemic awareness is related to reading achievement. The work of two researchers is noted in support of the explanation given in the first paragraph.

The second paragraph addresses the second question. The author describes each step in the instructional process. Following the description of each step in the instructional process (diagnostic instruction) is a sentence or two that give examples to support the description. The last sentence in the essay is a summary statement concerning phonemic awareness teaching.

# Domain 3/Assignment B

## Sample Essay

The student, Jane, is demonstrating a need to understand the role of prefixes and suffixes in decoding multisyllabic words. The instructional strategy the teacher would use in addressing this need is direct instruction of prefixes and suffixes. In addition, she would explain the meaning of prefixes and suffixes and how they would change the meaning of words. For example; *un–* means not, *–est* means most, and *–less* means without. The teacher would model reading a word with an affix by covering the prefix or suffix and having Jane decode the root word first. Guided practice may include repeatedly blending the prefix or suffix before adding it to the root word. This will build automaticity in decoding the affix. The student activity for independent practice would include dividing the prefix or suffix from the given root word by using a slash. The student would then do a word sort by creating a paper with two columns: words with prefixes and words with suffixes. Jane would then categorize words appropriately in the two columns. This process will be effective because students must be directly taught what is necessary to become accurate, fluent readers, (Charles H. Clark 1995). Practice toward automaticity in decoding will ensure that the student will reach grade-level fluency.

## Evaluating the Essay

The task addressed in the essay is "The Big Picture," tell what is happening, what the instructor will teach and have students practice, and why (rationale) the selected tasks meet the identified need. Using The Big Three as a guide, the author begins in the first sentence addressing the identified need. Examples are given related to each of the three steps. Examples add detail and help to make each step more understandable. Note, the identified need is to understand and use prefixes and suffixes. It is a skill need; therefore, the instructional strategy to use first is direct, explicit skill instruction.

# Domain 4/Assignment C

## Sample Essay

The understanding of vocabulary terms helps students have a clear conceptual meaning of important words to help in their reading development and cognitive processes. The best way for students to learn new words is by reading. Teachers can: (1) begin by reading a sentence from the book that contains the word *injustice,* and ask the students to use contextual clues and their prior knowledge to try to figure out what it means; (2) ask students to use the word *injustice* in their own sentences; (3) provide students with exposure to the new word by hearing the word repeated in different contexts; (4) help students by restating the word, providing examples using "word parts" with descriptions and clues about the definition; and (5) teachers can help students to learn and use reference aids (i.e. classroom or online dictionary).

## Evaluating the Essay

The essay fulfills the task by describing strategies and resources. It is effective because it identifies vocabulary as the appropriate domain. The writer gives specific details about vocabulary strategies. Instructional strategies included reading out loud, using the vocabulary word in a variety of contexts, providing additional exposure to the word, learning word parts (prefixes and suffixes), and using a dictionary or other reference guide. The essay clearly points out that using many strategies to meet the diverse needs of individual students will help target the gaps with direct instruction in identified needs.

# Domain 5/Assignment D

## Sample Essay

Literal comprehension is "reading the lines." It is identifying factual ideas that are explicitly stated. This could include the comprehension strategies such as identifying main idea, details, or cause-and-effect. Literal comprehension involves answering who, where, what, and when questions. Memory questions and recall are often used to determine literal comprehension.

Inferential comprehension is about inferring, figuring out ideas that are implied in a text. Inferential questions, "reading between the lines," require students to think beyond the facts of the text. In inferential comprehension questions the student is often asked to answer how and why questions. Comprehension strategies appropriate for this "what is implied" level of comprehension include drawing conclusions and making predictions. Inferential comprehension is about implied meanings. Interpretive questions (a higher level than memory/recall) as well as applying facts to new contexts aid students in practicing inferential comprehension.

Evaluative comprehension requires the reader to make a judgment about the text and to base these judgments on what he or she knows/understands both literally and inferentially. Making distinctions e.g., fact/opinion, identifying propaganda, identifying bias, helps students in evaluative comprehension. Comprehension strategies such as distinguishing between facts and opinions, reacting to a text's content, characters, and use of language are all appropriate strategies for evaluative comprehension. In evaluative comprehension students ask higher order questions, analyze new situations with new knowledge, synthesize information among texts, and evaluate texts.

## Evaluating the Essay

The essay clearly fulfills the two tasks. The first task is to describe the three levels and the second task is to describe two comprehension strategies appropriate to teach each level. The author chose to write three paragraphs. Each paragraph addresses a level of comprehension. First, there is a description of what the level is—a definition. Following the description of the level is the description of two comprehension strategies appropriate for that level. The last sentence in each paragraph gives a snapshot view of the level of comprehension.

# Case Study Information

**Your case-study essay should have included some of the following information.**

Since you are asked to identify three strengths and weaknesses and describe two teaching strategies, you will not be able to respond to every issue presented in this case study. You must select the weaknesses that are the most prominent, the most severe, and the most basic. To find strengths, look at the student's interest survey to find out what she likes to do, and what she says she is good at doing. Then, look at the teacher's comments for strengths.

In determining the most salient weaknesses, look for concerns that show up in more than one piece of data. In this case study, fluency was slow both on Tara's phonics tests and on her running record. Tara had difficulty with decoding basic words on both her phonics test and running record. You would recommend that Tara work on reading fluency, and suggest one or more strategies for working on fluency. She could also be working on decoding basic words at the same time, by practicing reading easy material and decodable books.

Tara had difficulty with spelling on her spelling assessment and in her writing samples. Furthermore, on her interest survey, she wrote that she wants to be a better speller. Specifically, she has difficulty spelling words with long vowels, as evidenced in her spelling test and writing samples. You would identify her spelling stage in the Beginning Within Word stage and you could recommend that she work on long vowel spelling patterns through word study, activities, spelling games, and study of common spelling patterns. You might also suggest activities in which Tara contrasts words with long vowels and words with short vowels.

Examine Tara's running record to see what information you can get from it. It was a fourth-grade selection, and she read it at the instructional level, so her instructional level is fourth grade. Since she is in sixth grade, she is two years behind in reading, so she needs help. Her comprehension was good, so that is a strength, as she is able to comprehend at a higher level. On the running record, Tara had trouble decoding multisyllabic words, as well as on her phonics tests. She does not possess strategies for decoding multisyllabic words and would benefit from practice in decoding them. On her running record, you can also see that her decoding errors are mostly substitutions and that she uses the beginning of the word to decode without attending to the rest of the word. She is using visual cues without attending to meaning. She needs to be taught to look at the whole word and read for meaning as well. The assessments definitely suggest that Tara would benefit from direct instruction and practice in her word recognition skills.

To improve Tara's decoding and fluency, you could suggest that she practice reading daily from books that are at her independent level. Additionally, reading a lot will help her improve her spelling and writing because she will be getting much needed exposure to the correct spellings of words, and to good written structures. To capitalize on her strengths, she could read books on topics about which she is interested. You can get her interests from the interest survey. For Tara it would be cheerleading, sports, mysteries, and instructional books. On her writing samples, Tara wrote about those topics, and she should continue to do so, and she should be encouraged to write mysteries and instructions. Tara's self-correction rate on her running record was low, so she needs to be encouraged to self-monitor her reading and read for meaning.

Next, look at the other assessment data. From the phonics assessments, you learned that Tara had difficulty reading nonsense words with short vowel sounds, multisyllabic words, and words with diphthongs. You would want to leave the diphthongs alone for now, because you need to work on the multisyllabic words and long vowel words identified in the other assessments first. Tara's difficulty with short-vowel nonsense words indicates that she reads words better in context than out of context.

From the writing samples you learned that Tara's sentences are simple, and she doesn't include many details. Once again, reading a lot will help her to see good writing patterns and formats. You could suggest writing lessons in which Tara would add details to sentences or fill in sentence frames with various formats. You also could suggest that Tara use graphic organizers or story planning charts to plan her writing, and as part of her prewriting.

# Analyzing Your Test Results

Use the following charts to carefully analyze your results and spot your strengths and weaknesses. Complete the process of analyzing each subject area and each individual question for Practice Test 2. Examine your results for trends in types of error (repeated errors) or poor results in specific subject areas. This re-examination and analysis is of tremendous importance for effective test preparation.

## Practice Test 2 Analysis Sheets

| Multiple-Choice Questions | | | | |
|---|---|---|---|---|
| | Possible | Completed | Right | Wrong |
| Domain 1 | 11 | | | |
| Domain 2 | 22 | | | |
| Domain 3 | 6 | | | |
| Domain 4 | 18 | | | |
| Domain 5 | 13 | | | |
| Total: | 70 | | | |

## Analysis/Tally Sheet for Multiple-Choice Questions

One of the most important parts of test preparation is analyzing why you missed a question so that you can reduce the number of mistakes. Now that you've taken Practice Test 2 and corrected your answers, carefully tally your multiple-choice mistakes by marking in the proper column.

| Reasons for Mistakes | | | | |
|---|---|---|---|---|
| | Total Mistakes | Simple Mistake | Misread Question | Lack of Knowledge |
| Domain 1 | | | | |
| Domain 2 | | | | |
| Domain 3 | | | | |
| Domain 4 | | | | |
| Domain 5 | | | | |
| Total: | | | | |

# Open-Ended Questions (The Essays)

See the discussion of essay scoring beginning on page 2 to evaluate your essays. Have someone knowledgeable in reading instruction read and evaluate your responses using the checklists that follow.

# Domain 2/Assignment A

# RICA Practice Essay Evaluation Form

**Use this checklist to evaluate your essay:**

1.  To what extent does this response reflect an **understanding of the relevant content** and academic knowledge from the applicable RICA domain?

    | **thorough** | **adequate** | **limited or no** |
    |---|---|---|
    | understanding | understanding | understanding |

2.  To what extent does this response **fulfill the purpose of the assignment?**

    | **completely** | **adequately** | **partially** |
    |---|---|---|
    | fulfills | fulfills | fulfills or fails to |

3.  To what extent does this essay **respond to the given task(s)?**

    | **fully** | **adequately** | **limited or inadequately** |
    |---|---|---|
    | responds | responds | responds |

4.  How **accurate** is the response?

    | **very** | **generally** | **inaccurate** |
    |---|---|---|
    | accurate | accurate | |

5.  Does the response **demonstrate an effective application** of the relevant content and academic knowledge from the applicable RICA domain?

    | **yes** | **reasonably** | **no** |
    |---|---|---|
    | effective | effective | ineffective and inaccurate |

6.  To what extent does the response **provide supporting examples, evidence, and rationale** based on the relevant content and academic knowledge from the applicable RICA domain?

    | **strong** | **adequate** | **limited or no** |
    |---|---|---|
    | support | support | support |

# Domain 3/Assignment B

# RICA Practice Essay Evaluation Form

**Use this checklist to evaluate your essay:**

1. To what extent does this response reflect an **understanding of the relevant content** and academic knowledge from the applicable RICA domain?

   | **thorough** | **adequate** | **limited or no** |
   |---|---|---|
   | understanding | understanding | understanding |

2. To what extent does this response **fulfill the purpose of the assignment?**

   | **completely** | **adequately** | **partially** |
   |---|---|---|
   | fulfills | fulfills | fulfills or fails to |

3. To what extent does this essay **respond to the given task(s)?**

   | **fully** | **adequately** | **limited or inadequately** |
   |---|---|---|
   | responds | responds | responds |

4. How **accurate** is the response?

   | **very** | **generally** | **inaccurate** |
   |---|---|---|
   | accurate | accurate | |

5. Does the response **demonstrate an effective application** of the relevant content and academic knowledge from the applicable RICA domain?

   | **yes** | **reasonably** | **no** |
   |---|---|---|
   | effective | effective | ineffective and inaccurate |

6. To what extent does the response **provide supporting examples, evidence, and rationale** based on the relevant content and academic knowledge from the applicable RICA domain?

   | **strong** | **adequate** | **limited or no** |
   |---|---|---|
   | support | support | support |

# Domain 4/Assignment C

# RICA Practice Essay Evaluation Form

**Use this checklist to evaluate your essay:**

1. To what extent does this response reflect an **understanding of the relevant content** and academic knowledge from the applicable RICA domain?

   | **thorough** | **adequate** | **limited or no** |
   |---|---|---|
   | understanding | understanding | understanding |

2. To what extent does this response **fulfill the purpose of the assignment?**

   | **completely** | **adequately** | **partially** |
   |---|---|---|
   | fulfills | fulfills | fulfills or fails to |

3. To what extent does this essay **respond to the given task(s)?**

   | **fully** | **adequately** | **limited or inadequately** |
   |---|---|---|
   | responds | responds | responds |

4. How **accurate** is the response?

   | **very** | **generally** | **inaccurate** |
   |---|---|---|
   | accurate | accurate | |

5. Does the response **demonstrate an effective application** of the relevant content and academic knowledge from the applicable RICA domain?

   | **yes** | **reasonably** | **no** |
   |---|---|---|
   | effective | effective | ineffective and inaccurate |

6. To what extent does the response **provide supporting examples, evidence, and rationale** based on the relevant content and academic knowledge from the applicable RICA domain?

   | **strong** | **adequate** | **limited or no** |
   |---|---|---|
   | support | support | support |

## Domain 5/Assignment D

# RICA Practice Essay Evaluation Form

**Use this checklist to evaluate your essay:**

1. To what extent does this response reflect an **understanding of the relevant content** and academic knowledge from the applicable RICA domain?

   | **thorough** | **adequate** | **limited or no** |
   |---|---|---|
   | understanding | understanding | understanding |

2. To what extent does this response **fulfill the purpose of the assignment?**

   | **completely** | **adequately** | **partially** |
   |---|---|---|
   | fulfills | fulfills | fulfills or fails to |

3. To what extent does this essay **respond to the given task(s)?**

   | **fully** | **adequately** | **limited or inadequately** |
   |---|---|---|
   | responds | responds | responds |

4. How **accurate** is the response?

   | **very** | **generally** | **inaccurate** |
   |---|---|---|
   | accurate | accurate | |

5. Does the response **demonstrate an effective application** of the relevant content and academic knowledge from the applicable RICA domain?

   | **yes** | **reasonably** | **no** |
   |---|---|---|
   | effective | effective | ineffective and inaccurate |

6. To what extent does the response **provide supporting examples, evidence, and rationale** based on the relevant content and academic knowledge from the applicable RICA domain?

   | **strong** | **adequate** | **limited or no** |
   |---|---|---|
   | support | support | support |

# Case Study/Assignment E

# RICA Practice Case Study Evaluation Form

**Use this checklist to evaluate your essay:**

1. To what extent does this response reflect an **understanding of the relevant content** and academic knowledge from the applicable RICA domain?

   | **thorough** | **adequate** | **limited** | **little or no** |
   |---|---|---|---|
   | understanding | understanding | understanding | understanding |

2. To what extent does this response **fulfill the purpose of the assignment?**

   | **completely** | **adequately** | **partially** | **fails to fulfill** |
   |---|---|---|---|
   | fulfills | fulfills | fulfills | |

3. To what extent does this essay **respond to the given task(s)?**

   | **fully** | **adequately** | **limited** | **inadequately** |
   |---|---|---|---|
   | responds | responds | responds | responds |

4. How **accurate** is the response?

   | **very** | **generally** | **partially** | **inaccurate** |
   |---|---|---|---|
   | accurate | accurate | accurate | |

5. Does the response **demonstrate an effective application** of the relevant content and academic knowledge from the applicable RICA domain?

   | **yes** | **reasonably** | **limited** | **no** |
   |---|---|---|---|
   | effective | effective | generally ineffective | inaccurate and ineffective |

6. To what extent does the response **provide supporting examples, evidence, and rationale** based on the relevant content and academic knowledge from the applicable RICA domain?

   | **strong** | **adequate** | **limited** | **little or no** |
   |---|---|---|---|
   | support | support | support | support |

# Essay Review

Compare your essays to the ones given and review the Evaluation Forms, which you have had a reader complete, for each assignment. From this information, circle what you feel is the appropriate level of response for each assignment. This should help give you some general guidelines for your review.

| Open-Ended Questions | | | |
|---|---|---|---|
| Level of Response | | | |
| Assignment A (Domain 2) | good | average | poor |
| Assignment B (Domain 3) | good | average | poor |
| Assignment C (Domain 4) | good | average | poor |
| Assignment D (Domain 5) | good | average | poor |
| Assignment E (Case Study) | good | average | poor |

# FINAL PREPARATION AND SOURCES

This short section is designed to help you put everything together to do your best on the RICA test. The Final Touches emphasize what you should do as you get close to the test day.

This section also acknowledges the sources of the assessments, tests, surveys, inventories, lists, glossaries, and charts used in this book.

# The Final Touches

1. Make sure that you are familiar with the testing center location and nearby parking facilities.

2. Spend the last week of preparation on a general review of key concepts and test-taking strategies and techniques.

3. Don't cram the night before the exam. It is a waste of time!

4. Arrive at the testing center in plenty of time. At least 30 minutes early.

5. Remember to bring the proper materials: identification, admission ticket, four or five sharpened No. 2 pencils, an eraser, and a watch.

6. Start off crisply, working the questions you know first, and then go back and try to answer the others.

7. On the multiple-choice questions, try to eliminate one or more choices before you guess, but make sure that you fill in all the answers. There is no penalty for guessing!

8. Underline key words in the questions. Write out important information and make notations on diagrams. Take advantage of being permitted to write in the test booklet.

9. On multiple-choice questions, cross out incorrect choices immediately: This can keep you from reconsidering a choice that you have already eliminated.

10. Make sure that you answer what is being asked.

11. On the open-ended assignments (essays), take a few minutes to jot down notes to organize your thoughts. Remember, you are writing a response to the task(s) and to show the readers how much you know about the given assignment.

12. On the essay assignments, even if you don't know the answer, at least try to give a partial response. Always write something; you could get partial credit.

13. Don't get stuck on any one question. Never spend more than $1\frac{1}{2}$ minutes on a multiple-choice question. Spend about 15 minutes each on Assignments A and B, and about 30 minutes each on Assignments C and D. Be sure to leave about an hour for Assignment E, the case study.

14. The key to getting a good score on the RICA Written Examination is reviewing properly, practicing, and getting the questions right that you can and should get right. A careful review of Parts I and II of this book will help you focus during the final week before the exam.

# Sources

Sincere appreciation is given to the following authors and companies for allowing the use of their assessments, tests, surveys, inventories, lists, glossaries, and charts from their outstanding works.

Page 63, Word Recognition Assessment: San Diego Quick Assessment—Record Form from "The Grades Word List: Quick Gauge of Reading Ability" by Margaret La Pray. Copyright 1969 M.H. La Pray and the International Reading Association. Copyright 1999 by CORE.

Page 65, Informal Reading Assessment: Fry Oral Reading Test—Record Form from "Building Reading Success 4–8" by Edward Fry, Ph.D. Copyright 1995 by Edward Fry. Copyright 1999 by CORE.

Page 67, Fluency Assessment: Grade 5 Probe 3 from "Collections for Young Scholars" Volume 5, Book I copyright 1995.

Pages 69–70, Phonics Test: Cunningham Names Test by Patricia Cunningham form California Reading Professional Development Institute copyright 1999.

Page 73, Qualitative Spelling Inventory: Upper Elementary Spelling Inventory by Bear, Donald R.; Invernizzi, Marcia; Templeton, Shane R.; Johnston, Francine; Words Their Way: Word Study for Phonics, Vocabulary, and Spelling Instruction, 1st Edition copyright 1996. Reprinted by permission of Pearson Education, Inc., Upper Saddle River, NJ.

Page 85, Home Survey: My Child as a Reader and Writer—copyright 1996 Wright Group Publishing, Inc.

Page 87, Student Survey: Myself as a Reader—copyright 1996 Wright Group Publishing, Inc.

Pages 89–90, Running Record: Book Evaluation—The Busy Mosquito from Early Detection of Reading Difficulties (Heinemann).

Page 92, High Frequency Words: Fry's Sight Word Recording Sheet by Edward Fry, Ph.D. Copyright 1995 by Edward Fry.

Pages 139–144, Glossary of Terms and Concepts Source: California Department of Education, 1430 N Street, Sacramento, CA 95814. The Guide to the California Reading Initiative of 1996 is out of print and no longer represents California Department of Education Policy.

Page 145, BPST: Beginning Phonic Skills Test by John Shefelbine (2006), California State University, Sacramento.

Pages 145–154, CSET: Multiple Subjects Test Prep by Jerry Bobrom. Ph.D., Wiley Publishing, Inc.: Hoboken, New Jersey, Feb. 2009.

Pages 145–154, Put Reading First: The Research Building Blocks for Teaching Children to Read, Kindergarten through Grade 3, 2nd ed. National Institute for Literacy, June 2003.

Page 197, Reading Attitude Survey: Assessment Handbook.

Page 199, Family Survey: Assessment Handbook.

Pages 201–202, Running Record: Moon Mouse from Early Detection of Reading Difficulties (Heinemann).

Page 270, Running Record: from Early Detection of Reading Difficulties (Heinemann).

Page 275, Writing Samples: Elementary Inventory Error Guide.